CW01301601

The Politics of Common Sense

This book offers a refreshingly different perspective on Pakistan – it documents the evolution of the country's structure of power over the past four decades, and in particular how the military dictatorship headed by General Zia ul Haq (1977–88) – whose rule has been almost exclusively associated with a narrow agenda of Islamisation – transformed the political field through a combination of coercion and consent-production.

The Zia regime – and its successors – have inculcated within society at large a 'common sense' privileging the cultivation of patronage ties and the concurrent demeaning of counter-hegemonic political practices which had threatened the structure of power in the decade before the military coup in 1977.

The book demonstrates how the politics of 'common sense' has been consolidated in the past three decades through the agency of emergent social forces such as traders and merchants, as well as the religio-political organisations that gained influence during the 1980s. While these constituencies thrived on the back of the dictatorship, their rise is also organic inasmuch as capital has penetrated into society at large, leading to (often unplanned) urbanisation and the proliferation of informal market networks, initially in the secondary and tertiary sectors of the agrarian economy but more and more extending to manufacturing and service sectors.

The rise of individuals and networks 'from below' accords the patronage-based system its resilience – the similarities in background and outlook between the mass of working people and the political and economic entrepreneurs that act as intermediaries in a vertically-organised structure of power blunt counter-hegemonic impulses, religion often serving as the final source of legitimacy in a world that revolves around the ruthless accumulation of power and capital.

Aasim Sajjad Akhtar teaches at the National Institute of Pakistan Studies, Quaid-i-Azam University. Previously, he was at the Lahore University of Management Sciences. He has published widely on subjects as diverse as peasant movements, imperialism, informality and state theory.

The Politics of Common Sense
State, Society and Culture in Pakistan

Aasim Sajjad Akhtar

CAMBRIDGE UNIVERSITY PRESS

CAMBRIDGE
UNIVERSITY PRESS

University Printing House, Cambridge CB2 8BS, United Kingdom

One Liberty Plaza, 20th Floor, New York, NY 10006, USA

477 Williamstown Road, Port Melbourne, vic 3207, Australia

314 to 321, 3rd Floor, Plot No.3, Splendor Forum, Jasola District Centre, New Delhi 110025, India

79 Anson Road, #06–04/06, Singapore 079906

Cambridge University Press is part of the University of Cambridge.

It furthers the University's mission by disseminating knowledge in the pursuit of education, learning and research at the highest international levels of excellence.

www.cambridge.org
Information on this title: www.cambridge.org/9781107155664

© Aasim Sajjad Akhtar 2018

This publication is in copyright. Subject to statutory exception and to the provisions of relevant collective licensing agreements, no reproduction of any part may take place without the written permission of Cambridge University Press.

First published 2018
Reprint 2019

Printed in India by Thomson Press India Ltd.

A catalogue record for this publication is available from the British Library

Library of Congress Cataloging-in-Publication Data
Names: Akhtar, Aasim Sajjad, author.
Title: The politics of 'common sense' : state, society and culture in Pakistan / Aasim Sajjad Akhtar.
Description: Delhi : Cambridge University Press, 2017. | Includes bibliographical references and index.
Identifiers: LCCN 2017035552 | ISBN 9781107155664 (hardback : alkaline paper)
Subjects: LCSH: Pakistan--Politics and government. | Power (Social sciences)--Pakistan. | Patronage, Political--Pakistan. | Pakistan--Social conditions. | Pakistan--History.
Classification: LCC DS389 .A49 2017 | DDC 954.91--dc23 LC record available at https://lccn.loc.gov/2017035552

ISBN 978-1-107-15566-4 Hardback

Cambridge University Press has no responsibility for the persistence or accuracy of URLs for external or third-party internet websites referred to in this publication, and does not guarantee that any content on such websites is, or will remain, accurate or appropriate.

For Amar
Who truly is forever

Contents

Preface   *ix*
Acknowledgments   *xii*

1. Introduction   1
2. The Structure of Power 'From Above'   31
3. Accumulation in Practice   62
4. The Many Faces of Islam   94
5. The Nation that Never Became   116
6. The Subordinate Classes: Beyond Common Sense?   132
7. Epilogue: What does a Counter-hegemonic Politics Look Like?   161

Glossary   *175*
Bibliography   *179*
Index   *195*

Preface

While the plethora of literature being produced on Pakistan these days might suggest otherwise, writing a book about the country's politics, history and culture is a task fraught with difficulty. Quite aside from the popular stereotypes and misleading scholarship that one feels compelled to debunk, there has been little grounded research on state and society over a period of three decades which renders dated even substantive literature serving as a point of departure. The constant recourse to material produced in a different time and place can impede our understanding of the present as much as it helps to enhance it.

The task becomes even more challenging in an environment often hostile to 'traditionalist' conceptual and empirical debates about class, state and the like. Embodying this challenge is the work of Antonio Gramsci. On the one hand, Gramsci's ideas have very much become part of the mainstream (western) academy. On the other hand, this mainstreaming equates to Gramsci being invoked exclusively as a scholar of the discursive realm, separated by academic fashion from the materialist concerns which underlay his own efforts.

This tendency can be explained in part by the changing mores of western societies. As reiterated in this book time and again, Pakistan has also changed dramatically over the past few decades, and efforts to theorize state and society are doomed to futility without recognition of this (ongoing) process of change. The work of note on Pakistan to have emerged in recent times is based on this recognition, as well as the imperative of being critical of Eurocentric conceptual apparatuses. Yet, I sometimes feel that for all the 'newness' of such approaches, the proneness to aping trends in the western academy remains intact.

In this book, I have tried to generate insights in the mould of new-age postcolonial scholars that have grown up being suspicious of conceptual approaches associated with their predecessors, whilst insisting that it is still worth thinking about what this earlier generation uncovered. In short, we must not throw the baby out with the bath water. In practice, this means a book that tries to cover a lot of bases in a 'grand theorizing' way which is increasingly uncommon. I recognize the shortcomings of such an approach, but I take this risk consciously. Let me explain.

What draws me to Gramsci is that, instead of a cold-blooded analysis of social and political forms, his method facilitates a much more grounded understanding of why people – and by this, I mean all sorts of people, even if Gramsci's emphasis is typically on the lowest orders of society – are motivated to action (or not) by different political imaginaries. Gramsci's ideological commitments demand that his analysis is always imbued by the question of how political imaginaries sustaining the status quo can be displaced by transformative ones.

In what circumstances, Gramsci asks, is the 'national popular collective will' generated? In short, Gramsci never steers too far from the political imperative of developing a shared vision of an egalitarian and just society. This, for him, is a prerequisite to building such a society.

For almost two decades, I have interacted extensively with working people across ethnic, religious and gender backgrounds, governing elites, the well-to-do chattering classes, religious functionaries, small and medium entrepreneurs, and professional groups such as journalists and lawyers. Most of these interactions have been while being active with social movements and everyday political struggles. The knowledge of society, its mores and the everyday considerations informing political action that I have thus acquired have not been from a 'neutral' vantage point. My political commitments have impelled me to think deeply about how and why the potentialities for counter-hegemonic politics have declined so sharply over the past 2-3 decades.

To state the obvious, politics in Pakistan is very different today than a generation or so ago. Indeed, the meaning and practice of politics has changed irrevocably all over the world following the demise of 'actually existing socialism' (and attendant proclamations of the *End of History*). I waded directly into active politics while capitalist triumphalism was unchallenged at the end of the 1990s. The incredible exposure afforded to me by political activism allowed me to experience– feel, even – the texture of a political field that has changed greatly since the heyday of radicalism in the 1960s and 1970s.

I have thus attempted to put together a somewhat grand narrative of continuity and change that can improve our understanding of contemporary political economy, social mores and the daily play of power relations. The purpose, as noted already, is to sketch a picture of Pakistan that builds upon the seminal treatises of the past and incorporates new empirical realities, all while critically engaging with innovative approaches popular in the contemporary period.

In truth, it does not take much to improve upon the scant literature on Pakistan that raises interesting questions and derives meaningful insights.

Accordingly, the major contribution that this book makes is to systematically demonstrate how the urban commercial classes and the religious right have forced their way into a structure of power which is based on the passive consent of the subordinate classes. While there have been many impressionistic offerings about the religious right and the intermediate classes over the years, linking their emergence to wider developments is important if we are to avoid either under- or over-stating their significance.

By illustrating how these emergent social forces are the major protagonists of the everyday politics of patronage in Pakistan, I hope to direct attention away from overemphasized and 'culturalized' themes like religious militancy and 'rogue' state behaviour. As is the case when trying to build a 'grand narrative' of state and society on the whole, there is also hazard in bringing under emphasized aspects of social and political life to the fore at the expense of overemphasized ones. But this, again, is a risk worth taking.

In the final analysis, I hope this book, with other efforts, helps scholarship on Pakistan turn a bit of a corner. Over the past few years, I have been fortunate to witness first hand the emergence of a number of young critical scholars educated in Pakistan and abroad. Despite the deep and pervasive legacy of dictatorship and the 'global restoration of class power', I am hopeful that this number will grow to become a critical mass capable of challenging the hegemonic intellectual – and political – order that prevails in contemporary Pakistan.

Acknowledgments

It would not be possible for me thank all the many people that have been sources of support and inspiration over the years that this book was written. As an accidental academic that took on a day job allowing me the most possible leeway to fulfil my political commitments, I have been privileged to know and learn from many comrades over the course of a political struggle that is almost two decades old. Quite aside from my being terrified at leaving out even one name that matters, it is also in many ways appropriate that I do not name anyone. The struggle for a more just and equal world has persisted for almost as long as human society itself, and many have come and gone along the way. The vast majority of those who have given of themselves for the cause of human emancipation have remained nameless. So it will be in the future too. To the many who have journeyed with me in the present – I do not need to name you for you to know how important you have been to me.

I thank my students at the Lahore University of Management Sciences, where I taught between 2003–09, and Quaid-i Azam University in Islamabad, where I still teach today. I have been lucky to come across so many vibrant young people who inspire tremendous hope for the future. I have always enjoyed the classroom and it has been a major site of learning for me over the years as I have tried to make sense of the social order in Pakistan. Some of my students have become friends as our paths have criss-crossed, and I am the richer for it.

It is difficult for me to separate intellectual from political influences, but it was as a doctoral student – which I was for a very brief time – that I first recognized what it means to think deeply about words and the ideas hidden within them. For that, I must thank Sudipta Kaviraj, who was able to relate to my political leanings, yet encourage me to experiment. Matthew Nelson was generous and extremely efficient, and the environment at SOAS suited my kind perfectly, not least of all in allowing me in and out very quickly.

I must thank the editors at Cambridge University Press, and particularly Lucy Rhymer and Qudsiya Ahmed for taking on what turned out to be a rather long project. The production team in Delhi was very patient and put in many hours during the editing phase. Anonymous reviewers helped shape the book into the form that it has finally taken, while thanks are due to the handful of (again nameless) people who read portions and offered suggestions at different stages. I am particularly grateful for the extremely tedious logistical work done by Annam Azeem at my home institution of NIPS at QAU towards the bitter end when I was unwilling to even look at the manuscript.

I have joked with those close to me that this book was written by three different people, spread out over many years. The second of those people was based at the Institute of South Asian Studies (ISAS) on the National University of Singapore campus in the summer of 2014. I thank friends at ISAS for the opportunity they provided, and hope that I can eventually take them up on their repeated offers to return.

Being in Singapore allowed me to spend some time with my family, which justifiably protests that it has not seen enough of me over the years. Despite my choosing a radically different life trajectory to theirs, my parents, Ruby and Sajjad, have continued to do what parents do – offering support through thick and thin. My brothers Usman and Emaad, and Saba, Esa and Hasan – much love to you. My extended family saw more of me as a student than they see now, and while I have not been in touch with them as much as I could, they have been, and will always be, a big part of my world.

I do not count many intimate friends, and in recent years have only developed close ties with comrades in the struggle. I am lucky, however, to still be in touch with childhood friends from Singapore, and those who I made later as a teenager and (very) young adult in New Mexico and Chicago. AB and the bracas deserve special mention. I see most of them rarely now, but would like to believe that they all know how important they remain to me.

Finally, to the family that I became part of and is now my own. My grandparents – and *Nani* in particular – were the only family I had when I first moved back to Pakistan almost eighteen years ago. Soon afterwards, I became involved, perhaps inevitably through shared political commitments, with a kinship group (could not help it!) unlike anything I had ever come across before.

To Asha – thank you for sharing so much with me and helping me grow in the process; I am grateful that our journeys continue to be intertwined, not least of all because of our boy. Hajra has taught me dignity and grace, Pervez the value of remaining steadfast in one's commitments, and Neil's friendship has been the most unexpected, but a lovely surprise. And then there is Alia, who has taught me the most important lessons of all, helping me uncover all that being human and loving someone entails.

Last, but most definitely not least, there is Rumi. It is to you that I dedicate this book, the first version of which was written as you came into the world. I know that you will inherit even more difficult challenges than my generation has done and can only hope we bequeath you something to take forward. In the meantime, know that every passing day that I get to be your Abba, I am reminded that I am the luckiest person alive.

1

Introduction

> There is no human activity from which every form of intellectual participation can be excluded: homo faber cannot be separated from homo sapiens. Each man carries on some form of intellectual activity, that is, he is a philosopher, an artist, a man of taste, he participates in a particular conception of the world, has a conscious line of moral conduct, and therefore contributes to sustain a conception of the world or to modify it, that is, to bring into being new modes of thought.[1]
>
> Antonio Gramsci (1971: 9)

Pakistan is one of the most written about, yet least understood countries in the world. It is often reduced to a series of categories that obfuscate more than they illuminate. Both in journalistic and scholarly accounts, the imperative of comprehending complex political, economic and cultural dynamics is thwarted by the predominance of monolithic narrative tropes such as 'Islamic' and 'terrorism'.

The events of 9/11 and subsequent developments explain much of the security-oriented literature that has proliferated in recent years. This recent trend aside, most scholarly works on Pakistan's state and society have never strayed very far from descriptive macro-level accounts which detail, in chronological fashion, the continuities and changes associated with different political regimes.

These mainstream accounts are premised, overtly or otherwise, on static readings of state and society; the former often depicted as an island of modernity struggling to impose itself on a society whose cultural moorings are incompatible with the imperatives of socio-economic change and progressive politics.[2]

In fact, the relationship between state and society is far more complex than most academic treatments of Pakistan have generally acknowledged. Only by constructing a thoroughly historicized narrative in which the interplay between myriad economic, political and cultural moments is clearly enunciated can one make sense of the contemporary social order in Pakistan.

In contravention to both 'security studies' and mainstream political histories, a grounded brand of scholarship has emerged in recent years featuring both substantial empirical insights about state and society and novel theoretical approaches. This book is a modest attempt to add to this growing archive. In it, I chart how a particular conception of navigating the everyday – what I call the politics of common sense – has become hegemonic across the length and breadth of Pakistan's society over the past three decades.

In sum, I present a historical materialist analysis of the patronage-based structure of power in Pakistan, and particularly how it has changed since the late 1960s. In constructing this narrative, I employ the theoretical architecture of the revolutionary Italian thinker Antonio Gramsci, and also engage with classical and contemporary literature on post-colonial state and society.

The politics of common sense is essentially a strategy of accommodation, whereby the lower orders of society accede to a patronage-dominated political field. I argue this phase of accommodation can be traced back to the dictatorship of General Zia ul Haq (1977–88), during which the structure of power was rehabilitated following a decade of intense political upheaval (1967–77) when an anti-systemic politics of the left raged across the country.

The emergence of the politics of common sense in Pakistan in many ways mirrors global trends. The era of post-WWII radicalism, which arguably culminated in the early 1970s, was followed by what has been called the 'restoration of class power' in many parts of the world.[3] This restoration was in part due to the liberal deployment of coercive force by states, propertied classes and imperialist powers. In Pakistan's case at least the decline of an anti-systemic, left politics can also be attributed to concrete and sophisticated strategies of cooptation adopted by the Zia regime in accordance with rapidly changing economic and cultural conditions.

These strategies of consent-production have been consolidated in the subsequent three decades, while structural change has proceeded apace. The 'success' of the patronage machine that was fashioned during the Zia period is most evident in the agency of the subordinate classes and other exploited segments of Pakistan's society, but its significance is precisely in the fact that it is operative across the class (and ethnic) divide, and hence, hegemonic.

Accordingly, while I develop analytical insights about the political alignments of the subordinate classes, the book is also about dominant social forces, including the civil bureaucracy, landlords, industrialists and the military. These institutions and classes have been major players in Pakistan's political economy since the inception of the state (and often long before).

Other contenders for power have emerged in the period under study, namely the urbanized, commercial classes and religio-political forces. Aside from detailing their sociological evolution and relationships to one another, I show how this combination of the old guard and *nouveau riche* has – or not, as the case may be – secured consent from the subordinate classes.

In outlining this evolution of the political field, I demonstrate not only how class and social structures have changed over time, but also how the composition and institutional logic of the Pakistan state have undergone transformation. I argue, a la Gramsci, that the structure of power is a dialectical unity whereby state and society constitute two mutually reinforcing sides of the same coin.

The narrative is ordered by three crucial junctures which have shaped the contemporary social order. First, there is the colonial encounter. I will revisit a familiar theme – the colonial state's reification of parochial identities and dynamic responses of working people – so as to outline how a particular logic of practice evolved in society during British rule. This patronage-based political order was, I think, the most lasting of colonial legacies.

Second, I will highlight the widespread social changes and politicization that took place across the length and breadth of Pakistan's society in the 1960s which greatly impacted the social and political landscape for at least a decade afterwards. On the one hand, this great wave of radical politics was global in scope, ranging from the African decolonization movements and national liberation struggles in East Asia to popular upheavals in the capitalist west and revolutionary experiments in Latin America. On the other hand, there were major socio-economic and ideational changes taking place within Pakistan's society which explain the dramatic emergence of an indigenous radical politics of the left.

Third, I will discuss the period starting with the military coup of 1977 which featured the constitution of a regenerated ruling clique and the beginnings of a 'politics of common sense' that, though periodically challenged, has prevailed through to the present conjuncture.

The story that I will tell in the following pages about an exclusionary political-economic order inherited from colonialism, emergent challenges to this order from a cross-section of the popular classes, and finally the reassertion of a hegemonic politics of patronage from the late 1970s onwards, resonates to a degree with the narrative presented by Saadia Toor about culture and politics in Pakistan during the Cold War.[4] This book augments Toor's argument about the demonization of leftist political forces by emphasizing how the state and propertied classes devised new strategies of political control in the midst of rapid social change.

While I cannot claim that my observations are representative beyond Pakistan – it is a challenge to even represent the diversity of the Pakistan experience – I will refer occasionally to scholarship about other parts of the post-colonial world, and especially neighbouring India. This reflects the many shared continuities (and breaks) in post-colonial countries with the period of European rule, and particularly the structures of economic and political power inherited from colonialism. India offers the most obvious comparative insights for the Pakistani case, notwithstanding the considerably different trajectories of both countries since partition.

Comparative studies on the two successor states of the British Raj have long tried to explain why India became a relatively stable democracy while Pakistan repeatedly experienced authoritarian rule, a concern that continues to animate scholars to this day.[5] However, academic works on Indian politics, culture and economy have diversified greatly, both theoretically and empirically. The bird's-eye macro-level analyses of the state that preoccupied a previous generation have given way too much more nuanced and localized studies of how the state operates at an everyday level. There has also developed a substantial literature on informality and emergent classes in an increasingly urbanized society. All in all, the scope and breadth of social science and humanities literature on India is impressive.[6]

Such work is relatively sparse in Pakistan, and throughout the manuscript I draw upon what has come to the fore in recent times. I also refer to more dated literature, and particularly the work of Hamza Alavi on the state and political economy. This serves both as a point of departure and as a call to transcend increasingly obsolete frameworks and learn from developments in scholarship on state and society across other parts of the post-colonial world.

In line with such developments, I present here a historical analysis of Pakistan's political economy that is not focused exclusively on the machinations of 'big men', which has been a preoccupation of both mainstream approaches and even non-traditional ones such as that proffered by Alavi. My particular contribution is to embed a political economy framework for understanding Pakistan within its specific historical context.[7]

I must confess, however, that there is one major aspect of the story that remains untold in this book. Pakistan is amongst the most patriarchal societies in the world today, and the public sphere is exceedingly male-dominated.

I cannot therefore venture that what I call the politics of common sense accurately depicts the everyday reality of the mass of Pakistan's women. While, in later chapters, I provide details of popular political strategies which have been adopted by both men and women, mine is not a gendered analysis of the structure of power in Pakistan, a shortcoming that desperately needs to be addressed.

I should also note at the outset that Pakistan's state and society have been greatly influenced by imperialist powers, both during and after the Cold War. I do not want to understate the significance of this international dimension, and the dialectic between global/regional geo-politics and domestic developments.[8] However, I have chosen not to engage in a detailed analysis of what Alavi called the 'metropolitan bourgeoisie' and its sway over state and society, partly due to constraints of time and space, and also because I want to call attention to historically under-specified areas in the literature.

My attempt to chart the underlying logic of Pakistan's political order needs to be augmented in many other ways, but given the paucity of innovative theoretical approaches to understanding Pakistan's state and society in the literature, I am hopeful that this particular Gramsci-inspired effort will open up new avenues for future research.

Gramscian Building Blocks

As is now common knowledge, Gramsci offered a corrective to what was an emaciated understanding of popular culture in materialist canon. He argued that matters of consciousness and political action had to be grounded in an understanding of existing social forms rather than assuming that the trajectory of culture and politics would conform to scientifically calculable 'laws of development'. Gramsci was more concerned than most in the materialist tradition with understanding the terrain of social life on which class struggle actually played out. In other words, his focus was on the political and cultural fields and the manner in which objective class interests were culturally perceived and subjectively articulated.

For Gramsci, "common sense' means the incoherent set of generally held assumptions and beliefs common to any given society'.[9] The ruling class in a society seeks to mould common sense – the taken-for-granted way of doing things – such that those they govern acquiesce to the rules of the existing social order. This does not mean that the latter are deluded about the actions of those who dominate them. In other words, they are not victims of 'false consciousness', but, for myriad reasons, the unequal and unjust system of domination is resilient and common sense requires subordinates to negotiate their way through the system rather than defy it:

> ...Subalterns come to see the hierarchies of the world they inhabit as inevitable and inescapable. They may not like their subordination, but they cannot see how things could possibly be other than as they are.[10]

With the rise to prominence of post-structuralist schools of thought over the past few decades, 'recovering' the voice of the subaltern has become an almost ontological quest. While this book is not concerned with the postmodern turn *per se*, I want to assert at the outset that common sense cannot be understood exclusively as a system of signs, representation or cultural symbols. It is a worldview that is embedded in the historically constituted structures of capitalist modernity, and a politics which ebbs and flows in accordance with structural shifts. Through the course of the book I will repeatedly call attention to two foundational structures; the post-colonial state and capitalist exchange and productive relations. Only by uncovering these structural underpinnings of everyday life can one develop an understanding of contemporary social and political practice.

Intuition suggests that common sense today was not necessarily common sense yesterday, and will not necessarily be common sense tomorrow. Quite simply, Gramsci was restating what all of us already know. More often than not, however, our efforts to theorize the real world ignore – at our peril – the most obvious of details. And it is the obviousness of our lived culture – and the embeddedness of political action within it – that Gramsci sought to foreground.

In recent times, the much celebrated 'cultural turn' in social theory has been extended to the study of post-colonial states.[11] At a fundamental level this is a welcome development given that most received theories about the state have been plagued by implicit ethnocentric bias or, as Sudipta Kaviraj puts it, the fact that the established conceptual apparatus is burdened with the baggage of specific historical embeddedness.[12] The recognition that there is a need to make both the terms we use and the ideas that inform them more contextually relevant (without digressing into relativism or abandoning praxis) is welcome.

Anthropologists have of course been striving for more than a century to understand the inner workings of (post) colonial societies. The colonial obsession for identifying exactly what was different about the 'natives' (for the purposes of administering them better) has given way to a sometimes torturous struggle to establish exactly how to conceptualize 'culture' and where to locate it on the larger map of post-colonial societies. For a significant part of the post-war period scholars of 'culture' were unable to recognize that 'politics' in the post-colony was not 'acultural' and needed to be conceptualized in dynamic rather than teleological ways. Post-structuralist conceptions of 'power' may have opened up remarkable new intellectual trajectories, but have not necessarily succeeded in theorizing culture, politics and economics in holistic terms.[13]

Notwithstanding the significance of the post-modern turn – inasmuch as this refers to the privileging of the everyday and discursive realms – there is a marked tendency within much contemporary scholarship to abstract from the real political and economic structures that shape working people's lives. In my understanding it is important to be cognizant of the specificity of all social life – a simple fact often overlooked by general, or structuralist, perspectives – as well as to supra-local political economy realities.[14]

To draw upon and then go beyond the insights that have been garnered by cultural theorists – that is, to understand the manner in which culture, politics and economics come together to explain the structures that exist and the agents that emerge from, reproduce, and sometimes challenge these structures – it is necessary to take seriously the study of history. I believe that satisfactory conceptualizations of social and political forms in the post-colony have remained elusive precisely because the tendency has been towards ahistorical analyses, in that culture has either been posited as unchanging and fixed, or completely invented.

A handful of contemporary scholars writing about Pakistan have made efforts to break the mould by bringing to the fore previously under-studied aspects of political economy, cultural history and statecraft. Matthew Hull's work on Islamabad's Capital Development Authority (CDA) highlights how the everyday state operates, and how it is thwarted by the wilful actions of the ordinary people who learn how to manipulate its formal modalities.[15] Naveeda Khan's work, based in Lahore, links sectarian contestations over 'proper' Islamic practice with the politics of mosque-building, again challenging monolithic conceptions of the conduct of both the state and ordinary Pakistanis.[16] Outside of major urban areas, Nosheen Ali has developed a body of work on the so-called Northern Areas,[17] focusing on cultural production – and particularly poetry – as a form of nationalist imagining.[18] I will invoke other such scholarship in due course to underline the possibilities of linking macro political economy concerns with more grounded questions of political subjectivity, in the process transgressing disciplinary boundaries and 'established' theoretical orthodoxies.

In building my case for a holistic understanding of the political, economic and cultural moments, I start with a brief history of the colonial period. While this book is primarily about processes of social change and evolving political forms since the 1970s, it is only possible to understand what has changed by first outlining the structural context inherited from colonialism.

The Colonial Rhythm

Kaviraj emphasizes that in pre-British India, the state was an 'alien' entity that did not command a presence beyond a symbolic or grand aura. In fact, it 'was traditionally seen as a necessarily limited and distinctly unpleasant part of the basic furniture of society'.[19] This suggests that the political field of most Indians was effectively autonomous of the state itself. In this respect alone, the colonial impact utterly changed the conception of the public and political and therefore social and political practice.

In the pre-British period, politics was 'self-contained' in that relationships of power were largely confined within the 'community' and only to a limited extent, between communities.[20] The breadth of the political field was dramatically enhanced under British rule. For example, disputes over land or other forms of social property – including women – were frequently mediated by the state, whether the police, courts or the administrative apparatus more generally. Even in cases where 'traditional' dispute resolution mechanisms such as local *panchayats* represented the primary means of resolving conflicts, it was often the case that the state in one or more of its forms was also invoked.[21]

The advent of British rule was thus a watershed in social and political practice in the subcontinent, with the state's enhanced interventions in social life. However, there was another major contributing factor to the dramatically increased complexity and scope of the political field: the logic of capital. As a direct corollary to the Indian social formation's exposure to and insertion into a burgeoning imperial economy evolved a multitude of power relationships that extended far beyond the realm of politics that had existed until that point.

Quite simply, the logic of capital became constitutive of the dynamics of power soon after the consolidation of British rule. The roles of existing social players on the Indian socio-economic stage were altered immensely; for instance, the increasing importance of usury in the Indian agrarian economy greatly enhanced the political and economic power of the *bania*.[22] The land*lord* who was transformed into land*owner* by fiat also experienced changes in status and functions.

The importance of the state grew manifold in the emergent dispensation. The landlord was transformed into landowner *by the state*, and not through a long-run process of organic economic change.[23] In no uncertain terms, the state first introduced private property in the formal, legal sense into the Indian social formation, and then directly facilitated many processes of class formation of a peculiarly colonial variety.

Colonial administrators often remained at pains to understand why land*owners* continued to function more like land*lords*. For Indians, economic efficiency and profitability was less important than sustaining political dependents. The 'meaning' of land in colonial India, encapsulated in the notion of 'land-to-rule', as opposed to the notion of 'land-to-own', persisted well into the post-colonial period.[24]

For the most part the colonial state acted in harmony with the larger imperial economy of which it was a part. Yet there remained throughout the colonial encounter a dialectical contradiction between 'order' and 'change', a feature of the post-colonial political order as well. At one level the British may have wanted to make the logic of capital dominant in the Indian social formation, but the imperative of stability – particularly after the Great Revolt in 1857 – sometimes overrode this principle. The colonial state directly facilitated the consolidation of a landed class endowed with formal property rights in Punjab and Sindh and instituted a legal framework through which land could be treated as private property in the classical, liberal guise. Yet, the same colonial state actively helped this landed class in circumventing the adverse effects of structural change through legislation such as the Punjab Alienation of Land Act 1901 and Sindh Encumbered Estates Act 1878, primarily because it feared for its own stability if its most prized allies were disenfranchised.[25]

The fact that the state had to ensure the political compliance of willing intermediaries meant that in many cases the British were impeding the same processes of social change that facilitated the consolidation of capitalism in Britain.[26]

In sum, the state and the logic of capital were both critical nodes of the 'new' political field. As a general rule, the state's power to promote or impede any particular social process was much more tangible than the 'invisible hand' of capital, although it is often difficult to separate the operation of either. In any case, the evolving configuration of social power was produced by of a unique combination of political-economic impulses deriving from the larger dynamics of a burgeoning capitalist world system and the governing impulses of the colonial state.

However, alongside the state's expanded reach and ability to foment social change, and even with the 'forcible integration of the segmentary productive regimes of rural India into an integrated economy', the internal logic of practice of Indian society was an autonomous factor in explaining the evolution of social forms and the nature of the political field.[27] The local unit of analysis in India, whether called the village or the community, featured established notions of common sense – most notably dyadic patron-client relations - which were conditioned by and conditioned the wider economic and political fields. The common sense of patron-client relations did not simply vanish following the establishment of British rule, but neither did it remain frozen in time.

I will show later in this chapter, and indeed the rest of the book, how common sense evolved over time. At this point I wish only to flag the need to pay constant attention to the conditioning role of the state and capital. Mapping the trajectory of what I call the politics of common sense is impossible without an appreciation of the dialectical relationship between accumulation of capital and accumulation of power, while recognizing that these processes of accumulation are embedded in particular cultural logics.

This analytical separation of three separate determinants of social power as it evolved beginning with the colonial period, i.e. India being inserted into the capitalist world economy; the substantially enhanced penetration of the state into social life; and political-cultural dynamics at the local level should not lend the impression that there is a simple determinism in any particular direction or that these are separate 'structures' as it were. Instead, evolving social forms and modes of politics in British India were, as they continued to be after the end of the Raj, subject to the structural constraints imposed by all three of these elements operating as a holistic and dialectical unity.[28]

The Historical Bloc

The form that this structure of power took in the post-colonial epoch is best captured by the Gramscian concept of the 'historical bloc'[29] – while Gramsci employed the term in the *Prison Notebooks* to refer to the prospective counter-hegemonic critical mass that could overturn the established structure of power, I adopt a more general reading. A historical bloc is a specific constellation of forces that has established hegemonic control at a particular conjuncture. The historical bloc can, therefore, be constituted by a cross-section of powerful actors exercising coercive control through state institutions coupled with consent at the various sites of civil society, or conversely be the counter-hegemonic critical mass to which reference was made above.

Following from this, my contention is that the long project of state formation in Pakistan did not establish rule of a particular dominant class, or even of the state as an (relatively) autonomous actor, but rather should be understood as an evolving assemblage of forces exercising power at different levels of the social formation. At the time of the country's creation, the civil bureaucracy and military assumed primacy within the historical bloc due to the specific conjuncture in which state formation took place.

As Jalal has famously pointed out, the new state's sovereignty came to be defined by its ability to develop adequate defence capacity to guard against India, which, Pakistan's state managers claimed, had not accepted the latter's existence.[30] Therefore, Pakistan retained the Raj's overbearing influence in charting the direction of the polity, economy and the social formation at large, and concocted an ideology to boot – protection of the subcontinent's Muslims from 'Hindu domination', or in other words the two-nation theory. The inordinate focus on defence had serious implications for the manner in which Pakistan was subjected to the rigours of a ruthless global economy and set the stage for its fateful alliance with the western bloc in the Cold War.

India-centrism ensured that the military came to occupy an exalted position within the polity soon after partition. Support for the 'national security' state was concentrated in northern and central Punjab and amongst Urdu-speaking migrants that had witnessed first-hand the horrors of partition violence. The sociological roots of militarism in post-colonial Pakistan can be found in the unique social contract established in colonial Punjab under the British, which I will discuss at greater length in subsequent chapters.[31] Crucially, the military's direct role in administration and its concurrent garnering of public resources was institutionalized in Punjab long before partition. This role was consolidated following the departure of the British with profound implications for the new state, the process of nation-building, and societal development.

In the immediate post-independence period, then, the civil-military apparatuses of the state arrogated to themselves the right to utilize and allocate public resources and exercise political power at will, always invoking the proverbial 'national interest' of defending the state from the ever-present threat of Indian expansionism in doing so. The undermining of the political process was both necessary and sufficient to ensure that the civil and military services established and then consolidated their power, with the balance of power within the civil-military combine shifting in favour of the latter over time. Crucial in this regard was the fact that the civil and military services were dominated by ethnic groups based in the western wing – Urdu-speakers and Punjabis most of all – to whom the prospect of a democratic political process represented a direct threat given that Bengalis based in the eastern wing constituted the ethnic majority.

The west Pakistan-dominated state bureaucracy presided over a period of intense capital accumulation, effectively concocting an industrialist class which, as a class without political power, relied entirely on state favours to prosper. Meanwhile, landed scions based largely in the western wing continued to enjoy considerable social power. The landed class dominated mainstream political parties and continued to be the major intermediary through which the state maintained social control. Even as the landed class started to suffer the transformative effects of capital's penetration into the countryside, its access to the state, ability to mediate disputes, and influence over the allocation of public resources, meant that it retained considerable political power.

Through the period before Ayub Khan's rise to power, the structure of power was centred around the ability of landed notables to engage the subordinate classes (and castes) in a politics of patronage that reinforced the governing logics institutionalized under colonialism. However, with the adoption of modernization policies by the first military regime, contradictions arose as capital penetrated farther and deeper into society. Migration, urbanization and other rapid developments gave rise to a new confrontational politics concentrated in towns and cities which led to the downfall of the Ayubian regime.[32]

As I will discuss in detail in subsequent chapters, this politics was spearheaded by industrial labour, students and, to a lesser extent, intermediate classes associated with the rapidly developing secondary and tertiary sectors of the agrarian economy. The organized labour and student movements were armed with the ideology of socialism, and spearheaded the effort to popularize a radical idiom of politics across a wide cross-section of society. While this burgeoning politics generated some real material gains for industrial workers, the peasantry and other segments of the subordinate classes, more significant was the change in the conception and practice of politics. Historically oppressed classes, castes and other segments of society could now be the subjects of a transformative politics and not bound by fate to powerful patrons acting in the name of 'tradition'.[33]

The 1970 general election marked the crystallization of the politics of class and ethnic-nationalism. While established landed aristocrats survived – some even prospered depending on their accommodation with the winning parties – there were more than just a handful of stunning victories for candidates defying status and class conventions. Both the Pakistan People's Party (PPP) and National Awami Party (NAP) – who respectively triumphed in Sindh/Punjab and NWFP/Balochistan – campaigned on broadly leftist political programmes, as did the Awami League in what was then still East Pakistan.

Held twenty-three years after independence, the country's first elections unleashed the political energies of the lower orders of society. The secession of East Pakistan proved the unviability of the *ancien* regime. The PPP came into power after the civil war and took charge of what remained of the country with both a unique opportunity and under tremendous pressure to fashion a new and democratic political dispensation.

The coalescing of progressive intellectuals, students, political activists and a cross-section of the subordinate classes had the makings of a counter-hegemonic historical bloc in its own right. There was within ruling circles and the propertied strata at large an acute fear of the leftist upsurge given the obvious potential of this constellation of progressive forces to overturn status quo. In the event, the PPP regime alienated much of its radical support base, and the left was finally crushed following the coming to power of General Zia-ul-Haq in 1977. The counter-hegemonic progressive consensus was thus unable to survive its embryonic beginnings.

The most underspecified aspect of the post-Bhutto conjuncture is the reassertion of class and state power, which I argue can be conceptualized as a reconstituted historical bloc. Tracing the constitution of this bloc and particularly the commercial middle classes and religio-political forces that were to become its major pillars demands an interrogation into the social changes that began with the Green Revolution in the 1950s and 1960s, the subject matter of Chapter 3.

Certainly the institutions of state and other dominant forces that constituted the historical bloc in 1947 have remained major players in the power game since the late 1970s. However, one of the central arguments of this book is that *the structure of power has changed and continues to evolve* with the emergence of new social and political forces.

Following the Zia junta's coming to power, it became apparent that the restoration of even a nominal democratic process would allow the transformative politics that had emerged in the preceding period to survive.

Thus, the *modus operandi* for both old and new contenders for power in the post-Bhutto period has been to prevent the re-emergence of an anti-systemic politics. In the immediate post-Bhutto period, the military regime overcame its lack of popular legitimacy by first conceiving of and then building a set of strategic alliances. This political strategy was backed up by a constant reassertion of the military's ultimate function: its coercive force.

Perhaps unsurprisingly, it was the usual suspects that were willing accomplices of the new military junta; a demoralized high bureaucracy alienated by the Bhutto regime's civil service reforms, an industrial bourgeoisie forever scarred by what it considered to be Bhutto's whimsical economic policies, and the landed class, that fit as seamlessly into Zia's schema of political engineering as it had done in all previous dispensations.[34] The Afghan War also set the stage for a consolidation of the historically consensual relationship between western imperialism and the military.

It was not all about continuity, however; it was in this period that religio-political forces garnered decisive space within the structure of power as the military junta chose to make an obscurantist Islam state ideology. The intermediate classes that had been the major protagonists in the anti-Bhutto upsurge were incorporated into the expanded historical bloc through the medium of heavily restricted local body elections, held every two years from 1979 to 1987. This allowed the military junta to garner a modicum of legitimacy whilst demobilizing class constituencies through manipulated 'democracy'.

The reconstituted historical bloc was united by the need to undermine the counter hegemonic power of the subordinate classes. This explains the remarkable stability of the Zia regime, even though it reneged on its promise of restoring democracy numerous times, beginning as early as three months after the July 1977 coup. In other words, the high bureaucracy and old propertied classes recognized that only a strong-arm period of military rule could counter the politics of class that had characterized the Bhutto years, while the Zia junta successfully co-opted new contenders for power.

The social and political logics that were institutionalized by the Zia junta, both similar and different from that which had come before, elevated the military to a position of unprecedented primary. The institution was able to use the infrastructure and resources of the state to serve its own independent corporate interests, whilst becoming the arbiter within the reconstituted historical bloc, thus occupying the most influential position in an ever expanding web of state patronage. This reassertion of the principle of 'personalization of power' which has been called the 'hallmark of Pakistan's political system' flew in the face of the more expansive mobilizations along class lines in the preceding period.[35]

In today's Pakistan *sifarish* (asking for favours) and *rishwat* (the 'payment' for favours) are commonplace. There is a certain lament about these cynical everyday practices in popular discourse, but the concern with the symptoms rarely translates into meaningful interrogation of underlying causes. In the popular memory *sifarish* and *rishwat* are attributable to a relatively recent 'cultural degeneration', in contrast to the more pristine society that apparently persisted in a bygone period. The post-Bhutto reassertion of a patronage principle in the polity, economy, and society at large is what much of this book is about. Rather than superficial 'culturalist' explanations, however, I emphasize the structural shifts that that have made *sifarish* and *rishwat* the dominant *modus operandi* in contemporary Pakistan.

I would like to reiterate here that the politics of common sense is predicated upon the state possessing the credible threat of coercion. Returning to Gramsci's schema, hegemony exists in the form of a complex dialectic of coercion and consent, in the complementary role of state as the repository of power and civil society as the terrain of common sense action. Scholars in the Arab context argue that 'the predominance of the "political" and the cruciality of the state is in some ways a function of the lack of class hegemony in society'. While it is true that no single class has been clearly dominant in Pakistan during and after the Zia years, I contend that existing power relations are hegemonic inasmuch as the politics of the subordinate classes resembles an 'anxiety from below to find a place in the complex vertical links of political power'.[36]

The post-Bhutto military regime successfully restated the idea of the state in the public mind in a manner that made it, at one and the same time, impersonal and dominant, but also accessible and personalized. In other words, for the politics of common sense to be truly hegemonic, the junta had to create a perception amongst the subordinate classes that confrontation of the kind that had become commonplace through the 1970s would be met with the severest of consequences and that relying on localized patronage networks leading to the state was 'rational' in the sense that 'class action' was unlikely to lead to a superior outcome.[37]

Common Sense: Theory and Practice

Put in another way, working people, ethnic and religious minorities and other historically excluded groups upon whose exploitation the structure of power rests have, in a manner of speaking, acceded to the prevailing rules of the game – not least of all because anti-systemic political options are few and far between. In borrowing the idea of 'common sense' from Gramsci I wish to highlight the acceptance of the lower orders of society that seeking out a patron to navigate an unjust structure of power is the way of the world – while this is a conception that is deeply-rooted and long precedes the period with which I am specifically concerned, the point to be emphasized is that the politics of patronage had to be reasserted as common sense in the face of the upsurge of radicalism in the 1960s and 1970s.

Crucial to this reassertion was the artefact of Islam, which constituted the Zia regime's *raison d'etre*. I will discuss in later chapters how religion has, over the past three decades, become both a source of social mobility and a language of legitimation. It is also worth noting that idealistic conceptions of cosmic order and morality have been associated with Islam and the Pakistan idea itself since the very inception of the state – if not before. Common sense, then, can also be said to be constitutive of this sacred genealogy, and I will return in Chapter 4 to the significance of this aspect of common sense to the relationship between religious rhetoric and changing patronage structures.

Crucially, Gramsci understood common sense not as hermetic, but as 'a product of history and a part of the historical process'.[38] The obvious implication, as I suggested earlier, is that common sense in a particular historical conjuncture contains sediments of the past and the seeds of the future. Reading between the lines one also finds that common sense is 'always half-way between folklore properly speaking and the philosophy, science, and economics of the specialists'.[39] Thus, when a particular social group, 'for reasons of submission and intellectual subordination, adopt[s] a conception which is not its own but is borrowed from another group', its 'own' conception is not evicted from the realm of consciousness, but remains dormant, the possibility of its re-emergence never completely foreclosed.[40] Throughout the *historical* process both conceptions of the world are constantly subject to mutual influence, and thus, transformation.

> ...[S]ubalterns might draw from both passive and active aspects of their culture without being entirely and permanently governed by one or the other, though negative, passive attributes [a]re likely, from the very fact of their subordination, to predominate. To put it another way, subaltern society [i]s engaged in a continuing dialectical tussle within itself, between its active and its passive voice, between acceptance and resistance, between isolation and collectivity, between disunity and cohesion.[41]

Understood thus, common sense is a complex totality, a means through which individual social actors operating as part of one or more collectivity, make sense of a historically constituted and unequal social world, a world in which a 'general direction [is] imposed on social life by the dominant fundamental group; consent is "historically" caused by the prestige (and consequent confidence) which the dominant group enjoys because of its position and function in the world of production'.[42]

Importantly, 'philosophy cannot be divorced from politics'. Further, 'philosophy in general does not in fact exist. Various philosophies or conceptions of the world exist, and one always makes a choice between them'.[43] Thus, the evolution of competing conceptions of the world and the political strategies we choose, is, in the final analysis, a function of the wider objective environment within which choices are to be made.

In the narrative presented here, the common sense of seeking out powerful patrons – which, in a predominantly agrarian social order were those who controlled land – faced a definitive challenge by the mid-1960s. Despite its internal differences, the political left posited the possibility of a world in which equal entitlements rather than personal ties to 'big men' determined one's conditions of existence.

At one level, this idea of change was completely novel inasmuch as left ideologies calling for a rejection of class, caste, gender and other social hierarchies represented a total break with the 'traditions' that made subordination appear an established fact of life. Yet, following Gramsci, at least some of the impetus for the lower orders' attraction towards the politics of the left came from within established notions of common sense. I detail in subsequent chapters how narratives of resistance that have always been part of the popular consciousness informed the political mobilizations of the 1960s and 1970s, as they do to this day.

This radical side of 'common sense' generated considerable alarm within ruling circles. For the most part scholars have emphasized the Zia regime's use of force to subdue leftist cadres, and the manner in which the 'Islamization' drive subjugated women and confessional groups outside the pale of 'official' Islam.[44] In my estimation, the most important aspect of the post-Bhutto dispensation was the rehabilitation of the submissive, patronage-based elements of common sense. Hence, by the mid-1980s, the socialist alternative which once seemed imminent had become a distant memory and the imperative of surviving the system by seeking out patrons – now of an increasingly varied character in a rapidly urbanizing society – resurfaced again as everyday common sense.

Kamran Asdar Ali's study of the Karachi Labour Movement in the early 1970s confirms how political affiliations and commitments changed dramatically for the city's working masses from the middle of that decade onwards.[45] Before the Zia period, Karachi was home to a vibrant industrial working class within which ethnic divisions were latent, but did not necessarily contradict the imperative of working class unity. From the late 1970s onwards with the decline of the left, the city has been transformed into a hotbed of ethnic conflict, in which class solidarity is but a relic of the past – indeed it is the city's working people whose guns are most often turned against one another.[46]

This is simply to say that common sense is complex and historically constituted rather than coherent and fixed. Accordingly, common sense can neither be romanticized (for representing an inclusive and egalitarian worldview) nor condemned (for being little more than 'false consciousness' and therefore containing no progressive dimension that may inform a new worldview).

While other scholars of contemporary Pakistan trying to forge new ground are not necessarily concerned with what I call common sense *per se*, locating emergent political subjectivities within the context of broader cultural, economic and political change is a shared imperative. Humeira Iqtidar, for instance, seeks to explain the 'secularizing' choices of women affiliated with religio-political organizations in the face of family and societal opposition.[47] What appear to be women's counter-intuitive decisions to veil themselves or become active with conservative organizations can, in fact, be thought of as declarations of independence in a modern world increasingly unencumbered by 'traditional' conventions.

I do not subscribe to Iqtidar's formulations – or to those of other peers to whom I have already made reference – largely because my commitment to class analysis and the potentialities for systemic transformation demand greater attention be paid to structuring forces such as state and capital. However, I share the impulse to conceptualize the political subject in ways that resonate with existing reality.

I am concerned not only with how subordinate classes understand the world, but also with why they come together – or not – and articulate a shared political project. This requires a look at how common sense has evolved over time and to trace the constant tug-of-war between competing conceptions of the world – intriguingly, dominant social forces have consistently drawn upon the same cultural repertoires of politics to reinforce their domination as social and political movements of working people have drawn upon to challenge this domination.[48]

The ability of the post-Zia historical bloc to propagate a cynical politics and delimit the imagination of an alternative social order – which is arguably the most important aspect of the politics of common sense – must be understood in holistic structural terms by reference to the state and its machinations, the intensifying penetration of capital into the social formation and to a constantly *contested* cultural toolkit.

Patronage in its Various Guises

In arguing that political order in Pakistan is structured by patronage ties, I am following in a long line of scholars of the post-colony that have both theorized political patronage and detailed its operation in a number of contexts across Asia, Africa and Latin America. A summary of this intellectual history is far too ambitious a task to try and accomplish here. While I refer below to selected scholarship, I am aided primarily by a recently published volume edited by Anastasia Pillavsky entitled *Patronage as Politics in South Asia* which brings to the fore most of the relevant debates on the subject in the South Asian context.[49] The tensions between my understanding of patronage and those presented in the above-mentioned volume help clarify the theoretical framework I employ through the course of this book as well as my understanding of how patronage structures have changed over time.

Pillavsky notes the classical features of patronage as having 'something to do with asymmetry of status and power, ...involv[ing] reciprocity, and ... rel[ying] on particular, intimate, face-to-face relations'.[50] She argues that the subject has had its heyday and is now considered somewhat passé, at least partially because the emphasis on the inequality inherent to patron-client systems means that patronage is often thought of, explicitly or otherwise, as 'a bad thing'.

Pillavsky correctly points out that this 'deeply ingrained moral aversion to patronage has frustrated the task of understanding it'.[51] However, time and again throughout both the introduction and the various case studies that constitute the volume, it is the dominant 'liberal-democratic' framework that is said to impede meaningful study of patronage, a framework of analysis in which patronage is either considered a residue of a pre-modern past and/ or evidence of the failure of the state to institutionalize the basic precepts of political modernity.

What gets lost in this otherwise accurate critique of the liberal academy is the fact that there have also been studies of patronage, its structural roots and the political subjectivities that are constructed around it, from more radical perspectives. Other than a brief, derisory mention of Marxist-inspired studies of patronage, the volume is generally silent on the linkages between patron-client relations at the micro-level and the dynamics of state power, capitalism and so on. For Pillavsky and other contributors to the volume, patronage is singularly a '*moral idiom* (emphasis in original)... an imperfect gloss for a widespread moral formulation which helps us escape the gridlock of liberal political heuristics and see the local actors' own normative imagination'.[52]

This book too presents a narrative outside the dominant liberal framework and with an emphasis on the objective worlds and subjective political choices of ordinary people, particularly those who function as 'clients' in the patron-client dyad. While I acknowledge that questions of inequality and power do not exhaust the discussion on patronage, it is nevertheless undeniable that these questions are central to the discussion, as much today as in the past.

That the imperative of a 'moral economy' have been at work at various times in both western and non-western societies is a generally accepted fact.[53] Yet, whatever the context, there is little evidence to suggest that subordinate classes have ever been ignorant of the inegalitarian and unjust nature of the social world that they inhabit. There have, after all, been innumerable revolts against authority throughout the history of settled society.

Pillavsky et al have chosen to focus on the moral discourses that circulate about patrons in society, whilst noting that these discourses rarely correspond to the reality of how powerful patrons operate in practice: 'To satisfy the patronal ideal, patrons must betray it'.[54] This dialectic is at the heart of Pillavsky et al argument, many aspects of which I share, particularly their detailing of how the actually existing political field functions as a personalized and permeable field of exchange rather than an impersonal legal-rational order *a la* Weber.

Taken out of its historical context, however, the accent of this argument changes entirely. A recent study on patronage in the Attock district of Pakistani Punjab would suggest that 'clients' are quite content to reinforce the unequal nature of their relationship with patrons:

> The majority of villagers have a vested interest in seeing the status quo maintained since it is through networks that problems are solved in Pakistan – not through laws or policies. A poor man who is the servant of an influential and powerful landlord is far better off than a poor man who is the servant of another poor man. Villagers reinforce the power of their landlords not because they are forced to do so, but because they can see the benefit of doing so.[55]

Such an exclusive emphasis on the 'positive', including performative, aspects of the patronage-based political order in South Asia betrays the fact that this order is not static, and has in fact undergone tremendous change over a prolonged period of time. Most importantly, ordinary people have had to adapt to the machinations of state, empire, and propertied classes. This is not to suggest that the lower orders of society should only be characterized by epithets such as 'oppressed' and 'subjugated'. However, patron-client ties are constitutive of the structure of power, and unpacking this structure is impossible without acknowledgment of the inegalitarian bases of patronage.

Most scholars of patron-client systems concur that modernity has transformed the structural basis of these systems. In terms of the colonial transformation (outlined above), the penetration of the state and capital into the social formation necessarily impacted the established logic of practice, and therefore, the political action of both dominant and subordinate classes.

The classical modernization theories (including orthodox Marxism) posited that the transformation of non-western societies would follow the broad pattern of Western Europe and North America. Hence, in part because of the 'push' provided by colonialism, non-western societies would eventually converge towards the compact modern social form – impersonal capitalist markets, legal-rational political systems and *Gessellschaft*.

In the 1960s and 1970s, when the newly independent countries appeared to 'stagnate', Weberians revamped earlier culturalist arguments, whereas Marxists asserted that the transition to capitalism was prolonged (due either to the machinations of imperialism or endogenous constraints, or a combination of both). Acknowledgment of the uniqueness of non-western modernity came much later – there now appears to be some begrudging consensus that the impersonal transactional practices of the western prototype did not, and probably will not, replace patronage-based social exchanges.

It was in order to fill the vacuum created by this failed prediction of modernization theorists that novel schools of thought such as the Subaltern Studies emerged. The appeal of the Subaltern claim that the nature and exercise of power in India (and other non-western societies) must be conceptualized in distinct ways from the history and trajectory of power in Europe is undeniable. Yet, neither modernization theory nor the 'culturalist' frameworks that have risen to prominence in the contemporary period are adequate to comprehend the dynamism of social forms that we encounter in today's post-colonial societies.

So, for instance, while on the one hand state personnel in Pakistan often espouse a rhetorical commitment to the principles of Weberian rationality – especially insofar as maintenance of the state's coercive apparatus is essential to the reproduction of power relations – on the other hand it is the (often illicit) access of dominant groups to state resources that greatly increases their power to act as dispensers of patronage across society.[56] This dialectic is neither an immutable cultural fact nor a question of institutional failure, but rather to be explained by the historical-structural patterns imposed by state and capital.

In a study of patronage and electoral practice in *both* India and England, Gilmartin finds that the idea of 'legitimate' influence – what was effectively political patronage – was prominent in both contexts, and was even written into law.[57] This implies that patron-client ties are not ahistorical cultural artefacts but a set of practices that have been significantly shaped by the technologies of the modern – both western and non-western – state.

Scholars such as Pillavsky et al tend to emphasize – implicitly or otherwise – the continuity of patron-client relations inasmuch as social and political exchanges appear to revolve around a deeply-rooted cultural logic. In fact, there has been a profound transformation in the basis of patron-client relations, both because of the deepening of capitalism and the legal, economic and administrative initiatives of the (post) colonial state.[58]

In this book, I highlight how the subordinate classes have acceded to a cynical patronage politics that has facilitated the consolidation of the historical bloc in the post-Bhutto period. Fundamental changes have taken place in the structure of society over the years which have shaped the evolution of an historically contingent politics of patronage, both as a strategic imposition 'from above' as well as a set of political choices 'from below'.

Conventionally, exchange relationships in the market are often understood as 'calculable, noncommittal and single-shot' exchanges focused exclusively on securing economic benefits.[59] In fact, market exchange in Pakistan often resembles a political relationship in which long-term considerations of both material and non-material kinds are operative. Yet in the final analysis, 'politics becomes a kind of business… is reduced to economics and recovers the depersonalized character inherent in the market'.[60]

In other words, starting with the Zia period the historical bloc has cultivated a complex relationship with the wider social formation, propagating a politics that has some bases in personal exchange relationships that persist from the pre-colonial period, but also changing forms and practices of the state, and evolving class relations. In doing so it has reinforced the historical pattern whereby – as Medard suggests is the case in the post-colonial African context – 'it is political resources which give access to economic resources'.[61]

Importantly, the subordinate classes have acceded to the politics of common sense knowing that it is a cynical 'exchange of organizational muscle for material benefits and is readily renegotiated if clients (or indeed entire factions) are offered better terms by other patrons or higher-level factions'.[62] Thinking about common sense politics in this way, I seek to show that working people accept the logic of the prevailing political field, but in a reflexive manner, which always leaves open the possibility of rebelling against it.

State, Capital and Patron-client Relations

In his recent formulation of subaltern politics in India, Partha Chatterjee has argued that 'institutions of the state, or at least governmental agencies (whether state or non-state), have become internal aspects of the [subaltern] community'.[63] By implication, in the early years after the end of colonial rule, and therefore necessarily during the British period as well, the state and/or governmental technologies were external to the worldview of working people. As noted earlier, I believe that institutions of the state transformed modes of social and political exchange during the colonial encounter itself. It is therefore difficult to maintain the claim that the 'subaltern community' was untouched by the state's role as mediator of disputes, repository of coercion, and guarantor/beneficiary of the codified private property regime.

Chatterjee argues that working people have learned to negotiate with the post-colonial state for a share of governmental welfare in the last three decades. However, an increasingly large body of scholarship has emphasized that ordinary Indians – or at least groups of Indians – were negotiating with the colonial state on the basis of ascribed caste (and tribal, linguistic, religious, etc.) identity soon after the creation of the 'ethnographic state'.[64] Whether they were negotiating for a share of public services which they understood to be their 'right' or they were simply coming into contact with the coercive and revenue-extracting arms of the colonial state is an important distinction. However, this does not take away from the fact that the state was entrenched within the worldview of the subordinate classes.

Scholars have drawn attention to the British obsession with classifying the Indian population – primarily through the census – so as to neatly separate Indians into ordered groups that could be administered efficiently.[65] The logic of maintaining public order in the aftermath of the Great Revolt of 1857 underlay this obsession. I wish to emphasize the dynamic reactions that this classification induced, and particularly the manner in which identities such as religion, caste, *biraderi*, *qaum*, etc. were forever politicized.

The nature of the British ethnographic exercise differed considerably within India. The areas that became part of modern-day Pakistan were all annexed to the Empire in and around the 1857 Revolt. Among the more significant and well documented impacts of this rather late insertion into the imperial body politic was the co-option of Punjabis and Pakhtuns into the British Indian Army. However, the state also modelled a new hydraulic society in central Punjab, upper Sindh and the Peshawar Valley by building a network of perennial irrigation canals between the 1880s and the first three decades of the twentieth century.[66] All this was accompanied by an extraordinary level of mapping and a reification of tribe similar to that of caste in eastern and northern India.

'British perceptions of north-western Indian social formations as primarily tribal and the subsequent ordering of the colonial state's patronage system to fit that definition created a vested interest in 'tribalism' even among clans more akin to the looser *biraderi* structures'.[67] In other words the state's insistence on forcing every Indian to fit within a particular classificatory scheme was not just passively accepted by Indians. It became clear that there were certain benefits to be garnered by being classified in particular ways.

Recent empirical work on the responses to the 1901 Punjab Alienation of Land Act is telling in this regard. Analyses of colonial reports detailing various aspects of land use and revenue collection in the canal colonies of western Punjab have established that eleven per cent of the population formally designated as 'non-agricultural' was successfully able to manipulate caste identity and acquire land by posing as 'agriculturalists'.[68]

A considerable literature on various African societies also indicates that the political strategies of the subordinate classes were highly responsive to colonial governmental technologies. Many scholars have discussed the attempts of the colonial state in African to employ 'custom' as a technology of rule and the responses these attempts engendered from local populations. These responses were not always uniform, but the net effect of the state's ordering pattern was the evolution of complex and perennially contested identity forms and patterns of social and political exchange.[69]

There is now a substantial body of literature that has built upon and critiqued the seminal theses of the 'invention of tradition'. The consensus appears to be that tradition was neither completely invented nor remained immune to the machinations of the modern (colonial) state.[70] Most of this literature problematizes terms such as 'tribe', 'caste', and 'ethnicity', but largely in terms of how the colonial state employed such identities and how the 'colonized' negotiated them. I believe it necessary to disaggregate the 'colonized' and establish how the subordinate classes – as opposed to dominant or intermediate classes – employed such identities (or not as the case may be).

The existing literature suggests that the political alignments of the subordinate classes were for the most part encapsulated within vertical identities. Subordinate classes had the option to either revolt against this oppressive order – Guha's well-known trichotomy of *sarkar, zamindar, sahurkar* – or survive within it. Revolt necessarily required that objective and subjective conditions conspire at particular historical conjunctures. Hence, common sense for the most part demanded that the subordinate classes learn the ropes of the system. I will argue through the course of this book that the state and propertied classes have consistently attempted to make it common sense for the subordinate classes to cultivate vertical relationships with caste, tribal, and *biraderi* super ordinates.

Even as the significance of ascriptive identities has changed in conjunction with the deepening of capital and urbanization, the established political order continues to reward, or at the very least provide some relief to, those embedded in patronage networks. Patrons apparently provide the best means of mediation with the state and the powerful more generally, as well as some facilitation in eking out subsistence under the constraints of the capitalist market.

The colonial intrusion forever transformed the patterns of social and political exchange by establishing a new political-economic structure represented by the colonial state and the (sometimes invisible) logic of capital. I believe that patrons (dominant social groups) were empowered decisively; first because the means of extra-economic coercion were enhanced (in the sense that established moral authority as well as the means of violence at the disposal of dominant groups were now reinforced by the coercive apparatus of the colonial state); and second because of the increasingly ubiquitous economic coercion of the market.

In this incredibly complex world the 'traditional' role of the patron became a self-fulfilling prophecy due to his ability to negotiate with the state and provide some respite from the vagaries of the market. Importantly, the analytical divide between extra-economic and economic coercion was decisively blurred. This was far from a 'failure' of the modernizing project; indeed 'colonialism could continue as a relation of power in the subcontinent only on the condition that the colonizing bourgeoisie should fail to live up to its own universalist project. The nature of the state it had created by the sword made this historically necessary'.[71]

As I hope to make clear in the next few chapters, there is no utility to establishing a binary of 'traditional' and 'modern' patron-client relations. Instead, it is necessary to understand how the patronage principle has ebbed and flowed as a organizing principle of modern rule. I wish to emphasize the social changes and political vicissitudes that led to the rise of a decidedly radical politics by the late 1960s to challenge the 'traditional' patron-client regime, the subsequent undermining of this politics, and finally the re-emergence of a regenerated patronage principle. In charting these ebbs and flows, I will foreground the deepening of capital within the social formation and the state's invasive (yet increasingly fragmented) role in almost all realms of social and political exchange.

As I have already pointed out, I am not claiming that – in Pillavsky's words – there is only a 'bad', oppressive side to patronage. I agree – and will show – that there are liberating dimensions of common sense through history that motivate progressive political strategies. Yet, there is little doubt that somewhat romantic accounts of patronage neglect the fact that it is, after all, a major plank of an exclusionary structure of power, and that the otherwise elective choices made by the lower orders of society to seek out patrons have to be put into their wider structural context.

It is to the state-centric structure of power that I turn next. In the final analysis, the state remains the repository of power in society and therefore the lynchpin of the patronage-based political order. The British institutionalized 'bureaucratic paternalism', and their protégé Pakistani high functionaries – civil and military – sought to ensure both that the politics of patronage remained supreme and that the state remained the primary dispenser of patronage. In the next chapter, I will trace how and why the state has remained so powerful – both as a material reality and as an ideological artefact – and thereby been at the heart of the politics of common sense.

To a large extent, the state apparatus has relied on the wilful support of propertied classes, both the mythical landed elite as well as big business based primarily in urban centres. I will demonstrate both how this consensus has developed and how it is punctuated by periodic crises, and the 'civil-military' conflict most of all. The social and economic changes of the past few decades have forever changed the constitution, interests and posture of the *ancien regime*, yet I will show that the 'old' propertied classes remain very much in the mix in collusion with the state despite the growing body of evidence (and commentary) that the latter is fragmenting, particularly in the neo-liberal era.

The 'old' propertied elite has been joined in the post-1977 period in what I have termed a 'reconstituted historical bloc' by segments of the intermediate classes that have risen to prominence with the growth of secondary and tertiary sectors of the agrarian economy, and subsequent processes of urbanization. The intermediate classes are arguably the most conspicuous symbols of the wider process of 'nativization' – that is the rise of vernacular or non-Anglicized political and economic interests – of the structure of power. Chapter 3 provides an overview of the broader economic and social changes that explain the rise of the intermediate classes, as well as the strategies that the latter employ to both accumulate power and capital which mark them out as the new patrons-of-choice for the subordinate classes.

In Chapter 4, I turn to an account of the other entrant into the reconstituted historical bloc, the religious right. While much of the chapter recounts the state patronage offered to the right-wing during the Zia years, and the manner in which it has become the face of 'defence of Islam' campaigns that have been ever-present since 1947, I also consider the longer-term cultural and political effects of the Zia regime's 'Islamization'. I develop a sociological account of the 'culture of politics' that has been championed by the right-wing and establish that this 'culture' is not at all contradictory to the politics of patronage. Finally I critically interrogate right-wing populism, and compare it to the left-wing upsurge of the previous period.

Throughout Pakistan's history, ethnic-nationalist movements have constituted the most vocal and organized form of resistance to the prevailing structure of power. The unitary state nationalist ideology built around the construct of 'Islam' has been consistently refuted by ethnic-nationalists who have demanded that Pakistan's identity be understood not as a unitary, religious one, but as an amalgam of diverse ethnic-linguistic groups with distinctive histories and cultures. In Chapter 5, I discuss the ethnic-nationalist politics of identity which remains the most potent anti-status quo form in Pakistan; Critical interrogation of ethnic-nationalism, however, confirms that it coincides for large segments of historically oppressed ethnic groups with the politics of common sense.

Finally, in Chapter 6, I discuss the heyday of radical politics in which class and ethnic-nationalist movements enjoyed substantial influence and the prevailing structure of power faced a systemic challenge. Even after the suppression of this transformative politics, and the subsequent institutionalization of a rehabilitated patronage machine, there was to be no return to 'traditional' alignments on the basis of ascriptive ties. Nevertheless, the Ziaist interregnum had deep impacts on many aspects of public culture which explain the relative stability of the politics of common sense. I offer in this chapter an interpretation of the coercion-consent dialectic in terms of various strategies and tactics of the subordinate classes in their engagement and periodic confrontation with dominant forces.

In the epilogue I offer some impressions on the future of the historical bloc and prospects for change. I return to the question of contradictions within the structure of power, particularly along the civil-military and westernized-vernacular fault lines, as well as the potentialities for a counter-hegemonic politics of our time.

Endnotes

1. Gramsci (1971: 9).
2. See, for instance, Lieven (2013).
3. Harvey (2005).
4. Toor (2011).
5. Jalal (1995); Tudor (2013).
6. For everyday state and society, see Fuller and Harris (2001); for informality see http://nceuis.nic.in/
7. I am influenced in this respect by the call for a 'critical cultural political economy'. See Sayer (2001).
8. Waseem (2002); Jalal (1990).
9. Gramsci (1971: 325–08).
10. Crehan (2013: 106).
11. Steinmetz (1999); Sharma and Gupta (2006).
12. Kaviraj (2005).
13. Spencer (1997).
14. For a good recent attempt to understand the post-colonial state and political economy of Pakistan (and India), see Amin-Khan (2012).
15. Hull (2012).
16. Khan (2009).
17. For most of Pakistan's history, the region adjacent to Kashmir was called the 'Federally Administered Northern Areas'; in 2009 it name was formally changed to Gilgit-Baltistan.
18. Ali (2008).
19. Kaviraj (2005a: 263).
20. Just as it is important to steer clear of unchanging and reified notions of bounded village economies, it is vital to avoid a parallel cultural or political construction of pre-British community. Sarkar (2000: 246–08) has noted that revisionist colonial historiography such as Subaltern Studies has romanticized notions of 'community'. In fact, before and even during British rule, there existed highly variegated forms of social organization across different regions of the subcontinent.
21. Invoking the state has a direct impact on 'informal' institutions, typically enhancing the bargaining power of one or both parties to the dispute. See Chaudhary (1999: 77–81) for a discussion on this dynamic of 'formal' and 'informal' mechanisms of justice in post-colonial Punjab.

22. Habib (1995: 334).
23. It can be argued that modern capitalism in Europe was the culmination of an organic process of societal change that that was spread out over hundreds of years. The modern western state developed alongside the capitalist mode of production. Conversely, the colonial state itself shaped the development of capitalism in non-western contexts.
24. Neale (1969).
25. Gilmartin (1988); Ansari (1992); (Nelson 2011).
26. Ali (2003).
27. Kaviraj (1994: 53).
28. Wacquant (1985) has coined the term 'organic causality' to capture this holism.
29. 'Structures and superstructures form an "historical bloc"...[there is a] necessary reciprocity between structure and superstructure, a reciprocity which is nothing other than the real dialectical process' (Gramsci, 1971: 366).
30. Jalal (1990).
31. Tan (2005).
32. Zaidi (2005a); Sayeed (1980).
33. Jones (2003).
34. Waseem (1994: 360–09).
35. Shafqat (1997: 82).
36. Ayubi (1995: 169–73).
37. Khan (2000: 576).
38. Gramsci (1971: 326).
39. Ibid, 326.
40. Ibid, 328.
41. Arnold (1984: 30).
42. Gramsci (1971: 12).
43. Gramsci (1971: 327).
44. See, for example, Weiss (2001) and Esposito (1988).
45. Ali (2005).
46. See also Laurent Gayer's (2014) excellent book on Karachi which meticulously documents the manner in which left-right political alignments in the 1960s and 1970s gave way to an ethnicized political environment from the 1980s onwards.
47. Iqtidar (2013).
48. 'In reality, contemporary cultures of the state are created by all social actors, including those from "below", even if their contribution does not necessarily contradict that of the powerful' (Bayart, 1991: 65).
49. Pillavsky (2014).
50. Ibid. 5.
51. Ibid.
52. Ibid. 4.
53. Thompson (1971); Scott (1976).
54. Pillavsky (2014: 25).

55. Lyon (2002: 184–05).
56. See Bayart (1993) for an exposition of similar processes in post-colonial Africa.
57. Gilmartin (2014).
58. For a detailed discussion of the class basis of patron-client relationships in the South Asian context, see Khan (1998; 2000).
59. Gellner (1977: 5–6).
60. Medard (1982: 181).
61. Ibid.
62. Khan (2000: 580).
63. Chatterjee (2008: 4).
64. Dirks (2001).
65. See Cohn (1996).
66. Ali (1988); Haines (2013).
67. Jalal (1995: 218).
68. Cassan (2011).
69. Berry (1992); Mamdani (1996).
70. Ranger and Hobsbawm (1983); Spear (2003).
71. Guha (1997: 64).

2

The Structure of Power 'From Above'

Scholarship on the Pakistan state in particular and the structure of power 'from above' more generally has historically centred around a handful of themes, including, but not limited to, the dominance of military over civilian apparatuses; an ethnically skewed structure of power; state sovereignty in the face of consistent intervention by foreign powers; and the fortunes of landed and other propertied classes.[1] At various points in the country's history, hypotheses about the very viability and continued existence of the state have also come to the fore.[2]

In this chapter, I develop a historical-sociological sketch of the Pakistan state and the propertied classes, building upon the theoretical foundations laid out in the introductory chapter. My basic argument is that though the structure of power in Pakistan appears to remain centred around the 'steel frame' established by the British, substantial changes have taken place over the past few decades that demand fresh interrogation of the institutional dynamics of the state as well as its sociological composition. In similar vein, the mythical 'feudal' elite of the British era has been significantly affected by the process of social change, to the point that classical characterizations of Pakistan's political economy are now largely obsolete.

Put simply, the structure of power in Pakistan as it has evolved since the later 1970s is far more complex than most mainstream scholarship suggests. For all the change that has taken place, however, the story that I tell in this chapter is also about continuity. Despite its increasingly fragmentary character, the state remains the repository of power in society, both because state functionaries continue to mediate access to political and economic resources, and due to the (coercive, economic and discursive) control exercised by what is often called the 'military establishment'. Even the propertied classes, therefore, perceive their interests to be served by proximity – and often deference – to an entrenched state apparatus.

As noted in the introductory chapter, the specific focus of this book is to explicate how Pakistan's patronage-based political order has undergone change, particularly since the late 1970s. It follows that there is a need to think much more deeply about how the structure of power operates 'from below' than most academic literature has traditionally done.[3]

An analytical engagement with the structure of power 'from below' cannot, however, take the place of more traditional concerns with the state, propertied classes and geo-politics. The theoretical tools that I borrow from Gramsci allow for a holistic framework that builds upon classical treatments and introduces new insights 'from below'.

I start with the seminal neo-Marxist treatise about Pakistan's structure of power written and developed in the 1970s and early 1980s. I then show how the existing state and structure of power 'from above' has evolved over the past few decades, and particularly what the patronage-based political order fashioned under the British – featuring both state institutions and 'big men' – looks like today. Finally, I discuss the military institution that emerged out of the shadow of the civil services to become the arbiter of power in Pakistan.

Classical Beginnings

Some forty-five years to the good, Hamza Alavi's pioneering theory of the 'overdeveloped' state continues to be amongst the most invoked theoretical and empirical statements on post-colonial Pakistan. Although state theory has come a long way since Alavi's writings, it is true that the 'overdeveloped' formulation *appears* to be remarkably resilient after all this time; at the very least, there have been very few substantive attempts over the decades to move beyond Alavi's theorization of the structure of power.[4]

Alavi's basic contention is that the post-colonial state is a primarily coercive apparatus directly inherited from the Raj – what he terms the all-powerful 'military-bureaucratic oligarchy'.[5] The oligarchy mediates the interests of three dominant classes, namely the landed class, the indigenous bourgeoisie, and the metropolitan bourgeoisie, while funnelling a major proportion of surplus to itself under the guise of 'development'.

For my purposes, what stands out about Alavi's theory is the characterization of society – including its dominant classes – as 'underdeveloped' *vis-a-vis* the state. This makes the formulation extremely functional and also very static inasmuch as it cannot account for the dynamism of a society that has undergone tremendous change. Even more problematic is the lack of explanation for why the structure of power is resilient, or in other words how it is legitimated 'from below'.

While Alavi improves upon the original 'overdeveloped' formulation in more empirical accounts that acknowledge transformations in class and other social structures, these empirical insights have not informed attempts to revise the theoretical formulation.[6] The focus remains on a narrative 'from above' and, therefore, the functionalist essence of the theory intact.

Similar formulations were put forth by many of Alavi's contemporaries in detailing the nature of the post-colonial state in Africa, all of which emphasized the competition between so called bureaucratic and petty bourgeoisies for control over the state, thereby suggesting that these constituted the dominant classes in most post-colonial social formations.[7] The state in this conception remains a primarily coercive apparatus, 'relatively autonomous' from society.[8] Thus, the question of legitimation of authority is underspecified in favour of a narrow theoretical emphasis on dominant class and institutional interests.

Ahmad's insightful formulation at least brings the political economy of dominant groups into greater focus.[9] He argues that the 'state bourgeoisie' steadily accumulates capital alongside the expansion of state power and functions. This state bourgeoisie follows in the footsteps of its colonial predecessor and is concerned first and foremost with consolidating its political power which in turn is a pre-condition for the enhancement of material interests.

In short, the dynamics of statecraft in colonial conditions are such that proximity to state power and resources conditions the accumulation of capital more generally, a point that I flagged in the introductory chapter. I would like to add that this dialectic of accumulating state power and capital means that that it is the norm for individual state functionaries to use their positions of influence to benefit themselves and their preferred choice of political clients.

This is not to suggest that the state has no coherence whatsoever. Much like its colonial predecessor, which endowed itself with the power to designate when and where it would allow the unfettered operation of capital, the Pakistan state has attempted to 'guide' the processes of class formation and social change.[10] Its ability to manipulate these larger processes – while never complete – has lessened over time, particularly with the imposition of neo-liberal policy dictates since the 1980s. Capital has penetrated deeper into Pakistan's society and has started to evince greater autonomy from the state, and the latter has appeared to fragment. Yet, state functionaries – if not the state as a coherent whole – are as influential as they have ever been.

In short, the kind of patronage politics that has become hegemonic since the late 1970s is built upon the axis of the state – both in its formal and informal manifestations. I will discuss below how the sociological and institutional bases of the state have changed over time. I first provide a snapshot of the wider social context within which the state has maintained centrality over the *longue durée*, and how this context has been transformed in recent decades.

'Big Men', Land and Social Transformation

The role of 'big men' in patronage based socio-political orders has been written about extensively across disciplinary boundaries. Much of the colonial project itself was designed and executed on the basis of assumptions about social and political norms operative within what was considered a relatively static, rural society. As long as colonialism remained intact, the classic orientalist caricature of India being a conglomeration of self-sufficient village republics endured. Given the significance of land on the socio-political landscape of colonial India the landed head of the village was designated as 'big man' of choice.[11]

To be sure, direct or indirect control over land which was the primary productive resource and an autonomous source of social prestige and power in a predominantly rural society was always going to be as crucial as any other single factor in determining the colonial configuration of power.[12] The protective measures undertaken by the British *vis-a-vis* their landed allies ensured that the latter were very favourably disposed towards the state. These landed castes and classes – colonial paternalism targeted not only 'big feudals' but also smaller proprietors hailing from 'agricultural castes' – were aware that the British needed their support to ensure the survival of colonialism in India, and that the colonial state in turn insulated them from the adverse effects of a deepening capitalism. The two allies had, in a manner of speaking, intertwining spheres of influence; the colonial administrators dealt with matters of policy, defence, economic management and revenue collection, whereas the rural notables had considerable freedom to adjudicate on local disputes: 'For *haris* and smallholders, *Waderos* were the real power in the land. The British authority, with its police and law courts, was remote, spiritually and also physically'.[13]

This is not to suggest that the relationship between civil administrators and landed notables was seamless.[14] There were conflicts, especially where landed notables insisted on more autonomy than state institutions were willing to concede.[15] In the final analysis, however, the state and landed notables were hand-in-glove, and this was no more evident than in the cooperation between the district administration and the landed influential(s) of the district: 'This two-pronged political system – feudalism and colonial bureaucracy – engendered a relatively permanent hierarchy within the community and centralized the political control of the bureaucracy'.[16]

The influence of landed notables endured into the post-colonial period. The new state inherited both the granary of the subcontinent – namely the canal colony regions in central Punjab – as well as the areas from which the majority of the military was recruited in the Punjab and NWFP, which meant that the authoritarian nexus of landed notables/upper peasantry and the civil-military 'steel frame', as discussed in the previous chapter, became the major edifice of an emergent post-colonial political economy.

Prior to Bhutto's civil service reforms of the 1970s, 'few individuals from non-landed families achieved prominence in government decision-making as either civilian or military bureaucrats; wealth in land, or some relation to wealth in land, appear(ed) to be a major, but not the only, requisite for political elite standing'.[17]

In the early years of Pakistan's existence, established landed families did not benefit from discriminatory legislation of the kind that the British had previously instituted to protect them from increasing exposure to the rigours of an ever-expanding international division of labour, at least insofar as industrialization became the stated objective of economic policy. However, the combination of landed notables' proclivity towards administrative rule and the fear of power shifting to the eastern wing in the event of countrywide elections reinforced the alliance between the highest echelons of the bureaucracy and the landed class.[18]

Following Ayub Khan's coup much was made of the 1959 land reforms that allegedly sought to break the back of 'big feudals' and promote a new capitalist farmer that harboured 'modern' sensibilities.[19] In the final analysis, however, the reforms did not greatly alter the dynamic of power in the rural social formation. Rather than enfranchising landless tenants (who had to pay for what land they did receive), the regime only succeeded in modestly reducing the size of the largest landholdings. Less than 1.3 per cent of total land was resumed – of which only a fraction was actually cultivable – with evasions commonplace.[20]

More substantial change was precipitated by Green Revolution technologies that were introduced progressively throughout the Ayub period, namely high-yield varieties of seeds, fertilizers, pesticides as well as farm machinery.

Established landed interests adapted to, and benefited from, the many changes that took place under the guise of the Green Revolution.[21] However, there were broader multiplier effects that had major long-term impacts on rural class relations and society at large – starting with the displacement of sharecropping tenants and their migration away from the rural farm economy.

Towards the end of the Ayub's dictatorship, the wider impacts of modernization and the increased availability of alternative livelihood sources for previously dependent sharecroppers started to become apparent in both rural and urban areas. The most lasting outcome was the emergence of commercially-minded 'intermediate' classes that were to become the face of the politics of common sense in decades to come. More immediately, a new, primarily urban, oppositional politics that broke with the established order came dramatically to the fore.

I will detail the sociology of the intermediate classes – and the popular political upsurge – in the chapters that follow. For the present purposes, while it can be reasonably argued that 'little was done to correct the politics of landholding and the influence of the landed class remained virtually unchecked' during the course of Ayub Khan's decade in power, a process of social transformation had been initiated that would not be reversed.[22]

The social change that began with the Green Revolution has, over time, led to a diversification of 'big men', with urban and rural capitalists of various shapes and sizes emerging to both complement and challenge the 'traditional' landed class. In a rapidly urbanizing society, the economic value of land as real estate has increased dramatically and in fact made it more of a marker of political power than ever before. In short, those who control land continue to exercise political influence.

Meanwhile, the formal state's control over land – and revenue from it – has waned considerably as capitalist modernity takes on an increasingly urban, service-dominated face. Yet, state functionaries continue to play a mediating role in land markets, which is to say that change has substantially impacted the state without necessarily reducing its centrality to political order in Pakistan. It is to the shape and form of an increasingly informalized state that I turn next.

An Anthropology of the State[23]

In trying to conceptualize the role of the state in Pakistan, and particularly its centrality to the politics of common sense, I think it is important to take into account the critical insights of theorists who seek to demystify the state and uncover 'the mask which prevents our seeing political practice as it is'.[24] In short, there is a case to be made for the conceptual blurring of the traditional state-society divide. However, this conceptual blurring is useful only insofar as the discursive construction of the state is linked to material realities. In other words, discourse is not separable from the nature and operation of state power (and its interrelationship with class and other forms of power). If the material and ideational power of the actually existing state are not understood thoroughly and dialectically, much more is obfuscated than illuminated.[25]

This was made clear to me by an informant from a *katchi abadi* in Islamabad during a brutal eviction that took place in July 2015. As his home was being demolished Niaz Ali noted:

> These people [the low-level state functionaries bulldozing the mud houses] are from within us (*hum me se hain*) and in normal times (*aam haalat mei*) interact with us very differently, but when they put on their uniforms they become almost possessed (*weshi ban jate hain*) and treat us like we are the scum of the earth. How is it that someone from our own class becomes our mortal enemy (*jani dushman*)?

Based largely on the Indian experience, a burgeoning literature has developed on the 'everyday state' which focuses on the routinized negotiations between ordinary people and state functionaries.[26] This body of work has added a great deal of insight into the actual workings of power at the micro-level, as well as how ordinary people experience and perceive the state.

For my purposes this literature is particularly useful because it can shed light on how oppressive structures of power are propped up 'from below', replete with contradictions and crises. So, for instance, Niaz Ali's insights confirm that the traditional state-society binary is indeed blurred insofar as state functionaries at the lower levels hail from very similar backgrounds to the working people with whom they come into contact, thereby facilitating social and political exchanges like *rishwat* and *sifarish* that constitute contemporary common sense. Yet, Niaz Ali also emphasizes that these same state functionaries can, in many circumstances, use their authority to target the poor and voiceless despite their shared class backgrounds.

In focusing on the 'blurred' everyday and discursive realms we must not lose sight of the fact that state functionaries often act to sustain a strict state-society binary, at least as far as the subordinate classes are concerned. State functionaries exercise power, but do so discriminately, often exempting the rich and powerful from the censure and violence that is regularly meted out to those without requisite 'connections' within the state apparatus.

Below I disaggregate the real state into high and low bureaucracies, in part to highlight the varying practices of state functionaries *vis-a-vis* different classes, ethnic groups and so on. Historically, the personnel who comprise the state at the higher and lower echelons have tended to hail from distinct class and ethnic backgrounds, which partly explains the differences in self-perception and daily practice of high and low bureaucracies. In suggesting the need for a dichotomous conceptualization of the real state, I am also calling attention to the fact that formal policies enacted in the higher echelons rarely resemble the actual practice of the state at the lower level.

This dichotomy in how the state actually works has a parallel in the framing of the 'state-idea' by working people; on the one hand the state is inaccessible and all-powerful, on the other it is permeable and personalized (albeit oppressive when necessary). Accordingly, an idealized and abstract conception of the state is sustained alongside the real practices of the low bureaucracy with which working people are familiar.[27] I believe that dominant forces have, particularly in the post-1977 period, consistently attempted to maintain this material and discursive dichotomy as a fundamental building block of common sense politics.

In related vein, there is now growing recognition amongst scholars of the post-colony that the real state is characterized by fragmentation and possibly even complete incoherence inasmuch as class or institutional fractions articulate competing goals. There are, therefore, many 'unintended consequences' of established policy frameworks.[28] I agree that civilian state institutions in Pakistan have over the years become less coherent both in the design of policy and everyday functioning. Yet, this increasing 'fragmentation' has been coeval with the relatively calculated institutionalization of a project of organized power in the post-1977 period that I call the politics of common sense.

I quote, at length, an anthropologist of urban politics in Karachi to make my point clearer:

> Rather than looking at the state as an autonomous, unified and monitoring agency, it appears more fruitful to study the state as a particular part of society that is characterized by a relatively high degree of political activities, including competition over resources, exchange of information, ideological debates, and the use of physical coercion. One should not merely look for

causes of this increasing fragmentation of the state in the state apparatus itself, but rather take it as a reflection of a more far-reaching transition of society at large.[29]

This complexity of power relations means that state institutions (or functionaries) and propertied classes (or individuals hailing from these classes) can never mute any and all potential challenges to their dominance, and the 'vigorous self-activating culture of the people [that] constitutes an ever-present threat to official descriptions of reality'.[30] I outline in this and later chapters exactly how this dialectic of domination and resistance plays out in the face of what otherwise appear to be increasingly inchoate practices of state institutions and functionaries.

The Real State

In the introductory chapter, I asserted that British rule brought with it an expanded political field in which the state, as the main repository of power in society, became inextricably intertwined with almost all aspects of social life. As more and more basic facets of everyday life became linked to the state – including the resolution of disputes, control and distribution of resources, and delivery of services – its interventions in social life increased accordingly.

The state's role in social exchange has become even more pronounced in the post-colonial period, albeit differently in different regions. Perhaps more accurately, state functionaries have continued to be major conduits in the exercise of power. As noted above, the vast majority of scholarly analyses of the civil services implicitly assume uniformity in their composition and practice. State bureaucracies are, in fact, 'bottom-heavy' and the politics and practice of the officer corps are considerably different from the majority of government servants. In Pakistan well over 90 per cent of the bureaucracy is comprised of low-level functionaries that do not enjoy officer status.[31] Moreover, when conceiving of the bureaucracy, the stereotype of 'faceless bureaucrats' is misrepresentative because the lower echelons of the civil service are 'staffed by people with whom some kind of social relationship can or could exist'.[32]

In post-colonial societies such as Pakistan, capitalist development has generated limited formal employment opportunities in private industries and trades. Accordingly, the state has historically been one of the primary sites of formal employment for the subordinate classes.[33] In today's Pakistan employment in the public sector remains extremely coveted, particularly with the large and growing number of people who can no longer earn a living off the land, and the extremely tenuous nature of employment – including self-employment – under conditions of urban informality.

According to the Annual Statistical Bulletin of Federal Government Employees for the year 2012-13 conducted by the Pakistan Public Administration Research Centre (PPARC), there were a total of 446816 employees in government service spread out across 210 autonomous/semi-autonomous bodies/ corporations under the Federal Government.[34] Of this, the total number of Class I officers (BPS 17-22 or equivalent) was 22156, Class II officers (BPS 16 or equivalent) was 28260 while the total number of staff (BPS 1- 15 or equivalent) was 396400.[35]

A student graduate from one of the country's prominent public universities preparing to appear in the Central Superior Services (CSS) examinations (for induction into public service) explained the significance of a permanent position within the state bureaucracy:

> The truth is that 'public service' (*awam ki khidmat*) is not really the motivation for taking the CSS exam. If I were to become an AC (assistant commissioner) even in a district far away from my home it would be a tremendous source of power for my family because people would look at us differently – no one would pick a fight with us; in fact we could pick a fight with whomever we wanted because of the power that an official position in the bureaucracy brings with it. My family's honor (*izzat*) would be enormously enhanced and people would come asking us for favours (*sifarish*) all day long.[36]

While the informant above had aspirations to joining the officer corps of the state bureaucracy, it is at the lower levels of the administrative apparatus that most Pakistanis of modest means seek entry. The low bureaucracy – including, but not limited to, the *patwari*, sub-*tehsildar* and sub-inspector – is responsible for public dealing of all kinds, and this has remained true from the inception of the (colonial) state until the present day.

The *thana* and *katcheri* in particular feature centrally in the lives of the subordinate classes. In the course of this intense interaction with working people, and because it is endowed with the power to provide/withhold services, dispense/deny justice and provide/deny employment, the low bureaucracy actually shares in the power that is typically assumed to be exercised by the high bureaucracy. Therefore, the nature of the low bureaucracy's power, and the manner in which it is exercised, needs to be understood in its own right.

The High Bureaucracy

The high bureaucracy came to occupy a pre-eminent position in Pakistan's power structure in the immediate post-independence period. Various factors – the ruling party being comprised largely of migrants; the outmigration of large numbers of educated non-Muslims from the Pakistan areas; the vested interests of the bureaucracy itself – conspired to ensure that a predominantly Urdu-speaking bureaucracy developed symbiotic links with the predominantly Punjabi rural-military combine. The former was arguably the senior partner of the two until the 1970s.

Bhutto's civil service reforms once and for all tilted the balance of power within the civil-military services towards the latter.[37] The reforms ostensibly aimed to undermine the insular and autonomous nature of the high bureaucracy, and thus assert the authority of the political leadership over the administrative arm of the state. In fact, as many scholars have noted, Bhutto's efforts were contradictory and designed to increase his power by instituting loyalists at all decision-making levels. Nationalization of industry and most other major policy initiatives increased bureaucratic control over productive sectors of the economy, thereby expanding the opportunities for political appointees to distribute patronage.[38]

In effect, the Bhutto period marked a progressive politicization of the bureaucracy insofar as high bureaucrats' power over resource-allocation and the general direction of government diminished over time; at the very least the high bureaucracy could not act *independently* of the elected political leadership, or military top brass. Of particular significance was the introduction of the so-called principle of lateral entry into the officer corps, which not only undid the exclusivity of the high bureaucracy permanently, but also ensured that a new power sharing arrangement took shape at the centre in the form of 'an implicit compromise between politicians and bureaucrats'.[39]

While the military high command had selectively penetrated the civil service during the Ayub period, the high bureaucracy was far less threatened by direct military recruits than by lateral entrants under the Bhutto regime because of the inherent similarities in outlook and ethos of the civil and military services.[40] The shock of the 1973 Civil Service reforms was especially acute because the PPP's elected leadership – which was revelling in its new power over the high bureaucracy – comprised a number of individuals hailing from historically excluded classes, castes and ethnic groups.

The Zia regime thus inherited an expanded set of state institutions which accorded it unparalleled opportunities to dole out patronage. The high bureaucracy's paternalism had remained pronounced in the first two decades following the end of colonial rule; this now gave way to a concern with personal survival and a commitment to a new status quo in which the military was the ascendant power. Zia ensured the subservience of the bureaucracy by effecting a virtual revolution in its upper echelons through the induction of large numbers of serving and retired military officers who were loyal to the army chief.[41]

During the democratic interregnum of 1988–1999, the high bureaucracy became even more prone to politicization due to the highly unstable nature of each successive regime. In this sense whatever remained of the high bureaucracy's autonomy was further eroded as both of the (extremely weak) mainstream political parties attempted to manipulate administrative institutions to gain ascendancy over each other.[42] Each incoming government took the practice of installing loyalists in important positions to new heights. Career bureaucrats became even more adept at towing the line of the party in power. Resultantly, the high bureaucracy became increasingly incoherent in its functioning, which, as a matter of fact, reinforced the politics of common sense insofar as the cynical use and abuse of public resources intensified dramatically.

All governments in Pakistan following Bhutto's have been keen to keep the high bureaucracy 'onside' because it still exercises control over day-to-day matters of administration. Having said this, the high bureaucracy no longer espouses the elitism and self-righteousness that the civil service had imbibed from its colonial predecessor at the time of independence.[43] In the pre-1972 period, the high bureaucracy was unanimous in the conviction that politicians had no business in matters of administration, including revenue collection and law and order.

A now-retired federal secretary shared the following anecdote:

> We CSP officers were convinced that we should have a monopoly over decision-making, that we were best equipped to run the country. We even had that feeling of superiority like the British that everyone else, including the politicians, were just unable to think about the larger picture. I now see that this was problematic, but at the same time it meant that state policy was informed by a clear vision for the future. Everything was not ad hoc like it has become now.[44]

The erosion of the elitist spirit has been coeval with the high bureaucracy's changing composition. Very few members of the historically powerful English-educated propertied classes now take up positions in the high bureaucracy. This strata now prefers private sector occupations which are far more lucrative.[45] The opening up of the civil service has also made a dent, however small, in the historic preponderance of Urdu-speakers and Punjabis, mostly via the cumulative effects of provincial quota stipulations.

The transformation in the composition of the services has been described most aptly as a process of 'nativization' that is defined as 'the institutionalization of vernacular political interests in the state'.[46] I submit that the change in composition of the civil (and military) services is amongst the most significant transformations to have taken place in Pakistan over the past few decades. More than ever, individuals that populate the services hail from the same social backgrounds of the people that they seek to administer/control. This is a major contributing factor to common sense politics as the state has more and more become a permeable entity that can be breached by personal 'connections'.

The entire bureaucratic structure, given the increasingly less elitist character of its higher echelons, has become more adept at generating consent from the subordinate classes. In what follows, I will detail the process through which the logic of practice of the low bureaucracy has seeped through the length and breadth of the polity.

The Low Bureaucracy

While the class and ethnic composition of the high bureaucracy has changed over time, the low bureaucracy has always been staffed by members of the subordinate classes across ethnic boundaries (with women conspicuous by their absence). In a family seeking mobility alongwith stability, one son seeks to enter the police force, another induction into the army, and the third employment in a civilian government department.[47]

While a certain Weberian rationality is present in the higher bureaucratic structure, at least in the design of official policy and the rhetoric of legal impersonalism, it is almost entirely missing at the lower rungs of the bureaucratic structure. Instead, there exists a highly permeable and personalized structure inasmuch as *biraderi*, caste, ethnic or linguistic ties, or for that matter any kind of shared background, is regularly invoked in the business of the state.[48] This is not to suggest that impersonal dealings do not take place at the level of the low bureaucracy, or that invoking patrons is a guarantee against the use of coercion, but only that this is a far more overt feature of the bureaucratic structure at the lower than at the higher level.

To put it more succinctly, at the level of the low bureaucracy, the exchange of money or favours is not hidden from public view or considered immoral *per se*; in contrast, urban middle-classes often decry such practices as 'corrupt'. A low-grade employee in the Quetta Development Authority (QDA) was quite matter-of-fact about it all: 'Rich people (*amir log*) just do it secretly, whereas we ordinary people (*awam-un-nas*) don't deny that the whole system is based on give and take (*lein-dein*). Nobody in Pakistan is upright (*aik number*); anyone who doesn't accede to the system is considered stupid'.

Quite simply, a certain amoralism is associated with what is called 'corruption' inasmuch as the habitual exchange of money and favours is widespread.[49] As an ideal-type, the bureaucracy contains within it the pretence of uprightness and honesty; in practice, especially at the lower level, there is no need to hide how the state actually functions.

Jeffrey Witsoe's study of the Lalu Prasad regime in the Indian state of Bihar indicates that the lower orders of society can actually conceive of 'corruption' as a way of rectifying historical injustices.[50] In Bihar, historically underrepresented castes inducted into the state services went about deliberately thwarting codified rules and regulations. These practices built upon Lalu's wider political movement against caste privilege.

In my estimation, the practice of giving and receiving favours from personnel of the state – at either the higher or lower levels – cannot be explained as some kind of cultural trait. As I hinted at in the introductory chapter, a particular understanding of the 'public' was institutionalized through the course of colonial rule so that '[p]ublic office under colonialism... came to be associated with personal gain, putting in place a formal culture of rent-seeking that was never actively discouraged by the state'.[51]

A comparison with another post-colonial context might be instructive here. Many years ago, Ekeh wrote a quite straightforward yet seminal note on the 'two publics' in post-colonial countries of Africa.[52] He argued that the actually existing public sphere in post-colonial Africa was defined by personalized exchanges on the basis of established moral norms of reciprocity. Thus, the notion of an impersonal civic public sphere that European colonizers at least rhetorically claimed to have brought with them was never internalized by ordinary people. Ekeh's conceptualization missed an account of the macro-structural – and particularly political economy – context, but this, I feel, makes his argument only slightly less compelling. In fact, if Ekeh was attempting to illustrate that macro-structures such as the 'state' played, on the one hand, a distinctly transformational role, while, on the other hand, they were considered alien and inaccessible, and that this 'cultural' disjunct is crucial to understanding political practice, then his point was invaluable.

A similar point is made by an anthropologist working in rural (Pakistani) Punjab:

> The Pakistani State is not seen as something distinct from [society]. Individuals within the State mechanisms are still intricately tied to their human resource networks and their priority must be their network's agenda. Entry to the State processes is seen, therefore, not as a means of service for the general good, but as one strategy for resource capitalization for the good of a specific human resource network.[53]

It is important to bear in mind that there has been a significant change in the popular perception of the state through the post-colonial period. In the first thirty years after the state's inception, the high bureaucracy, while hardly considered responsive to the needs of people, was nevertheless perceived to be committed to a coherent project of political, economic and cultural reform. Over time however, especially during the Ayub period when public perceptions about the bureaucracy plummeted, the systematic practices of self-aggrandizement that had existed since the colonial period became even more rampant alongside erosion in the relatively pristine image of the civil services.

An employee in the National Institute of Health and long-time trade unionist made the point thus:

> When I first joined the service it was not so bad. Neither employees nor outsiders who we were dealing with looked to exploit any and every opportunity to enrich themselves. Trade unionism was about collective betterment (*ijtamai behtri*) – but no one has any belief anymore in the idea that there is a shared responsibility for anything. Anyone who gets the chance to secure personal benefits does so. Only those who don't get an opportunity are honest (*Sharif wohi hota ha jis ko mauqa nahin milta*).[54]

In the context of an unjust and exclusionary social order that benefits the dominant propertied classes in society as well as high officials within state institutions, the ever-intensifying cynicism at the lowest levels of officialdom is not surprising. It may instead be more accurate to think of it as a lack of conviction in the notional 'public interest'. In the eyes of the low bureaucrat – mirroring his higher counterpart – the state and its resources are not considered a trust of the people. Accordingly, in the post-Bhutto period, civil servants at all levels have been emboldened to capture these resources.

Let alone developments over the past few decades, the low bureaucracy was considered a crucial cog of the statist project since the establishment of the Raj. The colonial state believed firmly that its longevity was dependent on control over a largely rural social formation and this entailed not only a mutually beneficial relationship with rural notables, but an administrative structure that facilitated social order. From the inception of the colonial state, the low bureaucrat was recruited from within local society by design; intermediary administrative positions such as *zaildar, numberdar* and others were created by the state for this very purpose.[55] The low bureaucrat then interacted with the state's favoured landed proprietor(s) in the area, considered the ultimate authority in local matters, and both together secured the consent of the subordinate classes (and castes).

This regime of social control remained intact in the post-colonial period, but was soon challenged by the burgeoning mass politics revolving around more expansive identities such as class that emerged in the late 1960s. While this new politics was a product of the cities, it inevitably impacted the rural social formation. It was therefore essential for the Zia regime – in concert with the other members of the historical bloc – to re-establish a familiar mediatory politics based on the wide-ranging influence of the administrator at the local level. In fact, the Zia regime skilfully expanded the scope of the local state's functions by co-opting the rapidly emerging commercial classes into the web of state patronage. As will be discussed in due course, these new commercial segments hail from rural or peri-urban backgrounds and are therefore familiar with the logic of localized patronage politics built around the low bureaucracy.

The 'End' of the State as We Know It?

Cheema argues that a rule-based logic persisted in the way that the bureaucracy operated until the Bhutto period, and this was reflected in systematic patronage of large industrial houses and other coherent corporate groups.[56] However, following Bhutto's reforms and the subsequent institutionalization of a refurbished patronage politics under Zia ul Haq, this rule-based logic of the state started to unravel and the bureaucracy became more comfortable distributing patronage to factions at the local level. As such this analysis implies that the low bureaucracy's importance under Zia and afterwards was significantly enhanced insofar as it acted as the medium through which the 'non-rule' based logic took root. In short, accumulation of both power and capital at the local level was not possible without involvement of the low bureaucracy.

Interestingly, Cheema asserts that this qualitative change in political dynamics at the local level implies a weaker state insofar as it is less cohesive and rule-bound, and therefore prone to 'capture' by non-state actors. This seems to be a variant of the 'state fragmentation' hypothesis discussed earlier. I agree that state functionaries at both the higher and the lower levels have, over the past three decades, started to act more and more independently of, and sometimes in direct contradiction to, official policy.

However, I contend that this lack of coherence does not necessarily imply weakness. It is important to note that political transactions between the low bureaucracy and the subordinate classes in the form of *rishwat* and *sifarish* is not a phenomenon unique to the post-Bhutto period. However, under the PPP regime the distribution of state patronage became more widespread, and then intensified further under Zia ul Haq. Bhutto's reforms, as discussed above, were related to the regime's desire to undermine the authority of the high bureaucracy. The politicization of the bureaucracy all the way down to the local level was a side effect of the reforms.

For the Zia regime however, the localization of politics was a very conscious objective. The emphasis placed on generating consent at the local level for an authoritarian political-economic order was far from incidental, reflecting the military high command's commitment to eradicating the confrontational politics that was still lingering even after Bhutto's demise.

In no way can this development be considered one that *weakened* the state *per se* because some semblance of political order was restored after at least a decade. That the state has changed substantively in the subsequent period is indisputable; it is far more prone to capture by a wide array of social groups, and the involvement of state functionaries in 'informal activities' has increased greatly.[57] However, this dynamic of doling out parts of the economic and political pie to new contenders for power, alongside the increasingly hegemonic common sense that participation in a patronage network is the only meaningful way of navigating everyday state and society, has greatly undermined transformational visions of politics.

One of my primary arguments about the state has to do with its defining role in moulding the social formation. New developments in the post-colonial period have, at various times, both reinforced and challenged this role. The state has undoubtedly lost some of its power to direct the nature of change within the social formation, both because of certain policy regimes enforced by global capital and due to its own tendency to function in fragmentary ways. Yet dominant forces, state functionaries included, have both adapted to and adopted dynamic new practices so as to facilitate both the accumulation of power and the accumulation of capital.

In sum, the state's overwhelming role in social life, particularly in the lives of the subordinate classes, has been premised upon the sociological rootedness of the low bureaucracy since the British period. While much has changed at many levels, the increasingly blurred nature of the divide between state functionaries and the subordinate classes has been one of the major facets of political order in post-Bhutto Pakistan, and thus a bedrock of the politics of common sense.

Symbiosis

I have narrated above a story of change – shifts in the institutional logic and composition of the state have been accompanied by what Arif Hasan has called a 'revolutionary change in Pakistani society' as a rural, agrarian social formation has metamorphosed into an increasingly urbanized, service-oriented one.[58] However, I noted at the beginning of this chapter that change has been accompanied by a significant degree of continuity and this is evident most of all in the ongoing symbiosis between the state and the mythical landed class.

In the late 1960s and early 1970s it appeared as if landed interests were forever to be banished to the dustbin of history, but many landed families were incorporated into the fold of the PPP very soon after the 1970 elections and the landed class and low bureaucracy subsequently joined hands to undertake a spate of tenant evictions.[59]

I will discuss in the next chapter how the urban, intermediate classes were the face of the Zia regime (along with the religious right) – yet the junta's political engineering did not necessarily undermine landed interests. With some notable exceptions, the landed class' political loyalties lay with whoever was in power, and this was reflected both in its steady acquisition of power within the PPP after the party's coming to power in 1971, and also in the immediate abandonment of the party by numerous landed notables after Bhutto's ouster in July 1977; many joined one of the constituent members of the anti-PPP Pakistan National Alliance (PNA) expecting that the Zia regime would favour the alliance in any subsequent political accommodation.[60] In addition, following Bhutto's deposal, landlords started to freely evict tenants from their lands because they were freed from the impediments imposed upon them by left populism, quite aside from the imperatives of a deepening capitalism in agriculture.[61]

Nevertheless, the landed class had to acknowledge the rising power of the intermediate classes as well as adapt to considerable changes in the worldview of the subordinate classes. Specifically, 'a partnership with the state that ignored the rural middle and lower classes was no longer feasible'.[62] Ultimately, the landed class could maintain a privileged position so long as it was willing to accommodate new political actors into a system that had both changed and remained the same insofar as building factional alliances and the acquisition of state resources remained the *modus operandi*.

To take this point further, I return to the argument made in the introductory chapter about the persistence of pre-colonial politico-cultural forms. I have already noted that the British came across social identities that they proceeded to politicize and thus reify; these identities were articulated in a different manner prior to the emergence of the colonial state. In the first couple of decades following the creation of Pakistan, state managers continued to rely on the political order that the British had fashioned in which such 'primordial' identities were instrumentalized.

When Zia came to power, and faced with the imperative of crushing the wave of mass politics on which Bhutto rode to power, familiar and localized forms of patronage politics were revitalized. The new moneyed classes that had emerged following the intense modernization of the 1960s were able to gain access to the corridors of state power. This politics of patronage, however, also provided respite to the landed incumbents that had been the lynchpin of the political order since colonial times.

This does not mean that landed scions enjoy power and influence like in a bygone era, or that they will always retain a position of pre-eminence especially given the ongoing processes of urbanization that have changed the social landscape. Yet, so long as state institutions patronize entrenched classes and castes at the local level, thereby reinforcing these classes' and castes' established cultural and political influence, they will continue to be a beneficiary of common sense politics.[63]

I have already noted the folly of assuming that the spread of capitalist productive relations and technology – and concomitant processes of urbanization – necessarily produce the demise of landed power. Indeed, it is increasingly difficult to mark a clear dividing line between classes deriving their power from control in the agrarian as opposed to non-agrarian sectors. In part, this has to do with the nature of urbanization in Pakistan – and particularly in its most developed region, central Punjab – whereby innumerable peri-urban settlements have developed in what were previously rural regions.

Coeval with this process of urbanization is the transformation of land from a productive into a financial asset, with real estate development emerging as arguably the single biggest driver of growth since the turn of the century.[64] Even where agriculture remains the source of livelihood for working people, changes in tenure relations have intensified – tenant farms represented 41.7 per cent of all farms in 1960 and only 18.6 per cent of the total in 1990.[65] It is virtually impossible to quantify the spread of wage labour, but '[i]t is unlikely that many of the tenants are in a position to become owners, so most of them will probably have been changed into agricultural or rural wage labourers or have migrated to urban areas and towns'.[66]

The landed class has adapted to the imperatives of capital accumulation in the twenty-first century whilst consolidating its long-standing entrenchment in the structure of political power. In fact, it is now somewhat of a truism that many landed scions depict capital gains realized through non-agricultural investments as being generated from land since agricultural income is not taxed in Pakistan. In turn, many urban businessmen who have acquired land as a means of enhancing both capital stock and prestige claim that a majority of their income is derived from farm holdings.

Many 'old' landed magnates also have considerable interests in the secondary and tertiary agrarian economy in towns, or at least have explicit political links with traders and middlemen operating in the small-town economy. In the immediate aftermath of partition, many trading functions previously performed by Hindu business castes were taken over by agricultural castes.[67] In other words, members of landed families themselves became *mandi* merchants. By the same token, *mandi* merchants expanded their business interests on account of their links to landed influentials, the latter providing access to both the local and central state.

The head of an extremely powerful landed family in Sindh, and well-known politician Makhdoom Amin Fahim explains how yesterday's 'feudals' have adapted to changes in today's Pakistan:

> If you don't accept the changing times, you are lost. There are some old families that have lost a lot of clout both because they insist on keeping many things exactly the same, but the truth is that *haris* cannot be kept dependent like in the past; besides we can't run our estates without concern for economic efficiency – we prefer to hire wage labour than have to sustain entire families for generations on end. The point is that if you keep abreast with the times then you can remain influential, especially if you have constant access to jobs and other resources so that people 'need' you (*logon ko aap ki zuroorat parti rahe*).

The Military

While the predominant concern of the high bureaucracy and landed scions has been to arrest their waning influence, the military has clearly established itself as the arbiter in Pakistan's structure of power. Both the military's image and institutional interest have become virtually synonymous with the state itself.

Under the British and in the early years after independence, a majority of the army's officer corps hailed from relatively educated families with non-negligible means – the contempt thus evinced for politicians reflected a colonial paternalism that was at the heart of the political order fashioned under the Raj. This socialization meant, however, that the 'British' – and later 'American' – generation of officers maintained at least some commitment to the colonial mantra of civilian supremacy in matters of government.[68] Needless to say, civilian supremacy meant a working relationship with counterparts in the civil service, rather than answering to elected representatives of the unruly masses.

Accordingly, the military's encroachment into politics was gradual rather than dramatic. It has been argued that Ayub Khan's first military regime was effectively rule by the Civil Service of Pakistan (CSP), with only a handful of military officers actually occupying executive positions in government.[69] In related vein, the military's overt patronage of the religious right began in earnest in the lead-up to the 1970 general election, which suggests that religion was initially considered a unifying ideology within the forces rather than a tool of social and political engineering into which it was later transformed.[70]

Certainly, the military's exalted position in Pakistan is directly related to the 'ideology of the state' that has been cultivated by all governments and their organic intellectuals:

> The military-state relation conceptualizes a dialectical relationship between Islam, Pakistan and the military. Without Islam, Pakistan would not have been able to come into existence; without Pakistan the military would not be able to exist; and without the military, Islam and Pakistan would be threatened.[71]

While this dialectical relationship has its roots in the partition of the subcontinent in 1947, it was during the Zia years that the military's economic and political interests started to approximate what they are today. The military's self-characterization as guardian of the country's physical and ideological frontiers took on unprecedented meaning during Zia's 'Islamization' drive and led to its acquiring immense political, economic and ideological power. A former Director-General of the powerful Inter-Services Intelligence (ISI) and a major ideologue of *jihad*, General Hameed Gul told me: 'Pakistan is a garrison surrounded on all sides by hostile countries – if the army was not this powerful we would never have been able to survive, and of course we are soldiers of Islam (*Islam k sipahi hain*).'

Socialization within the military emphasizes the institution's unique and undisputed status, while emphasizing the parochialism of 'politics'.[72] This 'guardian of the state' image has also been cultivated systematically within society at large, through use of the media, moulding of the educational curriculum and, particularly since the Zia period, by statist religio-political forces. The demeaning of politics and politicians has been a deliberate strategy in this regard, with the military projecting itself as always ready and willing to defuse the perennial crises caused by 'irresponsible' politicians.[73]

I noted above that the civil service in an erstwhile era viewed itself as superior to politicians. Military officers shared this outlook, and have in fact become more convinced of their superiority over time while the high bureaucracy has, to an extent, lost its appetite to dictate to the occupants of elected office. I attribute this superiority complex to the close association of the military with the 'ideology of the state' and also to the military's economic autonomy (which means it is not beholden to governmental authority). This autonomy buttresses its command and control system due to the many economic incentives for the rank-and-file to profess loyalty to the cause.

Siddiqa's seminal study on the military's economic empire has confirmed the gradual encroachment of the institution into all sectors of the country's economy, building at least to some extent on the processes set in motion under colonial rule.[74] There are three major insights that can be drawn from this work.

The first has to do with the relationship between the three services. There is little doubt that the Air Force and Navy have been historically subservient to the Army in size and strength, political influence, and financial clout. On the face of it, there has been limited dissent within the forces on account of the Army's dominant position. It can be surmised that insofar as all of the forces share in the benefits of praetorianism, differences between them are limited, or at most, not voiced. Each of the services enjoys a monopoly over certain economic activities. The Pakistan Navy, for example, 'has a far more extensive presence in real estate development' than the Army.[75] Meanwhile, the Air Force has established a virtual monopoly over the aviation industry, including travel agencies.

A second inference can be made regarding the relationship between the higher and lower ranks. At different points over the past seven decades, junior officers have attempted coups against their superiors.[76] The majority of these coups have been unsuccessful, which suggests that the military's command and control system has ultimately remained robust in the face of internal dissent. Nevertheless, enough anecdotes circulate within society to suggest that dissent within the lower ranks has increased because of the incredible scale of accumulation by the top brass. Many junior officers appear to retain some idealism about the military's nation-building role, and also come into contact with the wider society more than their superiors. They therefore face the brunt of public reaction, especially during the latter stages of martial law adventures when censure of the institution intensifies.

However, it also appears to be true that the material benefits of the military's corporate activities have trickled down to both junior officers and the rank-and-file. Blom uses the term 'military syndicalism' to capture the nature of the evolving military corporate empire.[77] She argues that although the boundless accumulation of power and capital over the past two decades has been the cause of envy and competition within the military, internal dissent remains negligible, and that 'paradoxically, the military's 'privatization' contributes to its internal cohesion'.

A junior army officer confided in me (on the condition of anonymity):

> Yes we inwardly resent the generals and brigadiers who make a killing (*loot mar*) both while in service and then once they retire, but at the same time I cannot pretend that we mortals (*aam makhluq*) do not benefit from being part of the army. Even jawans (rank-and-file soldiers) get a piece of land when they retire, and some even get jobs in security companies run by ex-officers. Besides, how can you quantify the respect (*izzat*) we are accorded in society? As for those segments of society that don't respect us, they fear us.

Third, the military's corporate empire has allowed it to attain more bargaining power *vis a vis* mainstream political parties. The 'civil-military' divide is one of the defining features of the polity – elected governments and the propertied classes that dominate political parties have periodically challenged the power of the unelected apparatuses of the state, civil-military relations ebbing and flowing accordingly. Yet, the military-run companies which in economic terms 'crowd out' the civilian propertied strata operate mostly without impediment – the tried and tested strategy of elected governments has been, as Hasan Askari-Rizvi suggests, to give cover to the military's corporate initiatives so that the officer corps is not motivated to displace political parties and take over the reins of government directly.[78]

This book is not about the civil-military relations *per se*, which is, by any account, probably the most prolifically written about subject in the social science literature on Pakistan.[79] I will discuss the potentialities for political forces to finally eclipse the 'military establishment' in the epilogue, but it is important to note here that the military's power *vis-a-vis* political parties can at least partially be explained by the dominant tendency of propertied classes in Pakistan to define their political interests in terms of their proximity to state power rather than as a function of corporate class concerns.

Mainstream political parties, peopled by both older propertied classes and the *nouveau-riche*, often seek accommodation with the military because challenging the latter is fraught with danger; towing the 'national security' line is perceived as being the best way to serve the interests of party leaderships.[80]

In the final analysis, mainstream parties have never quite committed to mobilizing popular support and thereby causing a rupture in the military-dominated structure of power. In short, the politics of common sense applies to propertied classes as much as the lower orders of society. Sheikh Rasheed Ahmed, an influential politician from Rawalpindi who was closely associated with the Musharraf dictatorship put it thus: 'Look, this isn't the 1960s anymore. You can't really expect to whip up a popular movement and cut the military down to size. You can't be taken seriously if you are in jail while other politicians are garnering benefits from their association with the military. Raising slogans is one thing, but actually delivering services to your electorate is another.'

I have already pointed out that the Zia regime distinguished itself both by regenerating the patronage principle in the political mainstream and by visiting unprecedented repression on political elements that did not accede to the junta's dictates. Stephen Cohen has argued that it was during the 1980s that a 'Pakistani generation' of soldiers rose to the leadership of Pakistan's army which was distinct in class terms – and therefore values and political orientation – from the more elitist, westernized generations of the previous decades.[81] The 'Pakistani generation' tends to be more urbanized, but educated in non-elite schools, with slightly more representation from historically underrepresented regions/ethnic groups.[82] It harbours more anti-politics attitudes than previous generations, loathing those political elements outside of its control with whom it has little or no contact (in marked contrast to earlier generations of the officer corps which maintained social ties to both affluent politicians, and the high bureaucracy).

Importantly, the genesis of this generation of officers can be traced to the Bhutto period, during which the scars of the humiliation of 1971 were still raw. The fact that the military darkest hour – the surrender in Dhaka –marked

Bhutto's coming to power meant that the 'Pakistani generation' of army officers was deeply suspicious of mass politics and its attendant forms of rhetoric (such as Bhutto's refrain against 'fat and flabby generals').[83]

During the late 1960s and 1970s, the more limited forms of political expression that had been institutionalized under the British gave way to a society-wide mobilization which, both at the time, and particularly later, was viewed as being anathema to the interests of Pakistan, and its guardian, the military. This mobilization of society, and the subsequent results – most importantly the break-up of the state itself – deeply politicized the military officer corps.

General (Retired) Talat Masood offered the following reflections:

> You have to understand that army officers believe that their commitment to Pakistan is second to none. For them to have deal with the east Pakistan debacle and on top of this a popular politics in which the army was also blamed for Pakistan's break-up was deeply disturbing. They never wanted a situation like that developing again. Mass politics is difficult to control. Army men always want control.

It was of course precisely to prevent the possibility of power shifting to a mobilized electorate that the military (along with the other unelected institutions of state) repeatedly interrupted the political process prior to 1970. The 'establishment' eventually had to relent and allow the first general election, the result of which, the Yahya Khan regime believed, would be a hung parliament.[84] The actual poll result confirmed just how much of a threat mass politics posed to the status quo.

The systematic interventions of the military's intelligence apparatus in domestic politics reflect the institution's conviction that it is the arbiter in what is a divided polity. The direct interference of the 'agencies' in politics is designed to ensure the compliance of mainstream politicians and extends to victimization of less influential political dissidents.[85]

Starting with Bhutto's hanging, the unbridled use of force by the military and its intelligence apparatus has signalled to the subordinate classes that even members of the historical bloc are subject to the state's wrath. Over time, the ideological power of the state – and the 'agencies' – has been sustained through the 'producing and reproducing' of a state-society divide by the subordinate classes themselves mostly through the creation of, and propagation of myth.[86] In other words, the omnipotence of the intelligence agencies is at least partially explained by the hyperbole that circulates openly within the polity, which heightens perceptions of state power amongst the more political disenfranchized segments of society.

This is despite the evidence that the 'establishment' is far less cohesive than typically believed:

> ...[S]everal law and order forces run their own agency and often appear to be interested in each other as much as in anybody else. This also means that the state cannot be regarded as Big Brother, spying on its subjects through secret activities penetrating private places and thereby effectively keeping society under its thumb. It instead resembles a troubled, fragmented family of several brothers who are deeply distrustful of each other and cannot rely too much on each other in their dealings with the outside world.[87]

All told, the military's becoming virtually synonymous with the 'idea of Pakistan' has been decisive in sustaining the institution's power. Propertied classes with aspirations to political power contribute to the military myth under the pretext that it is not possible to breach the highest echelons of government by antagonizing the top brass. The politicization of religion during and after the Zia years has permitted the military to assert its 'guardian of the state' role even more forcefully.

I will return in Chapter 4 to this last point including the contradictions to which the policy of patronizing *jihadis* has given rise – for the present purposes I want to reiterate that the military's ideological, economic and political power has grown dramatically in the post-Bhutto conjuncture. It is no coincidence that it is in this same period that anti-systemic politics has been evicted from the societal mainstream. Seen in this way, the military is, in no uncertain terms, the major beneficiary of the politics of common sense.

Still the military's position of pre-eminence would not have been possible without the collaboration of other members of the post-Bhutto historical bloc. I turn next to the 'intermediate' classes who became, as the term suggests, the major intermediaries between the subordinate classes and the state in the refashioned patronage machine crafted by the Zia military junta.

Endnotes

1. For civil-military relations, see Siddiqa (2007), Shah (2014) and Ahmed (2003); for ethnic-nationalism and the state see Khan (2005) and Siddiqui (2012b); for landed and other propertied class analyses see M. H. Khan (2000), Khan (2000).
2. Ali (1983); Cohen (2011).

3. I noted in the introduction more nuanced studies on various aspects of Pakistani state and society, but very few of these deal specifically with the structure of power that prevails in the country.
4. A handful of scholars stand out in this regard: Pasha's (1997) theoretical formulation of the 'hyper-extended State', Hasan's (2002) empirics, and most recently Zaidi's (2014) efforts must be noted.
5. Alavi (1972b).
6. Alavi (1990).
7. Shivji (1976); Mamdani (1976); Saul (1974); Leys (1976).
8. It was on the theoretical question of 'relative autonomy' that arguably the most famous debate on the state raged for many years in the 1970s between Ralph Miliband (1977) and Nicolas Poulantzas (1980). 'The Miliband-Poulantzas debate left many Marxists with the uncomfortable reality of a still unresolved dichotomy at the core of Marxist political theory, and for many it brought an end to the idea that there is something called the Marxist theory of the state' (Barrow, 2002: 43).
9. Ahmad (1980).
10. I noted in the previous chapter how a particular state-capital relation evolved in the colonial context such that the state wilfully manipulated the manner in which capital penetrated (differentially) into the social formation. Harvey (2003) and Arrighi (2005) have theorized this dialectic within the context of an imperialist system by positing the existence of two separate impulses of imperialist power, namely capitalistic and territorial logics. The British selectively stimulated the capitalistic logic within the Indian social formation – thereby incorporating it into the burgeoning capitalist world-economy – while ensuring the sustenance of British political power within India, and indeed the rest of the Empire.
11. See Gilmartin (2015) for a discussion on the manner in which political order was crafted in Punjab around the 'village community'.
12. Having said this, it is important to bear in mind that the colonial project, particularly in regions like the Punjab, involved significant transformations in eco-systems based on forms of pastoral nomadism towards settled agriculture. The large-scale mobilization of water and land for this purpose, as well as enforced changes in the use of forest resources, were crucial in this regard.
13. Cheesman (1997: 91).
14. I should also point out that the 'landed' class was by no means a monolith – in the canal colony districts of Punjab, for instance, the majority of the majority of land was distributed to 'peasant' grantees (cf Ali, 1988).
15. Ansari (1992: 57–76) details the example of the Hur rebellion spearheaded by the *Pir* Pagaro.
16. Gadi (2003: 99).
17. LaPorte (1975: 92).
18. Following the partition, a modicum of administrative order was established only when provincial landed magnates pledged their allegiance to the federal government in Karachi.

19. Burki (1976) argues that a qualitatively new dynamic was generated in rural areas led by emergent capitalist farmers. Jalal (1994: 160) claims that to the extent that there was a *middle-sized* landlord that was favoured by the reforms, it was in the form of the retired military and civilian bureaucrat.
20. Khan et al (2007: 36).
21. Alavi (1983b: 239–241).
22. Ziring (1997: 85).
23. This sub-title owes itself to an edited volume by the same name; see Gupta and Sharma (2006).
24. Abrams (1988: 87).
25. See Gupta (1995) for the classic post-structuralist exposition and Jeffrey and Lerche (2000) for a critique of the purely discursive perspective.
26. See, for example, Fuller and Benei (2001).
27. Bayart (2000: 230) puts it thus for the African context: 'African political societies are duplicated between, on the one hand, a *pays legal*.... and on the other hand, a *pays reel*, where real power is wielded'.
28. Fernandez (2008)
29. Verkaaik (2001: 141).
30. Thompson (1995: 142).
31. Maddison (1971: 143).
32. Fuller and Harriss (2001: 15).
33. Alavi (1987).
34. Annual Statistical Bulletin of Federal Government Employees 2012–2013. Accessed on 12 February 2016. http://www.establishment.gov.pk/gop/index.php?q=aHR0cDovLzE5Mi4xNjguNzAuMTM2L2VzdGFiL3VzZXJmaWxlczEvZmlsZS9Fc3RhYmxpc2htZW50L3B1YmxpY2F0aW9uLzA0LTIwMTMlMjBGaW5hbCUyMFNUQVRJU1RJQ1MlMjAyMDEy LTIwMTMucGRm.
35. The Punjab Development Statistics issued by the Bureau of Statistics in 2014, showed that the total number of sanctioned posts in the budget estimates of the year 2011–12 were 418008. Of the total, the strength of the staff i.e. BPS 1–15 or equivalent was 369321; the total number of Class II officers was 11986; the total number of Class I officers was 35798; while there were 903 sanctioned posts for unclassified/special grade See Punjab Development Statistics (2014: 225). http://www.bos.gop.pk/system/files/Dev-2014.pdf. Accessed on 15 February 2016. Data issued by the Finance Department of Sindh regarding the sanctioned posts according to BPS for the year 2006–07 shows that the total number of posts was 206, 165. The total number of posts for BPS 1–15 or equivalent was 182677. The total number of posts for BPS 16 or equivalent was 4,217 while that of BPS 17–22 or equivalent was 17142. Department and BPS Wise Number of Posts 2006–07 (Provincial). Accessed on 15 February 2016. http://fdsindh.gov.pk/site/userfiles/1173179122_59387.pdf. The White Paper for the budget of the year 2012–13 issued by the Finance Department KPK lists the total number of sanctioned posts

as 386,630. Out of the total, the number of posts for BPS 1–15 or equivalent was 336752. The total number of posts for the BPS 16 or equivalent was 20913 while that of BPS 17–22 or equivalent was 26559. Government of Khyber Pakhtunkhwa Finance Department 'White Paper' (2012–13: 139). Accessed on 19 February 2016. http://www.financekpp.gov.pk/FD/attachments/article/7/White%20Paper%20Budget%202012-13.pdf. According to the Financial Manual (2008) issued by the Finance Department of Balochistan, the total number of sanctioned posts for that year was 158476. Of the total, the number of posts for BPS 1–15 or equivalent was 140916. The total number of posts for the BPS 16 or equivalent was 7712 while that of BPS 17-22 or equivalent was 9848. The Balochistan Finance Manual- Vol. II (2008: 810). Accessed on 20 February 2016. http://balochistan.gov.pk/index.php?option=com_docman&task=cat_view&gid=870&Itemid=677.
36. Interview with Zameen Khan.
37. Noman (1988); Alavi (1983a); Burki (1980).
38. Raza (1997); Ahmad (2000).
39. Kennedy (1988: 83).
40. Mahmood (1988: 54).
41. Zaidi (2005a: 502).
42. Chadda (2000).
43. British officers were part of Pakistan's high bureaucracy until 1960 which was a major reason for its self-confidence and continuing contempt of politicians, who, as was the case under the Raj, were perceived to disrupt smooth administration (Mahmood, 1988: 32).
44. Interview with Tasneem Noorani.
45. Shafqat (2011).
46. Pasha (1997: 196).
47. As I will document in later chapters, the subordinate classes can now also conceive of social mobility as religious functionaries and as small entrepreneurs (on the basis of monies generated from migrations and the like).
48. In the context of the Indian post-colonial experience, which bears considerable similarities to Pakistan, this phenomenon has been described by Kaviraj (1997: 235) as follows: 'Long-term historical memories and time tested ways of dealing with power of the political authority took their revenge on the modern state, bending the straight lines of rationalist liberal politics through a cultural refraction of administrative meaning'.
49. For an insightful discussion of the cultural constructions of 'corruption' in Africa, see Blundo (2006).
50. Witsoe (2013).
51. Javid(2011).
52. Ekeh (1975).
53. Lyon (2002: 188).
54. Interview with Noor Khan.

60   *The Politics of Common Sense*

55. Cheema et. al (2006).
56. Cheema (2003).
57. Noman (2001) has called this systematic use of state resources 'shadow privatization', while the literature more generally describes this as 'privatization of the state'. See Bayart (1993) for the most cogent exposition of this idea.
58. Hasan (2002b).
59. Jones (2003: 428).
60. Richter (1978: 411).
61. Rouse (1983: 264).
62. Cheema et al. (2006: 15).
63. See Martin (2015) for a very rich ethnographic account of the displacement of historically powerful landed families in the Punjabi district of Sargodha by a *nouveau-riche* landed class that has a much more modern and hands-on approach to local politics.
64. Harvey's (2003) theorization on the subject employs the concepts of 'spatio-temporal fixes' and 'accumulation of dispossession'.
65. Zaidi (2005a: 42).
66. Ibid 50.
67. Alavi (1990) writes: 'The vacuum left by Hindu traders was filled by Muslim landowners, owners of, perhaps, between 300 to 800 acres, especially in the Punjab, who took over their trading function'.
68. Cohen (1988).
69. Burki (1969).
70. Haqqani (2005).
71. Husain (1979: 133).
72. Shah (2014).
73. Siddiqi (1996).
74. Siddiqa (2007). I have, alongwith others, built upon this work in a separate study conducted in rural areas of Punjab. See Khan and Akhtar (2014).
75. Siddiqa (2007: 193).
76. Consider for example the serious internal condemnation of General Yahya Khan following the surrender in Dhaka in December 1971. Internal dissent was also evident in a series of assassination attempts on General Pervez Musharraf. The alleged perpetrators, many of whom were junior and mid-level officers were court-martialled and eventually sentenced to hang.
77. Blom (2005).
78. Rizvi (2003: 12).
79. See for example: Shah (2014); Paul (2014); Fair (2014); Rizvi (2003); Haqqani (2005); Siddiqa (2007); Aziz, (2007); Cloughley (2008).
80. There is arguably no better example of this than the person of Shah Mahmood Qureshi, an influential *pir*/landlord from the Multan area who has been associated, at one time or another, with at least three of the country's major parties. Qureshi

is also the head of the most prominent lobbying organization of landlords, the Farmers Association of Pakistan (FAP). The *modus operandi* of politicians like Qureshi appears to be to join whichever mainstream party is at any particular point in time better placed to access the state and its resources.

81. Cohen (1998) argues that the 'Pakistani generation' was preceded by 'British' and 'American' generations of soldiers.
82. Fair and Nawaz (2011).
83. Shafqat (1997: 167–81).
84. Ziring (1974: 414–15).
85. Khan (September 21, 2014); Malik (March 8, 2014); Mussadaq (March 2, 2014); *Express Tribune* (February 13, 2014); *Express Tribune (*March 11, 2014).
86. Mitchell (1991: 94–95).
87. Verkaaik (2001: 357).

3

Accumulation in Practice

The deepening of capitalism and rise to prominence of the 'middle' classes in post-colonial societies over the past few decades has now well and truly become one of the most important thematic concerns of scholars across disciplinary and geographical boundaries. And rightfully so – for too long class analyses of both western and non-western societies have focused on the 'polar' classes with all that has come in the 'middle' either relegated to the ranks of 'petty bourgeoisie' or, in more recent times, banished to the realm of the 'informal'.

The centrality of the intermediate strata in the Pakistani story of capitalist modernity is, however, still to be adequately understood, both conceptually and in empirical terms. An inordinately large segment of the intelligentsia as well as arm-chair critics continue to depict Pakistani society as predominantly 'feudal', thereby understating the extent of urbanization and the substantial political and economic clout of non-agricultural commercial classes.[1]

In many ways, the lack of attention paid to the intermediate strata in particular, and changes in the class structure at large, can be explained by the continuing reliance on 'traditional' analyses of the state. I have already mentioned the handful of recent studies that have attempted to capture the specificities of statecraft in contemporary Pakistan through novel theoretical lenses. Research work done on the evolving class structure of Pakistan's society lags further behind; recent efforts tend to rely on limited data and dated conceptual tools.[2] The need to engage in more detailed research on actually existing capitalism in Pakistan can be gauged from one of the few insightful studies on the middle class which estimates it to total almost one-third of the country's population of 187 million.[3]

In this chapter, I identify members of this burgeoning class, their sociological backgrounds, and explain their centrality to my narrative about common sense politics. In doing so I engage – although not exhaustively – with the scholarly literature on the intermediate classes, as well as recent theoretical debates on the nature of capitalist modernity in non-western contexts. In the final analysis

I demonstrate that the intermediate classes have become the major protagonists of the contemporary political economy of patronage.

New Contenders for Power

In the first two chapters, I highlighted the main features of the refurbished patronage machine that emerged in Pakistan during and after the Zia years. While this political order includes established players such as the civil and military bureaucracies and landed class, I contend that its most distinctive feature is the steady rise of new contenders for power, namely the intermediate classes and the religious right.

As pointed out already, Bhutto's attempts to undermine the civil bureaucracy by instituting loyalists at all levels of the administrative structure proved to be the first step in the expansion of the state's patronage function. The PPP interregnum was conspicuous for the fact that hitherto excluded social groups gained access to state institutions. Previously, the high bureaucracy's insular and elitist nature limited direct access to state patronage.

The state's patronage function was further enhanced by the post-Bhutto military regime, primarily through the medium of local body elections. This allowed for the extension of patronage to classes that had emerged as contenders for power due to the social changes engendered by capitalist modernization. These 'intermediate' classes could not initially compete in electoral contests at the national and provincial level, but were able to make inroads in local bodies. As mentioned in the previous chapter, landed magnates now had to compete for state patronage with the 'new' middle classes, a process that has, over time, led to what one scholar has termed the 'democratization' of patronage.[4]

The purpose of this deliberate manipulation of the political process was both to counter the politics of resistance that had existed through the Bhutto period and reassert a vertical hierarchy of power relations culminating in the patronage-distributing institutions and/or personnel of the state. Whereas in the past only 'traditional' landed patrons could navigate this system, political alignments could now be forged through the money and know-how of new intermediaries in a rapidly urbanizing society.

Operating largely through informal means,[5] small and medium scale entrepreneurs – the single most influential component of the intermediate classes – were, along with religio-political forces, the most important *political* ally of the Zia regime. Recognizing the opportunity accorded to them, the intermediate classes moved from the local level upward into the ranks of an emergent bourgeoisie, capturing Chambers of Commerce at the provincial and national level. Of even greater note was their rapid graduation to mainstream politics.[6]

This was all made possible by the suspension of the formal political process at the national and provincial levels by the Zia regime for eight years. It was in this intervening period that the intermediate classes gained a foothold in the political mainstream and emerged as an autonomous force when national and provincial assembly elections were eventually held on a non-party basis in 1985.

Importantly, the support provided to segments of the small and medium scale entrepreneurial class was an outcome of the Zia regime's perceived need for self-preservation and not a function of a clear and coherent economic policy. In other words, the state's political engineering allowed a class of small and medium entrepreneurs to acquire political power far in excess of that which it would otherwise have had, which in turn reinforced the intermediate classes' economic clout. The military regime did not necessarily conceive of its political accommodations with the intermediate classes as a means of providing impetus to industry. In fact, in the Zia period 'the only change in the government attitude [was] the acknowledgement of the existence of the small-scale sector, though with no tangible policy thrust'.[7] As Addleton argues, Pakistan's economy became increasingly decentralized during the 1980s and it was the capitalist dynamic undergirding this decentralization that, articulated with the political access offered by the military regime, precipitated the emergence of a 'nativized' bourgeoisie with lofty political ambitions.[8]

Intermediate Classes in Theory and History

The variously defined middle classes have long been a popular ideal-type in radical theorizing about the post-colonial state. As mentioned in Chapter 2, a majority of treatises in the 1970s and 1980s viewed the post-colonial state as the preserve of the 'bureaucratic' bourgeoisie. This class, as a rule, was not involved in processes of production and, unlike the 'traditional' bourgeoisie, supplied the functionaries of the state, professionals and managers.[9]

These segments, famously clumped together by Hamza Alavi under the term 'salariat', continue to exercise significant influence as state managers and in society more generally.[10] However, since the 1960s, a separate segment of the middle classes has emerged as a major economic and political force in many post-colonial countries. This segment is comprised of traders, merchants, transporters and various types of petty producers, most of whom are, or historically have been, linked to the secondary and tertiary sectors of the agrarian economy.

A growing body of scholarship describes this segment under the broad term 'intermediate classes'.[11] The intermediate classes are internally differentiated across urban and rural; organized and unorganized; and labour-exploiting and self-employed categories. My use of the term draws on the empirical work of Harriss-White (2003) in India who in turn has worked with and modified Kalecki's original formulations.[12]

Kalecki is interested in the dynamics of what he calls an intermediate regime – a (non-western) society still in transition to mature capitalism whereby the capital-labour relation is not dominant. Intermediate classes constitute the majority demographic group and thereby dominate the governmental coalition. The emphasis of most of this literature is on the stunted growth patterns demonstrated by intermediate regimes, which are attributed to the various rent-seeking practices and efficiency-reducing collusion of different segments of the intermediate classes.[13]

I do not engage exhaustively with such questions here; I will, however, digress briefly to address the question of whether or not Pakistan – and other post-colonial societies – can still be thought of as in a state of 'transition' to the western capitalist prototype. I noted in the introductory chapter the folly of remaining true to Eurocentric conceptions of historical change that base analyses of social and political forms in non-western contexts on the European ideal-type. Maurice Dobb, Robert Brenner and others associated with what was known within radical circles as the 'transition' debate were concerned with the shift from feudal to capitalist agriculture *in western Europe*, and England in particular.[14] The conditions within which capitalism emerged in non-western societies, including those subjected to European colonial rule, were, needless to say, entirely distinct from the western experience. This recognition gave rise to theorizations such as that of the 'passive revolution' in India, in which the transition to capitalism was conceptualized as a 'blocked dialectic'.[15]

The implicit assumption remained that capitalist modernity in the non-western world was a flawed version of the ideal-type, that '[c]apitalism in the third world [is] weak and inadequate, incapable of performing its hegemonic role'.[16] In fact, as is now increasingly acknowledged by the literature on multiple and alternate modernities[17] no one site of capitalist modernity necessarily converges with any other, notwithstanding the universalizing tendency of capital.

In effect, capital's relentless drive to universalize itself does not render irrelevant historical difference; relations of power, cultural dispositions and even the shape and form of production and exchange all need to be understood in their own right. For instance, it is impossible to ignore that a large number of working people in South Asia fall into the category of self-employed, neither selling their labour power nor exploiting that of others to consider this empirical reality a sign of 'backwardness' relative to the western capitalist prototype is both unhelpful and problematic.

It is beyond the scope of this chapter to attempt an exhaustive review of capitalism in non-western contexts, and the intermediate classes in particular. For my purposes it is sufficient to note that there is a dearth of substantive research on the subject in Pakistan although there would appear to be a parallel between the intermediate classes and what Pakistan's scholars and others have described as the middle classes.[18]

I start, therefore, by mobilizing some stylized facts that underlie why academic energies must be directed towards an analysis of the intermediate classes, and the wider dynamics of actually existing capitalism. Over the past three decades the growth of the informal economy has far exceeded that of the formal economy in terms of employment generation, value-added and growth in capital stock.[19] This implies that the 'bourgeoisie' in the post-Bhutto period has become very diverse in size, background, and methods of accumulation. The rise of the intermediate classes is reflected in the major structural shift in the economy towards the service sector. According to official statistics, the sector accounts for more than half of GDP, and is where approximately 40 per cent of the total labour force is based.[20]

Arguably the most crucial feature of the intermediate classes is their structural position outside formal accounting mechanisms. Preliminary figures suggest that at least 50 per cent of output is generated by the 'underground' economy.[21] As a general rule, information on the informal economy is sparse, and that available qualitative rather than quantitative. It is, therefore, possible only to venture vague estimates on the size of the informal economy, and the extent of the intermediate classes' influence over Pakistan's political economy. By way of comparison, in neighbouring India upwards of 80 per cent of economic activity is generated in the unaccounted sector of the economy.[22]

In this chapter, I chalk out the beginnings of what can become a comprehensive research agenda on the political economy of the intermediate classes. My focus is on the emergence of the intermediate class segment as a major contender for power in Pakistan since the 1960s.

Historical Underpinnings

The intermediate classes in Pakistan rose to prominence with the progressive mechanization of agriculture and development of agro-processing industries in the urbanizing areas around the agricultural plains in the northern and central regions of the Punjab, and to a lesser extent in Sindh, Khyber Pakhtunkhwa and Balochistan. The rural-urban migrations that were coeval with the Green Revolution in the 1960s, as well as migrations to the Gulf and other parts of the world from the early 1970s, reinforced emergent trends. These developments have over time had considerable multiplier effects that have further fuelled expansion of small and medium enterprises in towns and cities.

Labour was substantially mobile in the northwest of India even during the colonial period, mainly due to social engineering experiments conducted by the Raj, particularly canal colonization in Punjab.[23] At partition and immediately afterwards, migrations of unprecedented magnitude once again altered the face of the social formation. It has been argued that the 'aggressively upwardly mobile migrant culture' had a major bearing on the emergent forms of politics and broader social norms.[24]

I will discuss the influence of (various) historical migrations on the structure of power in later chapters. For the time being I wish only to point out that while the Green Revolution may have accelerated socio-economic change and more specifically heralded the emergence of the intermediate classes as a major political and economic force, this was, to a significant extent, a cumulative process dating back at least a century.

As I have noted numerous times already, both socio-economic change from below and the manipulations of the state encouraged the burgeoning intermediate classes to compete with the traditional propertied classes – and particularly landed scions – for economic and political clout. Towards the end of the 1960s the intermediate classes played a major role in the popular movement that ended the Ayubian dictatorship, especially in the small towns of Punjab.

This political upsurge swept the PPP to power, and the intermediate classes emerged as one of the most vocal elements of the broad cross-section of forces that were demanding change.[25] The Ayub regime's downfall confirmed that the prevailing 'political settlement' characterized by 'traditional' matrices of patronage could not accommodate historically underrepresented segments of society that were clamouring for a greater share of the economic and political pie.[26]

In this regard, Jones writes: 'Bhutto's genius lay first in perceiving that the people's aspirations were nationalist, participatory, and economic, not revolutionary, and secondly in understanding the implications of their massive voting power'.[27] In the event, the PPP resorted to the use of state patronage to meet the fierce demands of the intermediate classes, through induction into state enterprises, tax breaks and other means. In doing so, the populist regime perhaps unwittingly re-established state power.

I mentioned in the introductory chapter the need to think deeply about how and why 'traditional' patron-client relations have metamorphosed into contemporary forms of patronage rather than giving way to a substantively different logic of practice across class and other fault lines. Trying to understand this specificity of post-colonial modernity, I think, requires us to focus on the agency of the intermediate classes.

What is crucial about the 1960s and early 1970s is that there was, if only briefly, the rise to prominence of a subordinate class politics based on confrontation with dominant social forces. This politics was premised on the imperative of transforming the state into a vehicle for substantive social change, thus challenging the hitherto prevailing notion of the state as an immovable repository of power, engagement with which was only possible through established intermediaries.

Yet, at the same time that the subordinate classes were allowed to dream of revolution and social change, the emergent intermediate classes were looking to secure political power to match their growing economic clout. For a brief interregnum in the late 1960s and early 1970s, segments of the intermediate classes, themselves rising through the ranks of the subordinate classes, were committed to structural upheaval, but this commitment was soon to give way to a more pragmatic strategy of securing access to power and resources through accommodation with dominant forces.

In effect the populist 'consensus' started to dissipate soon after the PPP's coming to power, and especially so after the nationalization of agro-based small industry was initiated in 1975. This particular initiative pitched traders and merchants totally reliant on profits from such industries firmly against the government. The regime had evinced, till then, a *relative* bias towards small-scale industry, and therefore, by extension, the trading and merchant classes.[28] Ultimately however, the intermediate classes had aspirations that were unmatched by (the rather confused) policy frameworks articulated by the populist government, and with the onset of nationalization, the die was cast.

The intermediate classes would become the major lightning rod of anti-PPP sentiment, aligning with the opposition PNA, providing it with funds, and also galvanizing other disparate groups in the social formation into the anti-Bhutto movement. In fact, the radical potentialities that were apparent in the preceding decade and early part of the 1970s had by now almost completely petered out. The latent contradictions between the subordinate and intermediate classes on the one hand, and Punjab and other relatively underdeveloped regions on the other hand, were gradually coming to the fore.

In principle, there was still a possibility that the social upheaval witnessed through the Bhutto period would propel radical political movements forward. By crafting a refurbished patronage machine in which emergent classes became thoroughly integrated, the Zia regime ensured that any remaining pretense to radical transformation within the intermediate strata was once and for all co-opted.

The intermediate classes have come to occupy a central place in the reconstituted historical bloc from the late 1970s onwards. Intensely ruthless and upwardly mobile, they are distinct from the 'old' bourgeoisie whose political, economic and even cultural influence has waned in the period under study. Making sense of the linkages between the two confirms the narrative of continuity and change that I present in this book.

The Bourgeoisie, in All its Incarnations

In the immediate aftermath of Pakistan's creation, the high bureaucracy, in keeping with its urbanist, modernist outlook, privileged the cause of industry, considering it the key to the economic survival of the new state.[29] Pakistan's business community was comprised largely of Gujrati-speaking trading families settled in Karachi who enjoyed links – albeit tenuous – with the Urdu-speaking leadership in the new central government.[30]

The vast majority of Pakistan's industrial production in the early years following partition was built around a highly personalized relationship between the civil bureaucracy and an insular and family-based migrant business community. An autonomous 'industrial bourgeoisie' that sought to attain political office or representation in state institutions was conspicuous by its absence; the business community relied almost entirely on the largesse of the bureaucracy to enhance its interests.

The migrant bourgeoisie made little effort to integrate itself in society. Based primarily in and around Karachi with almost no mooring in the urban, let alone rural, social formation, the possibilities of this bourgeoisie championing an independent politics were necessarily limited.

The business community in India had historically been considered socially inferior to the professional classes and the landed gentry, and it would appear that this perception was internalized to some extent by both the Gujrati migrant (and Punjab based Chinioti) business communities in post-partition Pakistan.[31] As inward-looking communities that clearly believed themselves to be vulnerable to the whims of the bureaucracy and politicians hailing primarily from the landed class, the emphasis was on the solidarity and insularity of the group rather than a developed sense of wider class interests.

The most striking evidence in this regard was the proliferation of business associations constituted almost entirely by insular communities and most often groups of families related by blood or marriage. The associations' primary purpose was to secure their parochial interests *vis a vis* the state; they were, by all accounts, a 'testimony to the highly individualistic, personalized and fragmented character of the Pakistani business community'.[32] These associations tended to adopt more and more regionalist identities through the 1960s as Punjabis started to encroach into an industrial sector previously dominated by the Karachi-based migrant families. As the number of competitors within business circles increased, and smaller and medium sized entrepreneurs entered the market, the more established families withdrew from leadership positions, ostensibly because they considered themselves above the petty politics of elections.[33]

The disinclination of the clannish refugee business families to assert themselves politically – a function both of their traditional aloofness from the political sphere and the intimidating posture of the bureaucracy – was one of the main causes of their gradual eclipse by a new indigenous industrial element in Punjab that rose to prominence due to the economic modernization that took place in that province through the 1960s. The shifting of the federal capital from Karachi to Islamabad in 1960 also had a direct bearing on the access of the incumbent Karachi-based business families to state patronage. The Ayub regime was keen to expand its network of patronage into the Punjab, and cultivate a 'middle class' element in the faster urbanizing zones of the country.[34] Chinioti business families were already part of the industrialist class and they gained in prominence through the Ayubian decade. However, it was the tumult of Bhutto's nationalization that provided the primary impetus for a change in the constitution and politics of the indigenous bourgeoisie.

The primary impact of the nationalization policy was political inasmuch as it exposed the complete vulnerability of the business community to the caprice of a populist government. The first nationalization in 1972 targeted a number of heavy industries in which the Karachi-based business families were dominant. While the initial nationalizations had been expected, it was the series of nationalizations starting with the vegetable ghee industry in 1973, then the banks and finally the agro-processing industries in 1976 that constituted the most significant political blows to the industrialist class.

Most of the assets of big business were concentrated in the sugar and textile industries that remained largely unscathed. The industries which were nationalized comprised 18 per cent of total large-scale manufacturing and their contribution to exports was 8.3 per cent.[35] Whilst those who were stripped of their assets were compensated quite generously in economic terms, nationalization completely demoralized big business in a political sense with a 'diminution in official respect for leading industrial families'.[36]

Some business families remained close to and were patronized quite actively by the regime.[37] Nonetheless, the confidence of the industrial bourgeoisie was permanently shaken and the organic link between financial and industrial capital shattered. As a result, a significant number of the big business families moved their capital abroad, with another attendant effect being the fragmentation of many major business empires. Many families involved in industries such as steel rolling completely withdrew from industrial production and transitioned to trade which was perceived to be less vulnerable to the government's whims.

Younger generations of the Karachi-based families seriously undermined by nationalization admitted the folly of aloofness from the political process. One forty-something owner of a shipping company who was a child at the time said to me: 'We deserved what we got'. In other words, it became clear to big business that if and when it attempted to revive its economic fortunes, it would have to reduce its dependence on the high bureaucracy, develop more robust political networks and fashion its business strategies so as to retain some autonomy from the ruling regime.

In contrast to the 'old' bourgeoisie, the small and medium sized entrepreneur that emerged in the 1970s as a genuine social and political force was well-integrated into societal networks of patronage. On the basis of organic linkages, emergent intermediate trading and capitalist classes in the rapidly urbanizing areas of the country – mostly in the Punjab – would soon graduate into the ranks of the big bourgeoisie. Indeed, the success of Punjabi industry during and after the Bhutto period can be explained by the 'small firms' proximity to large enterprises'.[38] As opposed to the Karachi-based families, Punjabi industry is far more sociologically integrated with the local social formation, imbibing and influencing its culture, and therefore able both to understand and progress in local politics.[39]

The Pakhtun intermediate classes have also proven to be adept at developing social and political networks, like their Punjabi counterparts. The latter tend towards a more overt political posture, inasmuch as larger numbers of Punjabi urban entrepreneurs have risen through the ranks of mainstream parties and even won election to office, but Pakhtun entrepreneurs are not far behind, with many linked to mainstream parties like the Awami National Party (ANP) and Pakhtunkhwa Milli Awami Party (PkMAP).

The comparative political savvy of the intermediate classes – as I have already noted – has its genesis in the localized, political order concocted by the Zia junta. The Federal and Karachi Chambers of Commerce – originally the preserve of Gujarati and Urdu-speaking families – were gradually taken over by Punjabis through the 1980s and 1990s who were better positioned in local politics.[40] After 1982, for the first time, the annual incorporation of companies in Punjab exceeded that of Karachi.[41]

Since the 1980s, the Pakistan Muslim League of Nawaz Sharif has distinguished itself as the party of the urban entrepreneur in the most urbanized belt of the country – north and central Punjab. Given that the emergent bourgeoisie can now represent itself through the political party, it is, unlike the migrant bourgeoisie of the pre-Bhutto period, not totally reliant on the civil bureaucracy – or the military as the case may be – to gain access to the state.

In the aftermath of the Bhutto period, 'a bumper crop of businessmen... entered politics [and] made fortunes in business...without qualms of conscience'.[42] The emphasis of this 'bumper crop' has been to accumulate power and capital, but without anything like the corporate class posture that one might otherwise associate with business lobbies.[43] Liberal theorists often posit a correlation between democracy and the rise of the bourgeoisie.[44] However, in many post-colonial countries the correlation between these two is weak, whereas, in Pakistan it may even be argued that the converse is true. The emergence of a predominantly Punjabi entrepreneurial class during and after the Zia period has not led to a deepening of democratic norms and practices, but at best to the widening of the patronage field to incorporate those previously without status or influence.

Before continuing, I will digress briefly to indicate how my interpretation of the rise of the intermediate classes compares to the (rather scant) literature on the subject. Hasan argues that 'the manner in which the Pakistan state is structured and governed, the manner in which its fiscal system operates, and developed, conceived, managed and implemented, does not reflect the changed demographic, social, cultural and economic realities'.[45] Addleton builds on this basic point in suggesting that the Gulf migrations of the 1970s and 1980s seriously undermined the state's ability to monopolize economic decision-making.[46] Both of these accounts are reasonably accurate reflections of the macro political economy context since the late 1970s; the formal apparatus of the state has unquestionably lost some of its ability to direct the process of economic and social change in the face of substantive transformations mentioned above.

However, these empirics of capital accumulation in the unorganized sector aside, I maintain, in continuance of the argument made in Chapter 2, that the structure of power has not been weakened, but has successfully absorbed new players so as to subdue potential counter-hegemonic challenges. On the one hand the formal state may be fragmenting, but on the other hand the patronage-based political-economic order has become virtually hegemonic.

The intermediate classes grow in importance on a day-to-day basis with the rapid expansion of capital into spaces that the formal state is increasingly unable to regulate. In the spheres of both production and exchange, the subordinate classes are enmeshed in a web of patronage featuring individuals, families and business groups that have graduated into the ranks of the intermediate classes 'from below'. Those who become traders, merchants, contractors and the like are typically sons of tenant farmers, industrial workers and self-employed street vendors. The story of the intermediate classes in Pakistan is the story of capitalist modernity over the past few decades, with all of its intricacies and contingencies.

The Brave New World: Gulf Labour Migrations

There is virtual consensus amongst scholars that the Gulf migrations which started during the Bhutto period have had revolutionary impacts on Pakistan's society, and particularly the Punjabi and Pakhtun regions which have contributed the largest number of migrants.[47] Remittances have had a major bearing on the economy at large and considerably improved migrant families' economic and social status.[48] The basic explanation is a simple one: earnings of migrants in the Gulf – at least in the initial years of the 1970s – were eight to ten times higher than at home and thus pushed migrant families into a higher income bracket, allowing them to break out of dependent economic relationships and acquire a new-found economic and social freedom.[49]

Naturally, this economic and social freedom has had significant impacts on political alignments. For example, the traditional *kammi* in a prototypical village unit that acquires an income source outside the village is no longer confined to subordinate status to the *zamindar*, and can therefore seek out new political intermediaries to access the State.[50] To better understand the politics of such emergent individuals and families it is necessary to consider the multiplier effects of remittance incomes.

As a general rule, beneficiaries of remittances tend towards consumption rather than savings, with the exception being substantial investment in housing; the construction industry boomed throughout the 1980s along with transport and communications. Many returning migrants sought to set up small businesses or invest further in already existing family enterprises, and while not all were able to do so, considerable impetus was provided to small-scale industry as a result.[51] At least part of this impetus was demand-driven and export-oriented as light consumer durables had a market amongst migrants in the Gulf.

The relative and decentralized prosperity due to remittances was a major cause of political stability under the Zia regime; upward mobility of migrant families meant that there was little reason for beneficiaries to participate in agitation.[52] Geography had a heavy bearing on the nature of opposition during the Zia period: The Movement for Restoration of Democracy (MRD), the most potent resistance movement during the Zia period, was centred in rural Sindh, a region which supplied very few Gulf migrants. In contrast, rural NWFP and Punjab supplied the vast majority of migrants and accordingly only scattered expressions of resistance emerged in these regions.

On the whole, the Gulf migrations have stimulated consumerism and ostentatious displays of wealth, especially insofar as the possession of expensive goods and disposable income to spend on services is a means of increasing '*izzat*', or what could be called symbolic capital.[53] Returning migrants also tend to further enhance their standing in society by contributing money to religious causes; migrants regularly donate money to be allocated for mosque-building in the local neighbourhood.

One of my informants from a village in the Gujjar Khan tehsil of Rawalpindi district who spent a few years as an electrician in Saudi Arabia was quite matter-of-fact about his family's change in status on account of earnings from abroad:

> Look money talks. Before I went to Saudi Arabia we were nobody because our family was historically low-status (*hum peechay se kamzor they*). Our money can't change our background but by showing it off, and by demonstrating our religious commitment, we have acquired a new-found status that even the historically more influential families cannot match.[54]

Influx of money has played a part in breaking down 'joint' family structures as nuclear units become more independent.[55] This does not mean that family affiliations have disappeared. Rather, they are now invoked and operationalized in different ways as the 'traditional' village-based units have fragmented. For instance, when upwardly mobile individuals or families establish themselves in a small town or city, members of the larger kinship group seek out the more affluent family/*biraderi* members when in search of a job, financial help or access to the state.[56]

The process of atomization at the level of the family runs parallel to the spread of market exchange, and also explains in part the aggressive political alignments of individuals who have pushed their way up into the intermediate strata. The economic ambitions of the intermediate classes have grown since their political emergence during the PNA movement; the small enterprises run by many returned Gulf migrants have over time acquired concessions from the formal state including tax exemption and free or heavily subsidized use of utilities.

The highly variegated intermediate classes are primarily concerned with developing 'connections' at all levels of the patronage chain. Their instrumental and individuated politics is in keeping with the historical bloc's project in the post-Bhutto period.

The 'nativization' of state institutions mentioned in Chapter 2 has been coeval with the rise of the intermediate classes. The latter's social and political sensibilities are considerably more conservative than older propertied segments which is why the reconstituted historical bloc has acquired a more 'native' character in comparison to the pre-Bhutto period. I will discuss in the next chapter a kindred spirit of the intermediate classes, the religious right. Not by accident, it is the intermediate classes, alongside the religious right, that are the most militant defenders of the state ideology – Islam.

The Protagonists

As already noted, a confluence of interests developed between state functionaries and the intermediate classes in the informal manufacturing and service sectors during the Bhutto period. Under the Zia regime, this collusion became apparent in the election of intermediate class factions to political office, initially at the local level and over time to provincial and national assemblies as many small and medium-sized entrepreneurs graduated into the ranks of big businessmen.

However, the intermediate classes offer those below them in the patronage chain access to the 'everyday state' and market not only as elected representatives. Intermediate class patrons promise relief from the economic coercion of work, and the excesses of the *thana* and *katcheri*. A network of subordinate class clients is actively cultivated even by those intermediate class patrons that do not necessarily seek political office. In turn, these budding patrons are always available to respond to their clients' demands.

Why is it necessary to build such a network? I have tried to outline throughout the course of this book a logic of practice in society that has persisted throughout the modern period, and has evolved in new directions over the past three decades in accordance with widespread social change. The intermediate classes seek to create networks in a distinctly capitalist world far less homogenous and arguably even more ruthless than the rustic one of a bygone era. 'New' forms of dependency are emerging as 'traditional', knowable social relations give way to more distant and market-oriented forms.[57]

In what follows I discuss the sociological background, accumulation strategies and engagement with the 'everyday state and market' of selected intermediate class actors all of whom embody the blurred line between rural and urban. The details presented here are based on prolonged participant-observation at research sites as diverse as Okara, Charsadda, Badin, Sialkot, Faisalabad, Islamabad and Quetta. There is no necessary logic to my choice of protagonists except that their agencies reflect the complex and constantly shifting social context within which capitalist modernity in general, and the politics of common sense in particular, evolves.

The Arhti

The *arhti* is the lynchpin of the small town agrarian sector, the biggest undocumented component of the economy. Over the past few decades, the *arhti* has acquired substantial economic, political and, more generally, social power.

As middlemen between primary producers and agro-processing industries, *arhtis* have a link to all staging grounds of the agrarian economy including the village, the wholesale market, the retail market, transporters, mill owners and exporters.

Arhtis have been players in agricultural commodity markets since the British period, and even before the colonial interregnum. Until partition however, the money lending and trading 'middleman' hailed from the predominantly Hindu *bania* caste.[58] This made the *bania* into a hated figure amongst the peasantry and provided great impetus to the politicization of religious identities in the tumultuous last years of the Raj. Importantly, however, despite the *bania's* steadily increasing economic power, the social order that the British fashioned in the Indus Plains ensured for rural notables and state administrators a 'degree of entrenchment, of a continuum in the access of power, that those involved with trade, commerce and non-agricultural production were not able to contest'.[59]

Following the migration of Hindu business castes from the Pakistan areas within a few years of partition, the role of moneylender and trader was taken over by incoming migrants, and to a lesser extent, by indigenous landed families. Until the Green Revolution, the dynamics of power in the rural social formation remained largely intact, with the *arhti* an important, but still dependent figure. Following modernization in the 1960s, the *arhti* has emerged as a bonafide economic and political force.

The *arhti* is typically a small-time entrepreneur who thrives on the basis of economic savvy and political contacts. As small towns grew in the period after the Green Revolution, local *arhtis* started to replace those from bigger markets in cities who had otherwise controlled trade and transport. Thus emerged a highly complex network of middlemen linking the village, the local *mandi* and supra-local markets.

Arhtis can hail from both agricultural and non-agricultural castes; caste background has become progressively less important in determining one's occupation. Persistent migration after 1947 has affected class formation in many parts of the country, and particularly in Sindh. Punjabi and Muhajir *arhtis* have been settled in many Sindhi market towns for decades, and can be considered outsiders where they share little culturally with the local population. The relationships between *arhti* and farmer in such towns nevertheless resembles the norm in other parts of the country, variegated along a broad spectrum of impersonal economic coercion and historically evolved, personalized ties.

There are dozens and sometimes hundreds of *arhtis* in major wholesale grain and seed markets, most of them small-time dealers, with a handful exercising greater economic and political clout. It is these bigger *arhtis* that compete for control over the market and have links to major political figures in the area as well as state officials, religious functionaries and other local influentials. The relative power of different *arhtis* is determined by how long they have been active in the market, their links with the low bureaucracy, and the size of their clientele.

The first contact that the *arhti* has with the small farmer is as lender of inputs.[60] The small farmer does not necessarily come into direct contact with the *arhti*, often interacting with another middleman who maintains contacts down to the village level. This subsidiary of the *arhti* is typically a budding entrepreneur who has earned some money to invest in business and is attempting to expand his capital.

This local middleman purchases the farmer's standing crop at a fixed rate so that the farmer is able to make arrangements for his next sowing. Upon harvesting the village middleman then takes the crop to the *mandi* where he passes the produce onto the *arhti* for a small commission, while the *arhti* himself secures most of the interest payment. In less urbanized belts, the nexus is less complex, but there are almost inevitably many middlemen competing with and complementing one another up and down the value chain.

The interaction of *arhtis*/middlemen with the lowest castes and classes conforms to some relatively consistent patterns. As a general rule poor farmers are simply not given advances, ostensibly because they have no productive assets. Where market ethics are tempered more by the logic of reciprocity, it is possible that the farmer can eke out an advance through the intermediation of a slightly better off individual in the village, who more often than not is a part of the farmer's larger kinship group. A long and drawn out process of negotiation often ensues in which the middleman is often seen to be 'doing a favour' for the 'poor' borrower. This perception is crucial to the politics of common sense insofar as poor farmers typically think about their association with patrons - in this case the middleman/*arthi* – as an advantage enjoyed over class contemporaries. This is despite the fact that the relationship is clearly an exploitative one.

The manner in which *arhtis*/middlemen recover outstanding debts further illustrates the ubiquity of cash in the agrarian economy as well as the patronage ties that condition operation of the market. The *arhti* has to create a delicate balance between expanding his network of clients and overtly demonstrating his paternalism, particularly towards the very weak. It is in fact by maintaining this balance that the *arhti* can mobilize wider social networks to pressure debtors into paying up. An informant who deals in grain in the Punjabi town of Okara had the following to say:

> Running this business is not child's play (*bachon ka khel nahin ha*). You rely entirely on social networks and sometimes you have to appear more influential than you are so that debtors are scared of the consequences if they don't pay up. In those cases I don't involve myself personally and send messengers who tell tales of police harassment and violence. But then that is tempered by a reminder of how generous and loving I can be if the debtor cooperates.[61]

The *arhti*'s most crucial function is as regulator of the market. Farmers wishing to access the market can do so only through the particular *arhti* to whom they are already affiliated; there is no chance of simply entering the market and selling their produce at an open market rate. If even the village middleman attempts to bypass the existing hierarchy and access the *mandi* directly, he is subject to the wrath of the police and other local officials.

The official regulatory system within the market reflects the relative power of the *arhtis*. For example, licenses are issued to smaller *arhtis* by the local administration usually after the approval of market committees run by dominant *arhtis*.

This spatial power of the *arhti* shores up the dependent relationship with the subordinate classes in that there is a clear demarcation between the forces that exercise (economic and non-economic) coercion, and those that do not. The relationship between the artisanal castes and middlemen through which the former access the market is similarly personalized and exploitative, but is less regulated spatially. This is because traditional artisans such as carpenters, cobblers, and welders do not operate within the confines of an insulated unit and have long since started occupying variegated spaces to ply their trade (or in many cases, taken on a completely different occupation). However, access to the market, whether in terms of them being able to sell their labour, or products that have been commissioned to them, is still mediated by middlemen.

The *arhti* and other non-agriculturalists have emerged as the new motor force of the local agrarian economy which engenders resentment amongst many agriculturalists: '[D]rivers, loom-operators, mechanics, shopkeepers.... earn more than agriculturalists and work less'.[62]

In conclusion, I want to suggest that the popular perception of the *arhti* amongst small and landless farmers can be conceptualised in terms of competing ideal-types. On the one hand, the *arhti* exploits the poor while on the other the *arhti* is viewed as a benefactor of sorts. It is not uncommon for farmers coming into contact with *arhtis* to suggest that the latter is doing them a favour by issuing them seeds, fertilizers, or even cash before receiving anything from them. It is just as common for the *arhti* to be decried as a despot who is concerned with nothing other than personal gain.

Rather than thinking about the relationship between the subordinate and intermediate classes as discrete it is more accurate to conceive of it as a spectrum whereby both perception and reality are constantly in flux. On the one hand, there is the recognition of exploitation and the resulting indignation that comes with it, while on the other hand there is the feeling of gratitude and reciprocity that seems more in line with the prototypical patron-client relationship. These ideal-types broadly reflect the coercion versus consent dialectic that characterizes the politics of common sense.

Urban thekedaar

The *thekedaar* (sub contractor) is a counterpart of the *arhti* based in the urban service and small manufacturing sector. Not directly involved in productive activity, the *thekedaar* benefits from the flexibility of labour and fragmentation of production that are the defining features of urban informality. The analysis presented here is based on extended interactions with *thekedaars* doing house construction in Islamabad, *thekedaars* involved in the manufacturing of surgical instruments in Sialkot, and *thekedaars* embedded in the power looms industry in Faisalabad.

In house construction most *thekedaars* are also closely associated with real estate; they are either agents themselves or work closely with them. In other words, there is a symbiotic relationship between purchase/sale/renting of land and construction on this land. As noted in Chapter 2, land earlier used for agriculture in areas outside the city is gradually being incorporated within it and transformed into real estate. The growing number of real estate agents from modest class backgrounds speaks both to the diminishing opportunities to make a living in productive sectors of the economy, and the unending stream of low-income migrants into the city engaging in housing transactions – primarily rental.

The *thekedaar* in the relatively well-established surgical instruments and power looms industries has more deep-rooted links with his clientele as well as the industry more generally. In these industries the *thekedaar* often starts off as a *shagird* associated with an *ustad* in a certain trade and eventually builds up his own network of *shagirds* whilst also cultivating links with patrons above him. In house construction the institution of apprenticeship is less common, but budding entrepreneurs do often learn through association with established *thekedaars*.

In all cases, the *thekedaar*'s background can almost inevitably be traced back to the subordinate classes; as with all other segments of the intermediate classes that I have encountered, the urban *thekedaar* distinguishes himself through his enterprise, his understanding of the personalized logic of the market, and his desire and ability to cultivate relationships with state functionaries and patrons in the industry. While in the case of the *arhti* the spectrum is large, ranging from small/less influential to big/more influential, there is even more differentiation in the case of the urban *thekedaar*. Most *thekedaar*s will expand into other industries/services once they have become wealthy or politically influential enough to do so.[63]

The urban *thekedaar* operates within a highly dense network of competitors and potential clients, and is himself always in danger of being pushed 'back down' into the subordinate class position from which he emerged. Some *thekedaars* who are barely making a profit supplement their income through daily wage labour or a permanent job; more affluent *thekedaars* are often government employees operating as contractors on the side. On the whole, *thekedaari* is about 'survival of the fittest', as one *thekedaar* involved in house construction in Islamabad made clear:

> We have a reputation for being exploitative (*khoon chooste hain*), but the reality is that we are vulnerable to all sorts of shocks. We can get stopped and harassed by the police like any other poor person and we can suffer from one bad project. Sometimes we don't get work at all. And why doesn't anyone ever talk about how workers take advantage of us (*mazdoor humare sath hath karte hain*) – they often drag their feet and produce bad quality work. Ultimately we are no better off than them (*humari kaunsi mazdooron se bahut behtr haalat ha*).

Thekedaars operate by developing networks of labourers and artisans that they employ on a task-wise basis depending on the job. In the housing and construction industry, the *thekedaar* comes into contact with a variety of wholesalers and artisans.[64] In some cases clients give the contractor responsibility for all aspects of construction/renovation, while in other cases, home owners or tenants effectively act as sub-contractors themselves by seeking out workers/materials for each separate task.[65] In any case, the industry is dominated by sub-contracting. This means that artisans and unskilled labourers are extremely vulnerable as they are almost all hired on daily wage rates by individuals rather than by legal entities under a written contract. In effect the only 'security' they have is to become part of the clientele of their respective sub-contractor, which guarantees work on a regular enough basis for them to survive. The same patterns exist in sectors as diverse as incense stick-making (*agarbatti*), prawn shelling, carpet weaving and bori (sack) stitching.[66] In many of these sectors, 'workers view the provision of work as a favour extended to them by the subcontractors'.[67]

Importantly, *thekedaars* interact less with state functionaries than other segments of the intermediate classes. 'Connections' are nevertheless cultivated to some extent. For example, building regulations in Islamabad prohibit the construction of residential units in certain zones of the Islamabad Capital Territory (ICT). However, there are numerous violations of these zoning laws due to the wilful compliance with builders of concerned state functionaries. In such cases, the doing of a 'favour' for the concerned state official is a well-accepted practice, and factored into the total cost of any construction job. In the instances where the *thekedaar* is also involved in the sale/rent of real estate, the state becomes much more prominent because all land transactions involve the local *patwari*. The latter can even engineer totally fraudulent transactions which means that those *thekedaars*/real estate agents with close links to the *patwari* are extremely powerful; this is typically reflected in the size of their network of clients.

The *thekedaar* in the manufacturing industries of surgical instruments and power looms is generally more secure than his counterpart in construction because these industries have been operative for many decades and there is less scope for new entrants in the market. Both of these industries are export-oriented and the *thekedaar's* immediate patron is therefore an exporter (or the latter's agent).[68]

Manufacturing industries have been subject to immense fragmentation over the past few decades, and particularly after the Bhutto period. For example, Power looms, for instance, were previously located within a larger textile factory alongwith many other value-added processes. However, partially to break the back of organized labour and also because of the structural changes within the textile industry itself, power looms are now housed separately from spinning, threading, packaging and other stages of textile production.

Both industries are housed in small workshops set up in semi-residential/semi-industrial areas of the city. These small workshops have just about enough room for necessary hardware and accommodate up to ten workers.[69]

The working conditions are absolutely putrid, with children and adolescents comprising an extremely high proportion of the workforce. A huge surplus pool of labour is available to those who run each individual workshop. Typically, the *thekedaar* supplies labour to more than one workshop, and has established links with the owners of each workshop as well as the police and local administration. *Thekedaars* often function as the collective bargaining agent (CBA) of the workers. In other words, the *thekedaar* acts in a parallel capacity as a trade unionist, ostensibly struggling for the rights of the workers.

It is telling that sub-contractors structurally positioned to extract as much surplus from workers as possible are also positioned as defenders of working class interests. Workers hesitate to speak negatively of the *thekedaar*, ostensibly because they fear for their jobs. In effect, workers see no other means of protecting their meagre earnings but through their *thekedaar*.[70]

The *thekedaar* often rejects many of the finished implements, particularly in the case of surgical instruments. Since workers are paid on piecemeal rates, this translates into additional labour for the same wage. The *thekedaar* often does not pay the workers on time. In case of accidents in which workers are injured while operating the looms or cutting an implement, the *thekedaar* takes care of their medical needs. However, he then arbitrarily deducts a sum from their wage in lieu of the treatment. Workers have no recourse to all such abuses, and it is a cruel irony that the *thekedaar* himself claims to be protecting workers rights.

Ultimately, it is in the *thekedaar*'s, state functionaries' and workshop owner's interest to keep both industries functioning informally because this not only allows them to maintain their arbitrary power to extract surplus, but also prevents organized resistance by workers. Moreover, the large number of children and adolescents working in these industries is a contravention of child labour laws, and only by continuing to operate informally can the nexus of owner-*thekedaar*-state functionary avoid formal censure.

As was the case with the *arhti*, the subordinate classes' perception of the urban *thekedaar* is highly variable. For the most part, the relationship of the worker to the *thekedaar* in the informal manufacturing industries is less mediated by personal ties than that of the farmer/landless labourer to the middleman/*arhti* in the rural cash economy, with the *thekedaar* in housing and construction somewhere in between. Nevertheless, ascriptive ties play a part in many exchanges, and particularly in the hiring patterns of the *thekedaar*s. For example, in the informal marble industry in and around Islamabad, a large number of Pakhtun migrants are hired by Pakhtun owners, an arrangement which reflects the owners' preference for employees of their own ethnic group; the latter tend to be 'grateful' for the opportunity they have been provided.

The invocation of shared histories along ethnic, caste or other lines is not enduring in the sense that a Pakhtun *thekedaar* hiring a Pakhtun worker does not necessarily imply special treatment nor does it act as a guarantee of retention. Hiring patterns reflect the *thekedaar*'s preference for workers from tried and tested backgrounds that also share a sense of community – however limited – with other workers. So long as the worker perceives employment to be a function of his ability to remain part of the *thekedaar*'s network rather than a right to which he is entitled and for which he must engage in struggle with other workers, the politics of common sense prevails.

Transporters

The 'transport mafia' is the subject of much polemic and speculation in contemporary Pakistan. Rather than the business of transportation *per se*, it is the sheer volume of illicit goods that are transported across the country – and indeed across borders – that explain the widespread use of the term 'transport mafia'.

Transporters attempt to secure the patronage of state functionaries to sustain their accumulation strategies in more systematic ways than other intermediate class groups. Most represent their interests through established associations, even if the actual exchanges in which they are engaged are carried on outside the formal, legal realm.

An example would be the All-Pakistan Federation of Transporters, which, like most associations in the sector, is based in Karachi. Dumper trucks in the metropolis transport construction materials such as cement and bricks. Almost everyone associated with the industry, including owners, drivers, conductors and menial labourers, are Pakhtun.[71] On closer inspection, one finds that the industry is dominated by migrants from Waziristan.

Access to the industry is restricted by influential Waziristanis to their own community members. Potential investors from outside the community are discouraged, sometimes even by state functionaries that have links to the truck owners, and do not hesitate to use negative sanction against them. Migrants from Waziristan to Karachi flock to this particular industry as a means of finding employment, which naturally reinforces insularity. There is a large network of roadside hotels on major thoroughfares running up and down the country run by Waziristanis, which are in turn patronized by truck drivers.[72]

The politics of common sense thrives at least in part because of the insular nature of the industry. So, for example, when the driver of a dumper truck is involved in a traffic accident leading to loss of life or severe injuries, he is whisked away to Waziristan to avoid criminal proceedings and is allowed to return only when enough time has elapsed and it is considered safe to resume driving in the city. This contributes to a sense of gratitude amongst drivers, loaders and conductors who consider their employers to be well-meaning patrons committed to the interest of the 'community'.

Waziristan is one of the border regions of the country – part of the so-called Federally Administered Tribal Areas (FATA) – plagued by the smuggling of drugs and guns which was systematized during the Afghan War of the 1980s. This smuggling of contraband was not only condoned but was actively promoted by the Zia junta, and the army-run National Logistics Cell (NLC) was a major protagonist in the development of the transport regime that thrives to this day.[73]

Given that the truck industry employs a large number of Waziristanis,[74] that it is very insular, and that it enjoys considerable protection from state functionaries, it should not be surprising that formal transport businesses function as fronts to convert black into white money. It is in this sense that it seems valid to use the term 'mafia' to describe its operations.

A former truck driver admitted (on the condition of anonymity):

> It is true that a lot of the material that we carry is illegal, but then very powerful people are part of the smuggling industry. Look, I was just trying to earn a living at home in Miramshah and a number of members of my family (*kabila*) said they could get me work as a driver in Karachi. So I went there. If there was viable employment in my village, why would I go so far away and constantly have a sword dangling over my head (*talwar sar par latki rahti thi*) because I was transporting guns and drugs in fear of being caught?

The political interests of the dumper truck industry are often represented by the Pakhtun Loya Jirga in Karachi, in which the Pakhtun-dominated Awami National Party (ANP) is a major player. The Loya Jirga is essentially the common front of Pakhtun (economic and political) interests in the city and is considered a highly influential political body.[75] So, for example, after political violence in May 2007 in which a number of ANP activists lost their lives and many transporters suffered substantial loss of property, the Loya Jirga issued an ultimatum to the provincial government of Sindh to compensate the victims, threatening (and sometimes carrying out) strikes if its demands were not met.[76]

In response transporters acquired concessions from the government with regard to a handful of routes that had recently been made inaccessible. Moreover, the government handed out compensation to a number of transporters that have suffered losses due to strikes and political violence in years past.[77]

Transporters as a general rule tend to be as functional in their political alignments as any of the other intermediate class groups discussed here. Even in the case of the dumper truck owners, ethnic insularity does not preclude their aligning with parties or state functionaries that are not typically associated with 'Pakhtun' interests if a particular situation demands it.

Notably, this seems to be the one major segment of the intermediate classes which does not lend itself to upward mobility through the ranks of the subordinate classes in the sense that one can only become an owner if one has enough capital to do so; operating a single bus or truck, let alone being a driver or conductor, is simply not sufficient to become a major player in the industry.

Urban shopkeeper/trader

The state has often thought of this segment of the intermediate classes as its most important ally, at least in the aftermath of economic modernization in the 1960s. To be sure, it is the shopkeeper/trader that is the most politically vocal segment of the intermediate classes, and has often been at the forefront of popular agitation, especially in the form of 'defence of Islam' campaigns. Finally, and perhaps most importantly, shopkeeping is the most common means of upward mobility for the subordinate classes.[78]

With exceptions, there are three different levels of trade, starting at the highest tier with the wholesale traders who are also often exporters; followed by retail traders (big shopkeepers); and then small shopkeepers. I contend that small shopkeepers are not in the intermediate class category, yet the links between these three types of traders are significant. Similar to the genesis of all the intermediate classes, big shopkeepers and wholesale traders often emerge from the ranks of the small shopkeeper.

Traders rely primarily – although not exclusively – on family labour and generally evince a ruthless commitment to profiteering. While kinship matters in terms of access to patrons and even customers, it has become less and less salient a factor over time. Many wholesale markets operate on credit and it is more and more the case that credit is withheld from members of the same kinship group because this implies greater difficult in recovering loaned money.

Hence, while the patronage logic is deeply entrenched, it is far less mediated by ascriptive ties than in the past.

Traders and shopkeepers generally evade taxation, and most attempts to bring them into the tax net have met with severe resistance. Despite occasional confrontations, traders' interests are implicitly recognized by the state given that they effectively remain outside the tax net to this day. This explains traders' willingness to support whoever is in power, regardless of otherwise expressed loyalties. Any opposition to government policies does not extend to any long-term hostility to the state *per se*, because traders ultimately rely on the informal patronage of state functionaries to prosper:

> Those people who criticize us for our agitations against registration fail to realise that we carry the entire burden of the government's decision to levy the General Sales Tax (GST). We barely manage to secure a profit margin and then we are asked to pay 16 per cent of our revenues in tax? We are not rich and powerful (*hum badshah log nahin hain*) who can overlook such impositions. Of course we get favours from people we know in the police, CDA and WAPDA, but they are nothing compared to the benefits that regularly accrue to the bigwigs (*barre log*).[79]

Arguably the most distinctive feature of this segment is its mobilizational capacity. Traders and shopkeepers embody the relatively autonomous role of the intermediate classes insofar as they both demonstrate self-consciousness as a class, and also regularly act as one. Alongside the legal fraternity, traders are also the only genuinely effective associational group in Pakistan and, as mentioned above, often come to the fore during political mobilizations in urban areas, and particularly mobilizations around Islam.

This ideological bent can be traced back to the PNA movement that overthrew Bhutto. In that movement, traders were mobilizing against government policies felt to be harmful to their interests, particularly the nationalization of agro-processing industries. The mobilization was given a religious character, with participants seeking establishment of the *Nizam-e-Mustapha* (literally: System of the Prophet) in the country. Ever since, traders have tended to support religious causes alongside religio-political organizations. This has been true regardless of whether the economic interests of traders have mandated such mobilizations. It is, therefore, important to understand why traders participate so vigorously in such reactionary movements.

As pointed out earlier, many of those who set up businesses and became part of the intermediate classes had been migrants to the Gulf, heavily influenced by the Wahhabi Islam of Saudi Arabia and the Gulf states. They therefore internalized much of the 'Islamization' discourse of the Zia regime and started to perceive themselves as major defenders of Islamic causes. This is despite the fact that traders have not affiliated themselves exclusively with religio-political movements, and do not seem to have a commitment to any partisan ideology, typically towing the line of the sitting government. Nevertheless, their commitment to heroic campaigns in defence of Islam remains second to none.

There are two possible explanations for traders' attachment to religious ideology that I wish to draw out. The first is simply that traders and merchants tend to be more pious and committed to a 'pure' religious form that they wish to see established through the medium of the state. The second possible explanation, and the one I find more persuasive, is that religion serves an instrumental purpose for traders/merchants. On the one hand, being vocal supporters of the 'ideology of Pakistan' confirms the symbiotic relationship between the state and traders, and thereby facilitates the latter's informal accumulation practices. On the other hand, traders and merchants demonstrate their religiosity to customers as a means of providing legitimacy to their profiteering.[79]

To be sure, traders are able and willing to reconcile their commitment to capital accumulation with (apparently) deep religious beliefs. In fact, religious beliefs do not seem to be an impediment to the often cynical social exchanges that take place at all levels of society. The subordinate classes and even more affluent members of society that come into contact with traders rarely harbour positive sentiments towards them. The resentment at traders' profiteering, however, betrays the fact that this social segment has arguably imbibed contemporary common sense better than most.

The Face of Change

The intermediate classes are the face of a rapidly urbanizing society in which the market and its unique ethics are increasingly dominant while the state and its functionaries continue to play a mediating role. Instead of ushering the social formation towards the impersonal, rational-legal Weberian ideal-type, capitalism in Pakistan, as in many parts of the post-colonial world, is infused by a heavily personalized rationality which privileges practices outside the domain of formal legality. State functionaries maintain their centrality within the accumulation regime due to the mediated nature of market exchange.

The cumulative effect of this dialectic of state and capital is the appearance to the subordinate classes that upward social mobility is genuinely achievable if one accedes to the prevailing logic of patronage. In actual fact, for every one member of the subordinate classes that actually graduates into the ranks of the intermediate classes, there are many, many more that do not, and in most cases, are subject to more brutal forms of exploitation and/or exclusion than in the past.

While my narrative about the politics of common sense has focused on the reassertion of the state's coercive power under Zia and a concurrent institutionalization of patronage-based political practice, the most crucial element of this politics *forty years after the fall of Bhutto* is a ruthless 'survival of the fittest' mentality that is imparted to young people almost as virtue on the Gramscian terrain of civil society, from the home to school, the mosque and finally the workplace. The emphasis is on individual mobility with an attendant disregard for collective concerns. Those who defy the norm are ridiculed for wasting their time on 'unrealistic' pursuits.

I will consider in later chapters whether an expansive politics similar to that which thrived in the pre-Zia years can be rehabilitated and contemporary common sense transcended. I have already noted that common sense is itself complex and multi-faceted, and the question of identity is at the heart of this complexity. Given the penchant of various members of the historical bloc to constantly assert that Pakistan is an 'ideological' state, the role of religion has become ever more important in conditioning economic, political and cultural fields. It is hence to the politics of Islam that I turn next.

Endnotes

1. See Zaidi (2015): Section on feudalism.
2. See Rahman (2012).
3. Durr-e-Nayab (2011).
4. Wilder (1998: 200).
5. 'Informal' economic activities did not suddenly emerge in the 1970s; the interest generated in that decade in the 'informal' sector is explained by the academy and policymakers belatedly trying to make sense of a long-standing set of interrelated phenomena that we now know by the term 'informality'.
6. Cheema (2003).
7. Sayeed (1995: 143).
8. Addleton (1992).

9. Johnson (1985).
10. Alavi (1987).
11. Some scholars include the 'salariat' segments within the intermediate classes while others narrow the latter category down only to those directly accumulating capital.
12. Harriss-White (2003); Kalecki (1969). Also relevant are the India-specific formulations of Jha (1980) and Fox (1984).
13. Kalecki also emphasized three macro-structural pre-requisites to the establishment of an intermediate regime, namely an incomplete land reform that deprives the 'feudal' elite of its power; non-alignment in international relations which facilitates aid and assistance across the cold war divide; and a developmental posture for the state which allows it to siphon resources on political grounds.
14. Dobb (1963); Brenner (1976).
15. See for example, Arnold (1984); Chatterjee (1986); Chaudhri (1988): 19–23; Sanyal (2007); Kaviraj (1988).
16. Sanyal (2007: 7).
17. Feenberg(1995); Appadurai (1996); Berger, and Huntington (2002); Eisenstadt (2000).
18. Zaidi (2005a); Hasan (2002b)
19. Nadvi (1990), quoted in Zaidi (2005a). Importantly these figures reflect the situation only until the mid-1980s. However, Zaidi suggests that the trends are likely to have intensified.
20. GoP (2007).
21. Kemal and Qasim (2012).
22. Harriss-White (2003: 4).
23. Addleton (1992).
24. Hasan (2002b); see also Burki (1980) who claims that the modern, urban proclivities of migrants have had a tremendous impact on state and society.
25. Burki and Baxter (1975) used election data to prove that the PPP vote in 1970 was the highest in the more urbanized parts of Punjab in which the emergent intermediate classes were seeking out new forms of politics embodying their aspirations for upward social mobility.
26. Sayeed (1995: 86–90).
27. Jones (2003: 205).
28. Zaidi (2005a: 150).
29. As suggested in earlier chapters, state administrators' perspectives on the agrarian economy were guided as much by the imperative of maintaining social order as purely economic considerations; economic primacy was thus given to industry while political accommodation was emphasized in rural areas.
30. Alavi (1983a: 46).
31. Papanek (1968: 40–6).
32. Kochanek (1983: 119).
33. Ibid, 153–61.

34. Zaidi (2005a: 501).
35. Shafqat (1997: 133).
36. Noman (1988: 77-8).
37. LaPorte (1975: 111-2).
38. Zaidi (2005a: 138).
39. Weiss (1991: 11).
40. Kochanek (1996).
41. Rehman (1998: 69).
42. Rehman (1998: 118).
43. See Mushtaq Khan's (2000) conceptual work which is based on the premise that political factions in non-western countries are dominated by the intermediate classes but the latter do not act as a coherent class *per se*.
44. See Johnson (1985) for a vociferous rebuttal of this point of view and an assertion that in fact dictatorship is the most suitable political shell for capitalism.
45. Hasan (2002b: 7).
46. Addleton (1992).
47. Arif and Irfan (1997a; 1997b).
48. It is impossible to get a sense of the actual magnitude of remittances because a large number of migrants use the so-called *hundi* system to send money home. Official remittances exceeded US$2 billion per annum for the first three years of the 1980s which was more than official aid receipts (Tsakok, 1986). In the ten years between 1977 and 1987 more than US$20 billion was remitted through official channels (Zaidi, 2005a: 503).
49. Addleton (1992: 23).
50. Lefebvre's (1999: 166–68) study of migration impacts in two villages of northern Punjab highlights that this new-found 'freedom' can also be a double-edged sword insofar as *zamindars* desperate to maintain their hitherto unchallenged superiority react against *kammis* seen to be rebelling against the traditional social order. Amongst *kammis* that have not prospered in any meaningful way change invokes melancholic feelings for the traditional social order which is perceived to have guaranteed mutual security for *zamindar* and *kammi* alike.
51. Sayeed (1995: 139) writes: 'The important qualitative change that…the Bhutto interregnum brought about was to move small scale manufacturing out of exclusively agriculture servicing activities to the terrain of broader manufacturing in the larger urban agglomerations'.
52. Ibid, 103.
53. From a gender lens, research has been done on *gham-khadi* practices with attention to Pakhtun women in Pakistan and how remittances affect wedding practices and family status (Ahmed 2006).
54. Interview with Zulfikar Khan.
55. Lefebvre (1999: 209–14).
56. See Lyon's (2002) discussion on 'Gujjarism'.

57. Sayeed (1995: 142–43) makes the point that this new form of dependency extends even to consumption via 'segmented' markets. In other words the subordinate classes purchase goods and services provided by the small-scale informal sector as they cannot afford formal sector prices.
58. For the most authoritative study of the character of the Mughal and British rural political economy, and particularly the role of usury, see Habib (1995).
59. Ali (2001: 97).
60. Money lending *per se* is increasingly uncommon.
61. Interview with Liaquat Ali.
62. Hasan (2002b: 142–48).
63. I discussed in the previous chapter how the 'new' Punjabi bourgeoisie emerged from the small-scale sector and graduated into large scale industry/finance/services.
64. For example, a typical housing contractor comes into contact with masons, plumbers, electricians, carpenters, menial labourers, marble cutters, painters, polishers and transporters.
65. Who is building the house/conducting the renovations is of crucial importance in determining the nature of the sub contracting arrangement. In the case of affluent propertied classes, there is typically one contractor that is hired to complete the whole job. Those with lesser means tend to be much more 'hands-on'.
66. Khan et al. (2005).
67. Khan et al. (2005: 56).
68. See Nadvi (2003: 148) on the firms in the surgical instruments industry: 'Key production relationships for local firms include vertical ties with subcontractors and external buyers and loose horizontal links with other producers, particularly through the trade association.'
69. The figure of 10 is crucial because registration of a trade union with the Labour Department is possible only if the enterprise employs at least 10 workers. Most workshops are not formally registered as manufacturing enterprises.
70. The *thekedaar* provides protection from police, access to the Labour Department which (selectively) allocates social security cards, loans in the case of emergencies, and facilities for washing and cleaning workers' personal belongings.
71. The extent of ethnic insularity in this particular case exceeds that of most other segments of the industry.
72. This is a feature of all transporters throughout the country, including passenger transport on cross-country routes.
73. Haq (1996).
74. Perlez and Shah (2010).
75. Jirgas by definition are only constituted in times of crisis or other extra-ordinary junctures. It is not a body that convenes regularly.
76. See http://archives.dailytimes.com.pk/karachi/23-May-2007/loya-jirga-asked-to-consider-one-day-strike.

77. Notably, Pakhtun transporters were not the only beneficiaries of these concessions, even though they did constitute the majority.
78. Opportunities for upward mobility are also stark in highly dynamic sectors such as housing and construction. However, a member of the subordinate classes that comes into some money is most likely to invest in a small shop which brings him into contact with bigger retailers, wholesalers, importers/exporters, etc.
79. Interview with Ajmal Baloch.
80. For a comparative look at the Iranian 'bazaar' and the idiom of Islam, see Keshavarzian (2006).

4

❖

The Many Faces of Islam

> Pakistan is like Israel, an ideological state. Take out Judaism from Israel and it will collapse like a house of cards. Take Islam out of Pakistan and make it a secular state; it would collapse.[1]

Modern nationalism has many variants, but Pakistan is in unique company, being one of only two countries in which religious identity is the basis of membership in the political community.[2] The myth of a monolithic Pakistani nation united by the bonds of Islam was totally exposed by the successful secession of more than half the population of the country in 1971. Yet, instead of acknowledging the glaring holes in the official nation-building project, the state and propertied classes proceeded to reassert Pakistan's 'Islamic' essence ever more vigorously.[3]

In no uncertain terms, the instrumentalization of Islam has been a defining feature of Pakistan's political economy, particularly from the time that Zia-ul-Haq came to power. In this chapter, I will detail how religion has shaped the body-politic, and demonstrate that it is constitutive of common sense politics.

Various religio-political forces have come to exercise influence in the social and political mainstream and thereby been integrated into the structure of power over time. The religious right played a crucial role in undermining the radical political environment of the 1960s and 1970s, and it was subsequently rewarded by the Zia regime. The right's influence has increased in the subsequent period as attendant economic, political and cultural developments have proceeded apace.

Religio-political forces of both the parliamentary and militant variety now espouse a politics of resistance in lieu of the secular-left ideology that was more influential through the Bhutto period. This idiom of Islam as the language of the oppressed has been given impetus by the changed global environment since 9/11, and the growing perception that western powers – and client states in Muslim countries – are attacking 'Islam' in the name of democracy and human rights.

The claim that it is the fountainhead of popular resistance aside, the religious right's politics has not represented an affront to the everyday patronage regime in Pakistan. The Zia regime's policy of 'Islamization' gained at least superficial acceptance 'from below' both because of fear of the coercive apparatus of the state and because 'Islam' became an avenue for upward mobility in a society ravaged by inequality and injustice.

Islam as Myth

I noted at the beginning of this book that a spate of literature has been spawned on Islam under the backdrop of geo-political developments since 9/11. Most of this literature has focused on state strategies, both western and Pakistan's, *vis-a-vis* 'terrorism'. A handful of scholars have also deepened long-running debates on the peculiarity of Pakistani Islam – both as an ideological construct and a major determinant of social order. Insofar as these debates relate to my particular concern with political power, capital accumulation and Islam as a form of legitimation, I engage briefly here with some of the literature that has come to the fore in recent times.

It is now well-established that the use of Islam as an idiom of political mobilization during the last few decades of the British Raj served the largely instrumental purposes of relatively well-to-do Muslims in the old heartland of Mughal north India whose status as a constitutional minority had to be offset by political manoeuvring with their imperial masters.[4] As partition drew nearer, some of the propertied classes in the Muslim-majority regions of the subcontinent also decided to put in their lot with the cause of Muslim communalism. The resulting acquisition of a 'moth-eaten' Pakistan was hardly, as Ayesha Jalal famously suggested, the originally intended outcome, and the confused ideological character of the new state clearly reflected the inchoate interests that coalesced around its formation.[5]

The prevalent view of the Muslim nationalist movement as essentially 'elitist' has been challenged, to an extent, by scholars who have highlighted the popularity of the Pakistan 'idea'.[6] The *ulema* faction that broke away from the pro-Congress Jamiat-e-Ulema-e-Hind (JUH) to form the Jamiat-e-Ulema-e-Islam (JUI) played an important role in this popularization, but so did more secular political cadres, including those associated with the Communist Party of India.[7]

Quite irrespective of the representativeness – or lack thereof – of this 'popular' dimension and the political/social forces behind it, a narrative of Pakistan as a mythical homeland for the Muslims could – and would – be sustained after its creation. As I have noted, the new state's managers eschewed a democratic path for the country, and needed a myth to sustain the autocratic methods they adopted. It was thus that an 'ideology of Pakistan' would soon crystallize around the fantastical notion that Pakistan was a God-sent homeland for India's long-suffering Muslim minority. Cultivating the threat of a 'foreign hand' which sought to thwart the realization of the Pakistan idea was but a logical corollary.

Faisal Devji's treatise on the uncanny similarities between the Pakistan 'myth' and the Zionist project in historical Palestine explores the foundational logic of this ideology.[8] In doing so he clarifies the significant role played by migrants both in conceiving the idea of Pakistan and in its subsequent (flawed) realization. Other scholarship has also tried to 'make sense of Pakistan', while yet more has taken a look at the manner in which ordinary people – including those who did not migrate from India – continue to rhetoricize about 'Islamic' Pakistan as a cosmic order irrespective of their everyday practices.[9]

As I will detail in the next chapter, the myth was not even rhetorically accepted by many who, by an accident of history, became Pakistan's citizens, especially those supporting ethnic-national movements which sought to foreground identities other than religion, and whose economic and political aspirations were not met in the new state. For the purposes of this chapter, I want to emphasize that although ordinary Pakistanis may espouse an ideational commitment to the mythical sense of 'Pakistaniat' that the state has incessantly attempted to inculcate within society at large, they are constantly prone – and consciously so – to betraying the myth in their everyday efforts to negotiate organized power and the market.

Indeed, as Devji suggests, the grafting of an abstract idea almost dismissive of history and geography onto an actually existing social formation with its own distinctive mores gave rise to the ultimate contradiction – legitimacy to those religio-political organizations that were in fact opposed to the Pakistan idea at the outset. Foremost amongst these was Maulana Maudoodi's Jamaa't-e-Islamic (JI). Following a decade of upheaval (1967-77) during which the 'Islamic' essence of Pakistan was challenged 'from below' more than ever, it was the combination of a military dictatorship seeking social control under the guise of 'Islamization' and the JI as the vanguard of this ideological project that provided a veil of legitimacy to the regime of accumulation that I have designated as the politics of common sense.

Islamic or Secular State?

In the defining initial years of state formation, the JI emerged as the primary proponent of an 'Islamic' ideological state. The JI was perceived by its founder

Maudoodi to be an ideological-moral vanguard rather than a mainstream political party *per se*.[10] On the one hand, Maudoodi was opposed to the idea of a separate state on purely theological grounds because it was inimical to the universalism of the Islamic *ummah*. On the other hand, Maudoodi was clear that an explicitly religious organization such as the JI would flourish in a state created on the basis of one's allegiance to Islam. He made no secret of his contempt for the 'anglicized style and the secular beliefs of Jinnah', and generally believed that ultimately it was the JI and not the Muslim League that embodied the sensibilities of what would become the people of Pakistan.[11]

Ironically, by appealing to Islamic symbols in the chaotic period immediately prior to partition, manifest most obviously in the slogan *'Pakistan ka matlab kya? La illahaillallah'*,[12] the nationalist leadership, regardless of its secular roots or ideological pretensions, opened up a space for religious polemic in the new state.[13] In the aftermath of Jinnah's death, starting with the Objectives Resolution in 1949, the juridical structures of the state were given at least a partially Islamic colour, and the controversy over the character of the Pakistan state – theocratic or secular? – was thereby permanently etched into its politics.

In practice this did not mean that the secularity of the state structure or its managers was compromised *per se*, but that the Islamic idiom was more and more instrumentalized by those in the corridors of power.[14] Indeed, modern Islamist politics 'defies the facile religion versus secularism concept', and it is much more apt, particularly in Pakistan's case, to view Islam not as a challenge to the post-colonial state-building project, but rather as an ideational hinge of this very project.[15]

In the immediate post-partition period, the migrant community became a crucial cog in the state-nationalist wheel. Scholars have documented the immensely influential role of migrants in the new state and have pointed out that their political weight and economic power was disproportionate to their demographic strength. By emphasizing the purported threat of Indian expansionism – which reflected the deep psychological impacts of partition violence – the migrant population, especially in urban areas, infused the political discourse with religious metaphors.[16]

Accordingly, religio-political movements initially established a constituency in the primarily urban Urdu-speaking (Muhajir) community – much smaller than the Punjabi migrant population, but more amenable to millenarian slogans. The religious parties' 'depiction of the plight of the Muhajirs as comparable to those of the original Muhajirs, the companions of the Prophet who migrated with him from Mecca to Medina' ensured that a symbiotic relationship developed between these parties and the migrant community – both became vocal supporters of the unitary state project and opponents of the ethnic-nationalist challenges to this project.[17]

In the early years following partition, urban protest movements around 'Islamic' causes conditioned the tone and tenor of politics. Even when clamping down upon such protests, as in the case of the 1953 Ahmadi riots, the civil and military services were able to effectively manipulate the discourse over religion so as to associate Islam with the defence of the 'Pakistani nation'. Disputing this discourse was hence both seditious (*vis a vis* the state) and heretical (*vis a vis* religion). It was not until the Zia years, however, that Islam became a symbol of fear as state institutions started to directly regulate public and private norms, and empowered the religious right to do the same. In sum, the Zia regime marked a departure from previous governments in that the state's instrumentalization of Islam became more explicit and far-reaching.

Islamization

The state-led project has not always been without its fallouts. During the Ayub and Bhutto periods, the ideational force of Islam came into increasing contradiction with the secular accumulation strategies of state institutions and propertied classes. The Ayubian regime managed to largely co-opt religious forces, at least partially because the latter were yet to penetrate the higher echelons of the state as they would later do. The regime did not face decisive challenges from religio-political movements until the latter joined with the larger mass movement that eventually overthrew the dictatorship.[18] Bhutto, on the other hand, while successfully manipulating the dominant nationalist discourse to come into power, eventually suffered the consequences of his own jingoism.

During the tenure of the PPP, Pakistan reconfigured its foreign policy towards the Gulf, while domestically the government conceded more and more ground to religio-political forces, declaring Ahmadis non-Muslims, making Friday the weekly holiday, and banning alcohol, nightclubs and other 'un-Islamic' activities. Rather than positing an alternative nation-building project, the first PPP regime appeared to reaffirm the 'Islamic' essence of Pakistan following the secession of the eastern wing.

Under the Zia regime even more substantive cultural and political transformations were to take place under the guise of 'Islamization'. After toppling the Bhutto regime, and provided a mandate by the PNA movement that had called for the imposition of the 'Nizam-e-Mustafa', the Zia junta announced that it was restoring to Pakistan's its original 'Islamic' mission. Accordingly, the martial law regime invited Islamists into the governmental coalition, and embarked on a more insidious project designed to change the very character of the state structure through the induction of conservatives.[19]

In the very first cabinet that was put together by Zia, four ministers belonged to the JI. Hence emerged a new claimant to state power and the attendant opportunities for patronage that such power afforded. Educated segments of the 'vernacular' urban middle-classes – the main constituency of the JI – were in the same period entering the officer corps of both the military and the civil bureaucracy.[20]

The regime created new state institutions such as the Federal Shariat Court and Council of Islamic Ideology, which provided further opportunities for religio-political forces to enter the echelons of power. 126,000 mosque functionaries were co-opted into the state structure during the Zia years, while 3000 village *ulema* were hired as part-time school teachers.[21]

The long-term impacts of this expansion of state patronage to accommodate religio-political forces are now plain to see. Most notably, the security apparatus of the state – along with foreign states such as Saudi Arabia and Iran – has empowered any number of sectarian/militant organizations to achieve domestic and foreign policy objectives, and change social mores. The process of fragmentation within the state has resulted in intelligence operatives favouring different religious organizations in increasingly violent and unpredictable ways.[22]

Even after the *ulema* parties and the JI started to distance themselves from the regime after 1981, they continued to depict themselves as the vanguards of 'Islamization'. By virtue of this politico-cultural mandate, mainstream religious parties, as well as the large number of religious groups that operate outside the formal political sphere, have become major players in the power-sharing arrangement.

Since the end of the Zia era, the religious right has been directly implicated in making and breaking elected governments. Most notoriously, it was a crucial component of the Islami Jamhoori Ittehad (IJI) alliance which united the anti-PPP vote in 1988 and 1990.[23] Indeed, from the late 1970s onwards, the right's involvement with the covert operations of the state in Kashmir and Afghanistan have meant that it is often far more privy to crucial matters of policy than even elected governments.[24]

The Afghan war that raged throughout the Zia decade greatly enhanced the profile of the religious right and a state-society consensus was forged vis-a-vis the role of the *mujahideen* in particular, and religious functionaries more generally. This not only provided the Zia regime with much-needed legitimacy, but was another major factor in permanently altering the idiom of politics in Pakistan as virtually unlimited social and political space was rendered to the functionaries of *jihad*.

Recalling the political environment of the 1970s confirms just how significant the subsequent transformation in discourse and political practice has been. In the lead-up to the 1970 general election, the country was divided between the radical socialist and/or ethnic-nationalist programmes of the PPP and Awami League on the one hand, and the so-called 'Islam-pasand' programmes of the religious right on the other. Despite championing anything but 'Islamic' political ideas, the progressives won the elections handsomely, even accounting for the relatively clear support given to the 'Islam-pasand' parties by the Yahya regime.[25]

As late as 1975, Prime Minister Bhutto responded to a public slight on him by Pakistan National Alliance (PNA) chief Maulana Mufti Mahmud on the subject of␣Bhutto being a fond drinker by proclaiming at a huge public rally, *'Mai sharab zuroor pita hoon likin maulana sahib ki tarah awam ka khoon nahin pita'*.[26] By the 1990s, the political and discursive fields had been transformed – a thoroughly Islamized idiom of politics had become virtually hegemonic. No political party in contemporary Pakistan risks alienating itself by employing polemic like that of the PPP and Awami League in years past. A sitting member of the national assembly, speaking to me on the condition of anonymity, noted a particular irony in this regard:

> Come on, everyone knows that Jinnah Sahib drank alcohol. It's patently ridiculous (*paghal pan*) that we idolize him as the founder of our country and then make personal decisions such as whether to drink alcohol a marker of our ability to represent the people. But this is Zia's Pakistan – even if the vast majority of members (in the national assembly) do have a drink, they would never want their habit to be exposed because it would mean their political death (*syasi maut*).

Islamic or Secular Society?

Religio-political organizations started to make major inroads into the body-politic during the Bhutto period. For example, the Islami Jamiat-e-Tulabah

(IJT) – the JI's student wing – won numerous elections on university campuses against leftist incumbents.[27] Islam was to become the ideological lightning-rod to which anti-Bhutto activists were drawn and right-wing student groups the most mobilized elements of the opposition.

Following the dismissal of the PPP government, the IJT enjoyed substantial state patronage on account of its mutual interests with the regime. The IJT was committed to breaking the back of left-oriented student unions which constituted a major threat to the military junta. Accordingly, it was empowered to use force to intimidate and harass opponents, and, more generally, presided over a dramatic change in the culture of university campuses.[28] Forty years later, parochial sentiments – both religious and ethnic – have largely displaced expansive ideologies in educational institutions. Politics in general is considered an undesirable activity from which a majority of students stay aloof; it is unusual to encounter young people who believe that political activism can be a force for progressive change.[29]

The Zia regime attempted to transform the environment of educational institutions in *toto*, purging dissident intelligentsia, particularly those based in public sector universities, mostly under the guise of Martial Law Regulation 51. The 1981 university ordinance allowed the government a direct say in appointments, and was used to induct a whole new slate of 'Islam-pasand' educators.[30] The long-term impacts of the 'Islamization' of college and university campuses are explained by a professor of a public sector varsity (on the condition of anonymity) as follows:

> It has been almost three decades since the end of the Zia regime, but Jamaatis are as entrenched as ever. They run the academic associations and control the administration. Nobody can get hired without their approval. They provide cover to the shenanigans (*kartoot*) of the IJT whilst prohibiting activities of any students they suspect of harbouring progressive ideas. In principle the government of the day appoints the vice-chancellor. In practice, it is the Jamaatis who decide who sits in the top office of the university.

The trade union movement was the other major bastion of left populism targeted by the religious right. While left-wing progressives within the trade union movement faced state repression, unions affiliated with the JI had started to make their presence felt in all major public sector enterprises by the 1980s.[31] The National Labour Federation (NLF) was created as an umbrella organization of all JI-supported trade unions. The purpose was as much to challenge the historical dominance of the left within the industrial working class as it was to propagate Islam as ideology.[32] Parallel to trade unions based in urban areas was the Kissan Board, which sought to extend the influence of the JI to peasant collectivities, another stronghold of leftists until the 1970s.

The focus on student associations and class organizations reflected the regime's – and religious right's – strategy of weakening the bases of independent power exercised by counter-hegemonic forces, and particularly those that had been at the forefront of anti-status quo politics throughout the decade of upheaval. This strategy has no doubt been entirely successful as there has been no regeneration of these organic bases of politics in almost four decades since the end of Zia's martial law.

However, the impact of the Zia period extends far beyond the 'Islamization' of student and trade union activities. In my estimation the political and cultural repression that took place under the guise of Islamization had far-ranging impacts across the length and breadth of society. It can plausibly be argued that as important as any other aspect of 'Islamization' was the mandate that the state arrogated to itself and its designated watchdogs – religio-political movements– to intervene into the previously private domain of personal conduct.[33]

Most obvious was the dramatic shrinking of space for cultural expression. Music, for example, was deemed un-Islamic, while places where popular culture previously flourished, such as cinemas, open-air theatres, parks and the like, were outlawed. Undoubtedly the most acute impact was felt by women, whose bodies were made the focus of the state-sponsored transformation of public culture.[34] Religious minorities too felt the burden of being non-Muslims in a state that was hell-bent on infusing religiosity into every nook and cranny of social life.

The entire project of Islamization was based on the inculcation of fear within the subordinate classes, and especially the dread of being branded 'un-Islamic'.[35] This fear was inculcated through the enactment of legislation such as the Hudood Ordinances and the Blasphemy Law, but can arguably be traced back further to the process that began towards the end of the Bhutto period, during which the state arrogated to itself the mandate to interfere in the personal domain.[36]

Crucial to the 'success' of Islamization was that segment of the urban propertied classes which till this day perceives itself to be the vanguard of secular values.[37] Cultural space became highly regulated during the Zia years, and has become progressively more so in the subsequent period. Resultantly, rich and powerful Pakistanis sporting 'secular' lifestyles have become increasingly alienated from the larger society. This is manifest primarily in the creation of elite 'ghettoes' in posh residential zones of big cities. That this highly secular elite acquiesced to Zia's Islamization reflected its desire to be rid of the anti-systemic politics that had characterized the Bhutto period and an attendant willingness to accept a cultural reconfiguration of society.

Ultimately the secular elite has managed to retain much of its privilege, including its ostentatious lifestyle, but has also become more confined to its 'ghettoes'. During the 1990s, this same elite started to express concern about 'religious fundamentalism', a catchphrase which, after 2001, morphed into the broader and much more nebulous category of 'terrorism'. The secular elite's sensibilities and real material interests prevent it from engaging in a thoroughgoing critique of the structure of power in which the religious right is but one component. As an obscurantist conception of the righteous life has transformed social mores, and the threat of the left has diminished, the elite has contended itself with an exclusively cultural critique of Islamization. A former leftist heading a big NGO in Islamabad (who wished not to be named) offers the following impressions:

> People in this society just don't listen to reason. They will follow whichever mullah whips up a frenzy. It is pointless to think about mobilizing the 'working class' or anything like that now, people are mobilized by religion and this is why the few of us [secular-type] should close ranks.

This should not be taken to mean that the subordinate classes were any more inclined to accept the transformation of public culture by the Zia regime. In fact, 'Islamization' did not at all reflect the needs or aspirations of a wide cross-section of social forces. Many so-called 'un-Islamic' practices – at least insofar as this labelling has become commonplace since 1977 – continue unabated in society, including amongst the subordinate classes.

One of my informants hailing from a village in the Punjabi district of Okara said:

> Yaar, on the surface we claim that we are pure (*pak*), but the truth is that everything happens here (*sub chalta ha*). In every third household people are making tharra (home-made wine), boys and girls are enjoying themselves in the fields (*kheton me maze kar rahe hain*) and those with nothing else to do are playing cards (*tash khelte hain*).[38]

However, because of the supposed norms of behaviour that characterize an 'Islamic' society, the predominant trend in public is to adhere to the Ziaist model of religious observance.[39] This duality in private and public life is widespread; for example restrictions on women in the public sphere are widely accepted to be necessary yet watching explicitly sexual representations of women on TV is not considered an aberration.[40] Pasha captures this dynamic succinctly: '[The] basic paradoxes between the dictates of accumulation and the compulsions of establishing a moral order may well produce a bizarre mixture of self-righteousness and hypocrisy.'[41]

It is instructive to note here that the right-wing upsurge has not been limited only to religio-political organizations. The Muttahida Qaumi Movement (MQM) is perhaps the preeminent example of a relatively secular, right-wing organization which has also emerged as a major contender for power in the period under study. The MQM's emergence in many ways mirrors the religious right insofar as it enjoyed a relatively consensual relationship with the Zia regime and was instrumental in changing the political landscape of Karachi – the centre of the labour movement through the 1970s – by displacing a radical class politics with a parochial ethnic politics which foregrounded the separate identity and material interests of the Urdu-speaking population of urban Sindh.

To a significant extent, the MQM has displaced religio-political organizations as the party of influence within middle-class Muhajirs in Karachi,[42] which is to suggest that the rise of the religious right is far from a uniform process across different geographies. With notable exceptions, the impact of Islamization has been greater in urban areas, and understandably so given that it was the burgeoning mass political culture of the cities and small towns that the military junta wanted to arrest. While the impact of Islamization on rural areas has been less profound, the increasing exposure of rural areas to urban influences, both through Gulf migrants and popular culture more generally, has had not insignificant effects.[43]

The north and central regions of Punjab as well as many parts of Khyber Pakhtunkhwa have been sending migrants to the Gulf region for three decades, and one of the more conspicuous results has been returning migrants' greater propensity to Wahabbi practices. Small-town Punjab has been, alongside Pakhtun regions, one of the major recruiting grounds for *jihad* in Afghanistan and Kashmir (which is explained as much by the state's machinations as by the impetus generated due to migrations).[44] Amongst the ethnic Baloch, 'the most salient collective function of the faith seems to be as a mortar, temporarily applied to chinks in the political edifice during crisis situations'.[45] Ethnic Sindhis too have generally been less exposed to state-sponsored Islamization. Yet historically peaceful regions like Gilgit-Baltistan have been badly scarred by state-sponsored sectarianism which is to suggest that religio-political movements continue to spread across the length and breadth of society, and to transform it accordingly.

In the final analysis, 'Islamization' has been a crucial component of the politics of common sense inasmuch as it has de-legitimated resistance to class and state power under the pretext that such political ideologies and practices are un-Islamic. So, for instance, the land reform agenda that remained very prominent through the end of the Bhutto period was almost completely banished from the public realm in 1989 when the Zia-created Federal Shariat Court ruled that land reform was un-Islamic. Religio-political movements then proceeded to popularize this ruling, preaching that those demanding redistribution of land were defying divine injunction.

As I have defined it, the politics of common sense is a complex dialectic of coercion and consent; once it became untenable for the subordinate classes to challenge the state and propertied classes for fear of being deemed 'un-Islamic', their accession to a revitalized machine politics was almost inevitable. That the politics of patronage co-exists with overt ritualism is testament to the cynical duality in public and private life that has become widespread since the 1980s, details of which I discuss below.

The 'Non-Elite' Culture of Politics

The religious right – as well as a segment of the urban middle class that has imbibed its agenda – often invokes the *lack of Islam* as the major explanation for social ills and problems such as unemployment, inflation and the lack of basic amenities such as health and education. It is believed that these problems can be solved through the imposition of *Sharia't*, because Islam is perceived to be *mukammal zabta hayat*.[46] In fact, scratching beneath the surface it becomes clear that 'Shariatization' is a rhetorical ploy and that there is but a tenuous link between the right's slogans and the everyday material realities facing working people, as well as women confined within the home. In short, religio-political forces do not offer a coherent alternative to the status quo, but nevertheless distinguish themselves from other political contenders largely by their more expansive use of populist rhetoric.

The major pillar of the religious right's political discourse is a devastating cultural lambasting of western society and its '*Ladeeniat*'[47] which represents an effort to identify with the lifestyle of the subordinate classes whilst condemning the 'secular and westernized' elite that is depicted as the bane of Pakistan's social ills. In effect, this discourse builds upon the 'nativization' logic alluded to earlier in the sense that secular radicalism – including its intellectual resources – is now an alien concept to a wide cross-section of society. This cultural critique is a clever ploy to maintain the intellectual and political power of the right without interrogating socio-economic structures; it is, in many ways, a narrative which mirrors that proffered by the secular elite *vis a vis* the religious right.

Having said this, the religious parties have displaced the left radicalism of the 1960s and 1970s at least partially by relying on similar organizing methods – which includes highlighting the simple lifestyles of their cadres.[48] That many of the activists of religious parties with which working people come into contact are themselves from amongst the subordinate classes accords to the activist of the religio-political organization a certain legitimacy as s/he polemicies about the need to challenge dominant incumbents.

The cadre of political activists that were the engine for the politics of resistance in the late 1960s and 1970s also emerged from within the subordinate classes, or at the very least adopted lifestyles consistent with the politics they espoused. As student, trade unions and other secular-left organizations have been demobilized, progressives have struggled to rehabilitate the once organic relation they enjoyed with the subordinate classes. On the other hand, right-wing forces, both secular and religious, maintain a comprehensive infrastructure within students, workers, young professionals and the intermediate classes that facilitates entrenchment within the body-politic.

The white collar lower-middle class forms the major support base of the religious parties in small towns and larger cities and is both culturally and politically conservative.[49] Then there is the prototypical *madrassahh* student that typically hails from a rural background and is drawn to the *madrassahh* in some cases because of need and in others because this appears to parents to be the most viable option for education. More generally, the religious parties cultivate the allegiance of 'the intellectual "counter-elite", shopkeepers and small merchants tied to the petite bourgeoisie; and the unemployed youth and the poor'.[50]

The idiom 'Islam as politics' has become increasingly appealing to these disparate constituencies for varying reasons. What brings them all together is the accessibility of religio-political organizations; they provide a means of social mobility for a wide cross-section of "non-elite" groups because they are closely linked to the state and/or international networks, and therefore to their resources.[51]

The scale and depth of the networks cultivated by religious functionaries and/or activists of religio-political organizations can be gauged by the following anecdote: one of my informants – a low-level government employee hailing from the Islamabad suburb of Bari Imam – used the 'connections' of his local *mullah* in dealing with a domestic dispute (which by all accounts is one of the major issues for which the state is invoked by ordinary people):

> I thought my wife was involved with someone else so I went to the local prayer leader (*imam*) and asked for help. He contacted his friend in the JI, who went to the local *thana* and asked a sub-inspector (SI) friend of his to investigate. Upon confirming that my wife was having an affair, the SI lodged an FIR on my behalf. The man having an affair with my wife then pleaded with the SI to not go through with the case, after which I was offered money to withdraw the case. I then filed for divorce, again through the imam who fast-tracked the application through another contact of his at the Arbitration Council at the F-8 district courts. My wife's family had to pay up, I got my divorce and I feel very happy to have an imam in my neighbourhood who is so helpful.[52]

The differences within the 'non-elite' *vis a vis* what Islamization has meant should certainly not be understated. The idiom 'Islam as politics' is internalized in different ways by the three major social groups that constitute the religious right's core support. The intermediate classes tend to be much more 'street smart' in the sense that they, like the religious parties themselves, employ populist rhetoric with no intention of challenging the incumbent power structure, hoping simply to acquire greater access to power themselves. On the other hand, the 'counter-elite' and the very poor tend to be far more committed to the notion of an alternative 'Islamic' order.

While issues such as poverty, illiteracy and even women's rights are part of the religio-political movements' rhetorical repertoire, the focus of their politics – both in and out of power – remains explicitly 'Islamic' causes. The poor and the women are mobilized because of their dire socio-economic conditions and cultural suffocation, and despite the fact that religio-political movements have never undertaken sustained campaigns to actually address class and gender exploitation. A young man previously affiliated with a sectarian organization describes how he came to recognize the inconsistencies in the religious right's 'counter-elite' narrative:

> When I first joined the mullahs I thought that their entire struggle was for the glory of Islam, to make Pakistan into a model Muslim country and to fight against the Hindus and the Zionists (*yahood-u-nasara*). But soon it became clear to me that there was a lot more going on: party members and their families wanted jobs, influence in the local *thana* and *katcheri*, and even

government contracts to make money. It seemed pretty normal for everyone to do this. It was then that I realized that Islam had become a business (*mazhab karobar ban gya*), and that the real problems in society could not be explained in religious terms.[53]

Some scholars have recently suggested that women who affiliate themselves with non-*ulema* religio-political organizations enhance their agency significantly in what is an extremely male-dominated public sphere. I touched in the introduction upon Humeira Iqtidar's work on what she calls the 'secularizing' influences of the religious right on the lives of working-class women in Lahore, whereas Sadaf Ahmad has also challenged established notions of women's agency in her study of the middle-class Al-Huda movement.[54]

These works certainly clarify that it is dangerous to adhere to fixed notions about agency – and even liberation – on the basis of normative commitments to secularism. Furthermore, they demonstrate that the religious right encourages significant numbers of women to engage with the male-dominated public sphere. These facts aside, religio-political organizations have reinforced everyday common sense, whether by propagating Islam as a hegemonic ideology or immersing themselves – and encouraging ordinary people, including women to do the same – in the machine politics that I have termed hegemonic.

In my work on religious militancy in the Swat region of Khyber Pakhtunkhwa (KPK), I found that women initially mobilized in significant numbers to an overtly Islamic cause. Later, they disassociated themselves with that very cause having felt misled. What initially appeared to be an exhilarating alternative to status quo propagated through radio broadcasts for women stuck behind the walls of their homes eventually proved to be a false mirage that resulted in untold suffering in the form of displacement and the loss of sons who were recruited to the militant cause.[55]

Some religious organizations actually distance themselves from overtly political agendas as a means of attracting popular support. Take, for example, self-described 'non-political' religious organizations such as the Tablihghi Jamaa't (TJ). The TJ has developed a huge network of followers, not only in Pakistan, but around the world, and features a disproportionately high number of relatively well-to-do professionals in its network of devotees. It has indubitably contributed to the politicization of religion in Pakistan along with the more overt efforts of the religious parties.[56] While its lack of a formal structure precludes any attempt to quantify its impact, TJ devotees at the very least contribute money and other in-kind donations to 'Islamic' causes.

The religious right has also been quite successful in establishing charitable foundations. Most religio-political organizations have a well-developed welfare apparatus which provides monetary and in-kind assistance to relatively underprivileged populations, whilst also running health and education networks.[57] Of non-religious political forces, only the MQM has successfully established a welfare wing.

Changing Contours of Global Politics

All told, the religious right has succeeded in expanding the bases of its support, with considerable support from state institutions and foreign patrons. Given the already considerable centrality of religion to social life, it is perhaps unsurprising that an explicit political project based on the moral sway of religion has had such wide-ranging cultural and political impacts. In this regard, not only has the religious right adopted the populist organizing methods of leftist and nationalist forces, it has widely co-opted their slogans as well.

The *ulema* under the Raj demonstrated – to some extent and at varying times – a commitment to anti-imperialist struggle. This trend was partially revived by the JUI when it emerged as a mainstream political force towards the end of the 1960s. The JUI formed coalition governments with the secular, anti-imperialist National Awami Party (NAP) after the 1970 elections and for a long time ridiculed the JI as an agent of American imperialism.[58] Subsequently, however, religio-political groups came together under the umbrella of the Pakistan National Alliance (PNA) and consolidated their alliance with the military and foreign patrons during the Afghan *jihad*.

By the end of the Zia period, with the politics of resistance largely crushed, and the PPP steadily distancing itself from its leftist genesis, religio-political forces projected themselves as the genuine representatives of 'the people', replete with a cultural critique of 'western' modernity. The end of the Afghan War marked a distinct change in the rhetoric of the religio-political movements away from anti-communism to anti-imperialism, although both were conveniently identified with western secularism. Over time the right's claim to be the bastion of resistance to imperialism, and to a lesser extent, domestic tyrants, has intensified, helped by the lack of alternatives in the political mainstream.

A cursory look at the literature of religio-political movements confirms this (superficial) shift in focus towards 'anti-imperialism'. As already suggested, religio-political movements have historically emphasized personal morality, and the imperative of 'Islamization' of the state to transform social mores.[59] From the late 1980s onwards, there has been an added focus on sectarian issues, as religio-political movements have started competing with one another to prove their anti-Shi'a or anti-Sunni credentials (as the case may be). While the emphasis on 'Zionist conspiracy' has always been pronounced, since 2001 a great deal of rhetoric has centred around *'Amriki Samraj'*.[60]

As mentioned at the beginning of the chapter, the religious right has, since the early years of the country's existence, spearheaded often frenzied public dissent in the name of defending Islam. This state of affairs has intensified over the past three decades with the 'defence of Islam' motif still the dominant expression of street power. Take, for example, protests organized against the removal of the religion column from the passport and the alleged manipulation of the educational curriculum by Aga Khanis.[61] Media projection and the urban-centric nature of mainstream political discourse ensure that such protests gain some traction, especially in the absence of genuine anti-establishment causes.

But how much popular support do religio-political organizations actually enjoy? The right has enjoyed an increase in its profile in recent times because of the global discourse of 'anti-terrorism', which has apparently made Huntington's 'clash of civilizations' into a self-fulfilling prophecy. At the very least, some Pakistanis believe that 'Islam' is under attack and this has, in the absence of a clearly enunciated secular anti-imperialist politics, allowed the religious right to garner greater political and social space than at any other time in the recent past.

I still maintain, however, that, geo-political shifts have reinforced the contradictions between the generations-old idea of Pakistan as a repository for Islam and the everyday practices of ordinary people which conform not to timeless moral principles, but to the structuring forces of state and market.

Resistance or Co-option?

This chapter has outlined that, beyond epic invocations of Muslim unity, the religious right has sought to become party to rather than challenge the system of power that prevails in Pakistan. Particularly in urban settings, religio-political movements have been willing participants in factional and patronage-based politics, relying on the use of parochial identities and the promise of access to the state.[62]

As mentioned earlier, there is a close link between the intermediate classes and religio-political movements given that both claim to be 'oppositional' forces that seek to challenging the 'traditional elite'. In practice, both seek to expand their network of clients by providing preferential access to the *thana*, *katcheri* and so on. In short, they essentially offer to the subordinate classes an alternative means to access the state, navigate the market and, in the final analysis, claim a stake in the prevailing system, rather than a programme for challenging the politics of common sense.

A recent experience of the religious right in power bears this out. Between 2002 and 2007, the six-party religious alliance Muttahida Majlis-e-Amal (MMA) occupied the seat of provincial government in then NWFP. State patronage was used to reward stalwarts of the alliance, as well as the MMA's electoral constituencies. Among the favours issued by the government to its constituents were employment in public sector organizations, issuing of road and other construction contracts and even the import of duty free vehicles. The MMA government made no meaningful attempt to restructure political and economic institutions in the province, and the implementation of an 'Islamic' social order was limited to the banning of music in public transport vehicles and the removal of billboards depicting unveiled women.[63]

The experience of the religious right in power eroded its own claim to being morally and culturally superior to the '*ladeen* elite' that is the target of its incessant polemic. From the later part of the Zia interregnum, the right's claim to being from within 'the people' and opposed to the 'decadent lifestyles' of dominant social groups was preserved by the very fact that it remained largely distant from state power. In subsequent years, as the religious right has become more implicated in power politics, its self-righteous claims have become considerably more tenuous.

Yet, the idiom of Islam remains at the forefront of Pakistani politics, and is invoked by all and sundry as the ultimate fountainhead of statecraft. I have reiterated many times over that Islam has greatly conditioned Pakistan's politics since the very inception of the state. However, with the emergence of the religious parties as the default vanguard of Islam since the late 1970s and the state's attendant formal and informal delegation of power to the *maulvi* (which has given the latter the right to dictate morality in the public and private spheres), religio-political forces have acquired greater power than ever to shape public discourse. As part of an expanded historical bloc, these forces have reinforced the notion that the state's official ideology is nothing less than the defence of Islam.

If the Zia regime increased 'vernacular interests' access to the state, it also demobilized the subordinate classes by using the hegemonic power of religion along with the coercive force of the state apparatus. The 'Arabization' of many migrant villages, the war economy of *jihad* in Afghanistan and Kashmir, and a creeping dominance of intermediate classes in peri-urban and rural areas with a commitment to reactionary politics have been the parallel societal impulses to the state-led project.

As I will discuss presently, this strategy has not completely succeeded, even if it has given rise to a parallel claimant to a people-centred politics that features defiance of 'imperialism' and 'tyranny'. When the subordinate classes have challenged state, corporate or propertied class power, the right has attempted to co-opt any potential radicalism, more often than not under the guise of following the righteous, 'Islamic' path. While the religious right now faces challenges from other populist right-of-centre political forces, it remains at the forefront of most major political mobilizations, in no case attempting to truly challenge status quo.

Evaluating the Ziaist project as a whole, it is clear that religio-political forces played a crucial role as a new intermediary between the subordinate classes and the state, sometimes displacing traditional intermediaries but more often than not taking over the limited but growing political space occupied by counter-hegemonic forces. The religious right will continue to be part of the historical bloc, but it now faces a changed geo-political environment as well as contradictions in its self-depiction as 'pro-people' due to its integration into the patronage machine. Perhaps most of all, it has yet to succeed in realising the Pakistan 'idea' that has persisted since before the inception of the state. In the following chapter, I detail just how tenuous its claims to be the ears and eyes of a Muslim 'nation' truly are.

Endnotes

1. General Zia-ul-Haq, *The Economist*, December 12, 1981, quoted in Ali (1983: 133).
2. Khory (1997) notes that Urdu – the other major symbol of state nationalism – has historically been ascribed the status of a 'Muslim' language.
3. It was in the late 1970s that the deliberate doctoring of textbooks began; history was re-written to project the Islamic basis of Pakistan's creation (Hoodbhoy and Nayyar, 1985).
4. For a seminal study that interrogates the way in which Islam was politicized in the context of the property rights regime in Punjab, see Gilmartin (1979)
5. Jalal (1985).

6. See, for example, Talbot (1996).
7. The breakaway faction was led by Maulana Shabbir Ahmed Usmani who formed the JUI in 1945. See Moj (2015); for the role of the communists, see Ali (2015).
8. Devji (2013).
9. Shaikh (2009); Nelson (2011).
10. Nasr (1994).
11. Ibid, 20.
12. Literally: 'What is the meaning of Pakistan? That there is no God but Allah'.
13. For a materialist analysis of the Pakistan movement that debunks the myth that it was founded on millenarian grounds, see Alavi (1987).
14. For a discussion of the historical accommodation between the 'modernist' state elite and 'traditionalist' religious forces, see Akhtar et al (2006).
15. Nasr (2001: 14); Ahmed (2003).
16. Wright Jr (1974); Gayer (2014).
17. Nasr (1994: 89).
18. The religious lobby did protest vociferously against the regime's enactment of the Model Family Laws Ordinance in 1961, but at no point was there an irreversible confrontation between the two sides.
19. It should be pointed out that General Zia had started to change the ethos of the Pakistani military following his promotion to Chief of Army Staff in 1976. The emergence of this 'Pakistani generation' of military men was discussed in Chapter 2.
20. Ahmad (1974).
21. Ahmad (1998: 106).
22. Hussain (2007).
23. The IJI is known to have been given explicit support by intelligence agencies so as to keep the PPP from winning the 1990 election. A former DG ISI admitted as much in a signed affidavit presented to the Supreme Court (Haqqani, 2005: 219).
24. Ibid, 292–93
25. Ibid, 57–59
26. Literally: 'I drink alcohol, but at least I do not drink the people's blood like Maulana Sahib'.
27. Nasr (2001: 93–96)
28. Younger Jamaat-e-Islami cadres that participated in the Afghan *jihad* inducted guns and violence onto university campuses (ICG, 2002: 12).
29. Proponents of cricketer-turned politician Imran Khan's Pakistan Tehrik-e-Insaf (PTI) party would argue that 'youth' have been mobilized in significant numbers to the cause, but there is no definitive evidence to suggest a decisive shift in the political proclivities of the almost 120 million Pakistanis under the age of 23.
30. Noman (1988: 133)
31. Examples include the PREM Union in Pakistan Railways and the Staff Employees Union in WAPDA.
32. As a general rule, economic equality or redistribution has never been a major concern of the religious parties; the JI has experienced serious internal debate and

struggle which has seen it move from being a restricted and insular ideological organization to a more populist one in tune with the demands of working people.
33. Nasr (2001: 136–37)
34. Weiss (1994)
35. This is true in general and in terms of the growing influence of religio-political forces: '[T]he authorities in Pakistan are hard-pressed to contend with organizations that operate in the name of Islam and claim to be defending its interests: police action against [them] is seen as harassment of the true servants of the faith' (Nasr, 2002: 96).
36. The quite arbitrary use of the so-called Blasphemy law against hapless individuals – most of whom are non-Muslims – has become an endemic problem. See Siddique and Hayat (2008).
37. Hasan uses the term elite to refer to this strata – I understand it here to refer to the relatively educated and secular minded elements in the *pre-Bhutto* historical bloc.
38. Interview with Mohammad Ramzan.
39. It would be facile to suggest that the increase in religious orthodoxy is entirely a response to the perceived need to adhere to state-imposed sanctions. It is worth considering the Weberian notion that Puritanism is coeval with the deepening of capitalism; as was discussed at length in the previous chapter, the intermediate classes have been amongst the most devoted followers of religious causes which reflects the close relationship between capitalist modernization (within a specific cultural milieu) and the rise of religious orthodoxy.
40. Nelson (2011) has also touched upon this duality by showing that rural Punjabis are keen to be seen as committed to the Islamic law of inheritance, yet regularly attempt to bypass the same law in their engagements with politicians.
41. Pasha (1992: 124).
42. See Verkaaik (2001; 2004).
43. Kurin (1985).
44. During the Zia regime the government provided unprecedented support to seminaries, giving them zakat funds, and guaranteeing graduates opportunities after their education (Nasr, 2001: 142–43). While it would be erroneous to attribute the proliferation of *jihadi* tendencies solely to *madrassahs*, there is no doubt a close correlation between the rise in militancy and parochial *madrassah* education. For more on this topic see Hussain (2007).
45. Pastner (1996: 177).
46. Literally: a complete code for how to live one's life. The JI's literature constructs the Islamic code around an ethical system (*ikhlaqi*); a political system (*syasi*); a societal system (*maashrati*); an economic system (*iqtasadi*); and a spiritual system (*rohani*).
47. This literally translates into irreligiosity and is typically equated with secularism.
48. Ahmed (1986: 79) makes the interesting point that the populist 'mullah' 'watched and learned' from Bhutto during the 1970s and emerged as a political force only during and after this period.

49. Zaman (1998: 709) makes the compelling argument that 'the emergence of sectarian organizations has responded to the search of many people – including, but not only, returning labour migrants from abroad, for an urban religious identity, which would accompany, and perhaps facilitate, their quest for a middle-class status'.
50. Nasr (2001: 15).
51. For a more general perspective on the cadres and constituents of religio-political movements, see Ahmad (2006: 189).
52. Interview with Jalal Din.
53. Interview with Yasir Khan.
54. Iqtidar (2011); Ahmad (2009).
55. Akhtar (2010).
56. Metcalf (2001); Mamdani (2005: 134–35)
57. Such welfare organizations are involved in activities as diverse as collecting donations for victims of natural calamities, organizing food handouts during the fasting month of Ramzan, and providing free schooling to widows and orphans of men who have died during the course of *jihad*. Militant organizations such as the Lashkar-e-Tayyaba (most recently known as the Jamaa't-ud-Da'wa) openly operate welfare fronts such as the Falah-e-Insaniyat Foundation.
58. Pirzada (2000).
59. Ahmad (1998: 105) writes: 'Among the articles and write-ups on current affairs in the seven publications sponsored by the Jamaat-e-Islami, JUI, JUP, and JUAH during October 1984–November 1987, 33 per cent of them were on issues pertaining to personal morality and only 3 per cent on problems of socio-economic injustices in Pakistani society.'
60. Literally: American imperialism.
61. See for example *Dawn* (March 10, 2005; May 12, 2015).
62. The most widely quoted example of the rise of the religio-political movements in small-town Punjab is that of the Sipaha Sahaba in Jhang which has garnered support amongst the Sunni intermediate classes in opposition to Shia landed notables (Nasr 2002; Zaman 1998).
63. White (2008).

5

The Nation that Never Became

Notwithstanding the growing influence of Islam in Pakistan's body-politic, ethnicity rather than religion has been the primary marker of identity in large parts of the country both before and after 1947; outside of the dominant province Punjab, the so-called 'ideology of Pakistan' has always been seriously contested. Through the course of this book I have attempted to explain how the politics of common sense came to displace more expansive and transformative political idioms from the Zia period onwards. To truly make this hypothesis a viable one in what is a very ethnically divided country, it is necessary to probe the history of ethnic-nationalism and its relationship with the politics of common sense.

Contrary to official myth, the various ethnic-linguistic communities that came to comprise the new Muslim-majority state were not all flag bearers of the Pakistan movement. Most famously, Pakhtuns in the Peshawar Valley region largely supported the Congress-allied Khudai Khidmatgars.[1] After the creation of the country, Pakhtun nationalism retained its appeal in the Peshawar Valley and other parts of NWFP, as well as what is today northern Balochistan. Ethnic Sindhis had been protesting political and economic marginalization at the hands of migrants and allottees of state land since well before 1947, notwithstanding the passing of a formal resolution in favour of the Pakistan demand by the Sindh provincial assembly in the lead-up to Partition.[2] Balochistan, which was only formally recognized as a province in 1970, also had what at best could be called an ambivalent relationship to the new state. The Khan of the Kalat state, the large princely territory that comprised most of the Baloch people, repeatedly claimed that he was forced to accede to Pakistan at the barrel of a gun.[3]

In the event, the protestations of various ethnic-linguistic communities in west Pakistan were dramatically overshadowed by the conflict that erupted immediately after the establishment of the state between the Bengali majority based in east Pakistan and the civil and military bureaucracies dominated by Urdu-speakers and Punjabis respectively. Troubles began as early as 1948 following an infamous speech by Muhammad Ali Jinnah to students in Dhaka in which the country's founder insisted that Urdu would be the official language of the new state, even though Bangla was the native tongue of more than half of Pakistan's population. Student protests both before and after Jinnah's pronouncement eventually culminated in the Dhaka riots of February 1952 which left scores of students dead and marked the crystallization of the Bengali nationalist movement.

Language was only one of many acute grievances that caused a wedge to develop between west Pakistan's ruling clique and Bengali nationalists. The Karachi-based migrant industrialists discussed in Chapter 2 presided over what was essentially a relationship of economic colonialism between the two wings; export earnings from jute produced in the eastern wing were used to fund industrial enterprises based almost exclusively in the western wing. Meanwhile, the dismal representation of Bengalis in the permanent institutions of the state – relative to their overall population – was never meaningfully redressed.[4]

As I have already noted, the civil and military services along with the west Pakistan's propertied classes resisted the establishment of a democratic political process for more than two decades. When the country's first general election in 1970 resulted in an outright victory for the east Pakistan-based Awami League (AL), the Yahya military regime refused to hand over power to AL leader Mujibur Rahman and the simmering conflict hurtled towards its logical conclusion.

East Bengal eventually seceded from Pakistan after a nine-month civil war in which Pakistan's military was engaged by the full-fledged insurgent force, *Mukti Bahini*. This remains the only instance in the history of the modern nation state in which the majority of the population has seceded from a demographic minority.

Yet remarkably, little over a year after the PPP government of Zulfikar Ali Bhutto came to power following the military's ignominious fall from grace, another army operation had been launched against another dissenting ethnic-national community. The new populist government had managed in late 1972 to piece together enough support in parliament to conclude a new constitution which made many overtures to ethnic-nationalists under the guise of increasing provincial autonomy. The constitution was begrudgingly accepted by nationalists in the opposition, most notably the National Awami Party (NAP), which had formed coalition governments with the Jami'at-e-Ulama-Islam (JUI) in both the NWFP and Balochistan.

However, soon afterwards, the federal government claimed that the NAP regime in Balochistan was plotting a conspiracy to unseat the PPP at the centre. Bhutto dissolved the NAP-led Balochistan government, after which the NAP leadership openly voiced doubts about remaining part of the federation. The military was called into quell the rising tide of dissent, making another full-fledged insurgency into a self-fulfilling prophecy.

It was only five years later in 1978 following the deposal of the PPP Government by the Zia junta that a truce was called and the criminal charges lodged by Bhutto against the NAP leadership withdrawn. Yet by 2004, another insurgency had taken root in Balochistan, and the military was once again using its coercive power to put down 'enemies of the state'.

The full force of state power has been employed not only in erstwhile east Pakistan and Balochistan, but also in Sindh, most notably during the Movement for Restoration of Democracy (MRD) movement in 1983. Sindhis have never lived down the use of missiles and bombs against unarmed populations in the Moro region of the province at the height of the anti-dictatorship struggle. Even the Urdu-speaking community in urban areas of Sindh, which has historically enjoyed a symbiotic relationship with state power, experienced the brunt of the military's coercive force on a handful of occasions after the creation of the Muttahida Qaumi Movement (MQM) in the late 1980s.[5]

To be sure, ethnic-nationalism is an undeniable reality of Pakistan's political economy, fuelled by an undemocratic structure of power and the skewed ethnic composition of the civil and military services. In the first few decades after Pakistan's inception, Urdu-speakers were considered (at least) equal partners in the structure of power. However, since the Zia years the perception that the state is 'Punjabi-dominated' has gained increasing traction across the country.[6] In short, ethnic-linguistic identity remains as significant as any other fault line in the polity seventy years after the creation of the state.[7]

Nationalism in Theory and Practice

I have noted at various points the paucity of theoretical work on Pakistan's state and society and the imperative of moving beyond now dated seminal treatises. A similar quandary exists in the case of ethnic-nationalism in Pakistan. The most invoked explanation for the salience of ethnic-nationalist politics after the creation of Pakistan traces its genesis back to the Muslim nationalist movement in India which was dominated by Punjabi and Urdu-speaking white-collar professionals, or 'salariat'.[8] According to this account the differential access of ethnic-linguistic communities to the new state's economic and political resources explains all subsequent expressions of nationalism (or lack thereof).

This instrumentalist explanation is without doubt appealing. Punjabis and Urdu-speakers did take over the reins of the new state and the former continue to dominate state institutions and the economy almost seven decades later.[9] Nonetheless, it would be naïve to completely ignore what scholars associated with the 'perennialist' school of thought would assert are the cultural bases of nationalism.[10]

According to this line of thinking, nationalism cannot be reduced simply to a political movement that emerges as a corporate group lays claim to material resources under the guise of being a 'nation'. Instead national identity should be seen as rooted in historically shared symbols such as language, territory and broader aspects of culture.

I think that it is important not to lose sight of exactly how powerful the idea of a shared cultural past can be, even if it is a largely constructed one. This is particularly so in Pakistan where ethnic identity – for virtually everyone other than Punjabis – is so salient. I will discuss below the extent to which the ethnic-nationalist mythologies have remained intact in the face of substantive social change and integration, but there is something to be said for the fact that the idea of 'Sindhi-ness', for instance, is as powerful as it is. So while the nationalist idiom remains very prominent in large part because of (real and perceived) unevenness in the distribution of power and resources, there is nevertheless a crisis of identity in Pakistan that renders purely instrumental accounts of ethnic-nationalism unsatisfactory.

Having said this, in this chapter, I do not engage at length with larger debates over nationalism and limit my discussion to the politics of actually existing national movements. In this regard, the most useful conceptual distinction for Pakistan's case is that between 'state nationalism' and 'ethnic nationalism'.[11] The state has adhered to a unitary nationalist project which foregrounds Islam and Urdu, and has accordingly criminalized ethnic-linguistic communities that claim resources and demand a power-sharing arrangement that is akin to a multi-national federation. Ethnic nationalists might also be seeking control over the state, but their nationalism is, by definition, an ideology of resistance precisely because they are largely excluded from the exercise of power.

Symbiosis between Class and Ethnicity

The idiom of ethnic nationalism has been associated with an anti-status quo politics from the very inception of the state. It therefore shared a symbiotic relationship with the politics of class during the decade of upheaval (1967–77) that I have discussed at length through the course of the book. This symbiosis was most obvious in the composition and politics of the Awami League (AL) in erstwhile East Pakistan and the National Awami Party (NAP) which, as mentioned above, came to power in NWFP and Balochistan in west Pakistan.

The NAP, successor to the Red Shirts or Khudai Khidmatgar movement, was a unique amalgam of leftists and ethnic nationalists that at one and the same time was demanding an overhaul of the unitary state structure and propagating a politics of class in the interests of peasants and workers. The NAP's history as a party of medium-sized landowners in the Peshawar Valley was a major reason for its electoral victory in NWFP, whereas its leadership in Balochistan was comprised of historically powerful tribal chieftains who enjoyed substantial dependencies. The party's leftist component was nevertheless significant and its dismissal by the central government so soon after its assumption of the reins of government indicated the extent of its counter-hegemonic potentialities.[12]

In the other two provinces, Sindh and Punjab, the PPP was the dominant political force. As I have already discussed in previous chapters, the PPP championed a politics of class. However, in the Sindhi context, the party identified greatly with the ethnic-nationalist cause. Zulfikar Ali Bhutto's decision to make Sindhi the official language of the province and spearhead a host of other symbolic initiatives that promoted Sindhi culture meant that, in Bhutto's home province, the PPP took on a decidedly 'Sindhi' colour.[13]

The PPP's posture in Punjab was markedly different, which follows from its leader's long association with the Punjabi-dominated military establishment. Zulfikar Ali Bhutto resigned from his position as foreign minister under Auyb Khan following the Tashkent Agreement between India and Pakistan in January 1966. Adopting a typical state-nationalist position, Bhutto claimed that his former boss had 'sold out' the country.

For the next eighteen months, prior to the creation of the PPP in December 1967, Bhutto toured Punjab and drummed up anti-India sentiment. His jingoism endeared him to many young people, including the leftist National Students Federation (NSF) which, by virtue of its pro-China slant, was predisposed to anti-India sloganeering. NSF cadres played a significant role in generating political support for the PPP in Punjab in the lead-up to the 1970 general election.

After coming to power, Bhutto continued to play to the Punjabi gallery, talking up a 'thousand year war' with the designated arch-enemy, downplaying the country's sub-continental roots and reorienting foreign policy towards Muslim countries to the west. Following the Indian nuclear test of 1974, the Prime Minister launched Pakistan's programme with the promise that he would 'eat grass' so as to secure the bomb. Perhaps most crucially, Bhutto called in the military in Balochistan in 1973, an episode that reignited the flames of chauvinism in the Punjab against oppressed nations and helped rehabilitate the Punjabi-dominated military's prestige.

In short, whereas the symbiotic relationship between class and ethnicity was a major pillar of the politics of resistance through the 1970s, it was precisely the fact that this relationship was inverted in Punjab that set the stage for the restoration of state and class power. Under the Zia regime, ethnic-national movements other than in Sindh were either co-opted or subdued. With the gradual relegation of class to the periphery of political discourse and practice – in Pakistan and also much of the world – the symbiotic relationship between class and ethnicity has largely come undone. While ethnic-nationalism remains prominent on the political landscape, there is no coherent and organized political force like the NAP of yesteryear to unify working people of all oppressed nations and build a counter-hegemonic politics. Instead, xenophobic tendencies have risen to the surface within some ethnic-nationalist movements while leftist influences remain conspicuous by their absence.[14]

Proximity to the State

Notwithstanding the fragmentation of counter-hegemonic forces, ethnic-national movements remain a potent form of resistance to organized state power. Alongside older movements, Siraikis, the people of Gilgit-Baltistan and Hindko-speakers (based in the Hazara areas of Khyber Pakhtunkhwa) have intensified their political efforts for recognition and resources in the post-2008 period.[15] The posture of state institutions towards some of these movements, and particularly the ongoing use of coercive force against them by the military, confirms that they are considered a definitive threat to the formal structure of power and, as importantly, the 'ideology of the state'.

Most notable is the disappearing, killing and dumping of nationalists – and even those considered sympathetic to nationalist politics – in Balochistan, and to a lesser extent, Sindh. Thousands of Baloch have been disappeared since 2005, allegedly by Pakistan's intelligence agencies. In some cases, mutilated bodies encrusted with Pakistan's nationalist slogans have been discovered in roadside drains.[16]

Evidently, the security apparatus of the state remains fearful enough of ethnic-nationalism to employ its most potent ideological weapon - 'Islam' to blunt nationalism's popular appeal. I mentioned in the last chapter how religious functionaries patronized by the Zia regime and its foreign backers played a major role in 'Islamizing' Pakhtun regions that have historically been fertile breeding grounds of ethnic-nationalism. A similar state-sponsored effort is underway in contemporary Balochistan where many seminaries and religious organizations are being facilitated by the security apparatus to undermine the influence of Baloch nationalism.

A student at the Engineering University in Khuzdar told me of his experience:

> The authorities realized that many of us were being influenced by the Baloch Students Organization – Azad (a radical group believed to be linked to some militant nationalists). So they started bringing in Tableeghi Jamaa't preachers who would be given free access to the university premises and particularly the dormitories. The point was to wean the students away from the nationalist groups.[17]

As I suggested in the last chapter, the direct infusion of 'Islam' into the body-politic has been a major constitutive element of the politics of common sense. I have nevertheless maintained that it is in the realms of the everyday state and market – where know-how, status and money rather than ideology play the dominant role – that the consent of the passive majority is garnered.

As per the broader coercion-consent schema I have outlined in earlier chapters, I interrogate below whether the 'imagined community' that ethnic-nationalists claim is resisting a purportedly monolithic state actually exists in practice. In short, I want to suggest that the politics of common sense can, and does, co-exist with a politics of ethnic-nationalist resistance in many of the peripheral regions of the country.

However, first I must digress briefly to establish why a wide cross-section of Punjabi society has historically imagined the state as benign in stark comparison to the imaginary of the state in most of the non-Punjabi peripheries. I think it is necessary to consider this history because it provides much needed context to my claim about the uneasy co-existence of the politics of common sense and the politics of ethnic-nationalist resistance in large parts of the country.

Punjab under the British constituted a remarkable experiment in social engineering insofar as the construction of perennial irrigation canals in the western plains dramatically altered the social structure of the region and accordingly vested in the state unprecedented power to mould the social order.

The colonial project in Punjab was premised upon the firm belief that the northwest frontier of India was the crucial buffer that would protect the vast British empire – extending as far east as Australia and New Zealand – from potential aggressors to the west and the north. The rank and file of the British Indian army then, particularly after the 1880s, was derived disproportionately from the Punjab and the Pakhtuns of the Northwest Frontier.[18] The state proceeded to effectively buy the loyalty of this volunteer army through the systematic issuing of land grants in the canal colonies. The end result was the creation of a nexus of military-bureaucracy-landed proprietor that persisted long beyond the end of colonialism.[19]

A unique form of government was institutionalized by the second decade of the twentieth century, popularly known as the Punjab school of administration, in which 'authoritarian' tendencies were actively encouraged. Military men were inducted into positions of civilian authority in repudiation of the well-established colonial principle.[20] Even the electoral regime created and refined by the British from 1919 onwards reinforced the unique civil-military nexus. This regime was based on deeply ingrained principle of distribution of patronage and heavily skewed towards rural-military interests.[21] This nexus of power championed the tremendous social and economic modernization that took place in the province throughout the century of British rule (and has continued into the post-colonial period). Among other things, Punjab enjoyed the multiplier effects of cantonment towns, the highest density of railroad track in the subcontinent and a formidable road infrastructure.[22]

On the whole, the agriculturalist that was the mainstay of the social order benefited considerably from it and therefore could be counted upon to stand by the state. Meanwhile, the non-irrigated and relatively poor Potohar plateau in the northern part of the province was the major recruiting ground for the army, and was kept relatively underdeveloped so as to ensure the loyalty of the majority of the subaltern population that was almost entirely reliant on recruitment to the army for its livelihood.[23]

I noted in Chapter 2 that many of these colonial patterns of development and recruitment remained intact many decades later, albeit with some important changes. The idyllic and relatively ordered rural Punjab over which the British presided is now increasingly – some might say predominantly – urban. As I have demonstrated, urban Punjab is home to arguably the most upwardly mobile segments in the country in the form of intermediate classes. In effect, a significant number of Punjab's 'ordinary people' continue to remain beneficiaries of a rapidly changing social order in which patterns of development and the exercise of formal state power across the ethnic-linguistic divide nevertheless appear to remain quite stable.

This is not to suggest that Punjab is a monolith. Subordinate classes and castes, not to mention the vast majority of women, have remained subject to the vagaries of market and an extractive state apparatus since the colonial period. The low bureaucracy – and particularly the *thana, patwari* and *katcheri* – is navigated ruefully and often unsuccessfully by Punjabis without power, wealth and influence, just as it is by non-Punjabis. In the next chapter, I will describe both trials and tribulations of working Punjabis as well as prominent mobilizations that have resisted and state power.

It is nevertheless true that levels of social and economic deprivation in much of Punjab are noticeably lower than peripheral regions of the country. Poverty indicators in Sindh and Khyer Pakhtunkhwa roughly match the country-wide average of 33 per cent while Balochistan exceeds it; in comparison only 19 per cent of Punjab's population is considered poor, while the rural-urban divide is also considerably less acute than the other provinces (28 per cent rural households and 10 per cent urban households are poor). Finally, there is considerable variance between north/central Punjab and the Siraiki belt in the southern and western parts of the province; the Siraiki districts are considerably poorer than the Punjabi ones.[24]

Most significantly, the 'state-idea' in Punjab remains more powerful than anywhere else in the country. The worldview of most Punjabis across the class divide corresponds to the state nationalist discourse, especially with respect to the criminalization of ethnic minorities. The Baloch are regularly designated conspirators for demanding their rights, while in the post-9/11 era, Pakhtuns, most of whom themselves abhor religious militancy, are often all reduced to 'Taliban'. There are exceptions to the general rule, but it would be remiss to ignore what is effectively a consensus between a significant cross-section of Punjabi society and the formal state.

I do think it is important to note that this consensus is largely forged within an urban context in which the corporate media and heavily-controlled formal education system are very influential in framing issues and thereby constructing 'public opinion'. Accordingly, 'state nationalism' enjoys a captive audience within relatively educated professional segments and while Punjabis are the single biggest ethnic-linguistic group in this demographic, they are not the only one.

Yet, the proximity of Punjabi society to the formal state, both in terms of the benefits of development and *vis-a-vis* the 'state-idea', is not to be understated.

One of my informants from the Punjabi town of Sahiwal had the following insight:

> You can't neglect the fact that the statist worldview (*ryasti nuktanazar*) is most forcefully asserted in Punjab. Yes there is no doubt that we Punjabis are relatively better off than non-Punjabis, but there are enough working people in Punjab who are struggling to survive who have no love lost for the system (*nizam k ashiq nahin hain*). It's just that state nationalism is so deeply inculcated in them that they do not rebel and indeed often brand non-Punjabis as unpatriotic, just like the state wants.[25]

Conversely, a wide cross-section of Baloch and Sindhi society espouses commitment to the narratives and politics of ethnic nationalism. Even the Urdu-speaking Muhajirs of urban Sindh, once so committed to unitary state nationalism, are increasingly prone to seeing the state as captured by Punjabis and framing their politics accordingly.[26]

I now share some anecdotes to demonstrate the complex political economy and imaginary of different ethnic-linguistic groups. In so doing I hope to shed further light on the dialectic of resistance and common sense in actually existing Pakistan.

Contours of Change

Throughout the book, I have made a case for recognition of the rapid social changes that have taken place across the length and breadth of society, replete variations in time, space and place. In the context of this chapter, social change and resulting shifts in political alignments have been no more evident than in the case of Pakhtuns.

As the ethnic-linguistic group with arguably the most antagonistic relationship to the new state, it might have been expected that a majority of Pakhtuns would, over the medium to long-run, continue to resist state nationalism, in much the same way as say, the Baloch continue to do in the contemporary period. However, the otherwise conflictual relationship of Pakhtun nationalists with Pakistani state oligarchs in the early years, and the attendant coercive force used by the latter to subdue nationalist politics, tended to mask the fact that Pakhtuns were overrepresented in Pakistan's military, having been designated a 'martial race' by the British after the 1857 War of Independence.[27] The Peshawar Valley was one of the major recruiting grounds of the British Indian army in NWFP, along with Kohat district.

In the immediate post-partition period, the Pakhtun component in the Pakistani military continued to grow, and crossed 20 per cent at the turn of the century.[28] By the 1980s, representation of Pakhtuns in the civil apparatuses of the state had also increased considerably. Along with Punjabis and Muhajirs, Pakhtuns are now over-represented in the officer ranks of the civil bureaucracy.[29]

The growing economic integration of Pakhtuns into Pakistan's economy has been as significant as their integration into the state services. As noted in Chapter 3, the Pakhtun intermediate classes have become a formidable economic and political force both in Khyber Pakhtunkhwa and the rest of the country. Beyond transport, Pakhtuns dominate a number of service industries, and individual traders and merchants are found in agricultural commodity bazaars in innumerable small towns across the country. On the whole, Pakhtuns are easily the most mobile ethnic-linguistic community in the country; successive waves of migrations have made Karachi into the biggest Pakhtun city in the world; conservative estimates suggest that at least 3 million Pakhtuns live in the metropolis.[30]

Of course most Pakhtun migrants living in Karachi and other urban centres across the country, not to mention foreign cities, hail from the subordinate classes, and therefore can hardly be considered well-to-do. The example quoted in Chapter 2 of Pakhtun working-class families being evicted from a huge *katchi abadi* (squatter settlement) outside the capital Islamabad is indicative in this regard. My informant Niaz Ali noted:

> We Pakhtuns are subject to the worst kind of racial profiling and victimization. These days we are branded 'terrorists' by whoever feels like it. We leave our villages not because we want to, but because of war and suffering – we have to provide for our families amidst all of these conflicts that have destroyed our livelihoods. We come to the city and we are subject to even more harassment and violence.

It is beyond the scope of this book to critically interrogate the so-called 'war on terror' and the manner in which states all over the world have strengthened their coercive apparatus and criminalized certain populations in the name of countering 'terrorism'. For the purposes of this chapter, I wish only to emphasize that ordinary Pakhtuns have indeed suffered the brunt of Pakistan's incarnation of the 'war on terror'; political violence has become a daily affair in the so-called Federally Administered Tribal Areas (FATA) as well as settled parts of Khyber Pakhtunkhwa province.

While the anger and resentment of individuals like Niaz Ali confirms the deep sense of alienation of ordinary Pakhtuns from Pakistani officialdom, it has not necessarily led to greater assertion of Pakhtun ethnic-nationalism. This is despite the fact that Pakhtun victims of war or various forms of exclusion are increasingly more conscious of their 'Pakhtun-ness'. However, this does not necessarily equate to a politics of confrontation like that propagated by the Pakhtun nationalist movements in Pakistan's early years.

The evolution of the successor party of the Khudai Khidmatgars, still the largest Pakhtun nationalist party in the country, is testament to this fact. I mentioned earlier that the NAP was perceived by the state to be an anti-establishment political force through the 1970s. By all accounts, its current incarnation, the Awami National Party (ANP), continues to be viewed with great suspicion in the contemporary period.[31] Yet the ANP has to a significant extent disavowed its separatist beginnings; its leadership regularly voices its commitment to (a tempered) state nationalism, almost as if it wishes to convince sceptics within the permanent state apparatus that its nationalist commitments are no longer 'dangerous'.[32]

To the extent that the ANP still claims to be committed to restructuring the unitary state, in its everyday politics it is concerned with access to the *existing* state, which is, in turn, the principal demand of its supporters. This is the case both in Khyber Paktunkhwa, and in Karachi (where the ANP is widely considered to represent the Pakhtun intermediate classes).

Thus, the everyday politics of patronage, the various contours of which I have laid out in previous pages, is dominant in Pakhtun society as much as anywhere else in Pakistan. The ANP is not alone in espousing a political commitment to ethnic nationalism, whilst also reproducing the politics of common sense. The Pakhtunkhwa MilliAwami Party (PkMAP) became a coalition partner in the Balochistan provincial government following the general election of 2013, even while party chief Mahmood Khan Achakzai forcefully asserted his anti-establishment credentials.[33] A mid-level PkMAP leader spoke to me about the gap between rhetoric and reality:

> We cannot afford to be out of government for too long – people want jobs and other things that we can only provide if in power. And coming into power in Pakistan means doing a deal with the establishment. Of course we will continue to propagate anti-establishment slogans in public, but just chanting slogans does not help us meet people's everyday needs.[34]

Poor and politically weak Pakhtuns may be conscious and resentful of their social and political positions but continue to be largely guided by the common sense of seeking out those more powerful than them to help cope with their trials and tribulations. A former organizer of the Hashtanagar land rights movement (which I describe in greater detail in the next chapter) has the following to say:

> The truth is that people are more conscious of the system's injustice (*nizam ki na insafian*), but less convinced that anything can be gained by rebelling against it. In fact while thirty years ago there were very few of our kinsmen (*humare ilaqe ke log*) in positions of power – even at the lower echelons of the state – now there are dozens so most of us prefer to seek out the support of such powerful people rather than stake everything we have in the name of a principled politics.[35]

On the surface this common sense is not shared by the Baloch masses whose sympathies appear to be fuelling an ongoing insurgency against the state. I noted earlier the security apparatus' use of brutal force to quell successive insurgencies in Balochistan – in recent years the alienation felt by what in previous incarnations was a nationalist movement dominated by traditional 'big men' has filtered down to a much wider cross-section of Baloch society, and particularly educated middle-class segments.[36]

That many young people have abandoned 'normal' lives to join what is conceived as a struggle for national liberation would suggest that there is in Baloch society an alternative political imaginary to the common sense politics that I have detailed through the course of this book. Notwithstanding the intensification of ethnic nationalism, however, the mundane everyday social and political practices of many ordinary Baloch are not necessarily all that distinct from other Pakistanis.

An informant working at the Quetta Development Authority had the following to say:

> Of course we Baloch are conscious of the overall policies of the Pakistani state and all of us support the cause of Baloch resistance in some way or the other. But we also have to make ends meet in the here and now (*aaj k daur me zinda bhi rehna ha*). As many young people there are who want to join the resistance, there are many more who want jobs, security and all sorts of other things that only access to state resources can provide. I know because so many people come to me with *sifarish* every day.[37]

Counter-hegemonic ideologies and active political movements of resistance have to contend with the everyday compulsions of ordinary people seeking to survive the system, including those occupying the lowest rung of the subordinate classes. I noted in the introductory chapter how political consciousness is to be thought of as complex and multi-pronged rather than singular, and the case of the Baloch as the most alienated and excluded of all of Pakistan's ethnic-nations confirms as much.

As I will discuss in the next chapter, the limited expressions of counter-hegemonic politics in contemporary society cannot be explained by the persistence of an age-old 'false consciousness'; in fact the possibilities of expansive political action are never entirely foreclosed despite the dominance of submissive strands of common sense. I hold the same to be true in the case of ethnic-nationalist politics; it is in some sense an ideal to which the subordinate classes hailing from relatively excluded and exploited ethnic-linguistic communities aspire, but the existence of this ideal, and occasional expressions of it, do not preclude the existence or even irrefutability of everyday patronage and the compulsions of the politics of common sense.

In any case, ethnic nationalism is premised upon a rather romantic notion of an 'imagined community' which does not always correspond to complex realities of ethnic identity and ethnic-national politics.[38] Recent scholarship has pointed to the importance of acknowledging 'intra-ethnic' conflicts within Pakistan so as to understand the ebbs and flows of ethnic-nationalist movements, and also to ascertain their internal coherence.[39]

To take one example: the ethnic-national group generally referred to as 'Baloch' is comprised of two major linguistic communities, Balochi-speakers and Brahvi-speakers. There remain political differences across this, and, for that matter, other fault lines in Baloch society. However, the political imaginary of the 'Baloch nation' is inclusive of Brahvi-speakers as much as Balochi-speakers, and it can be argued that the political idea of an all-inclusive Baloch nation has grained traction over time, whereas earlier expressions of nationalist politics were driven by more parochial loyalties, such as that to tribe.[40]

Regardless of the coherence and internal composition of ethnic-nationalist movements, it is clear that the project of state nationalism has never succeeded in redressing the ethnic-linguistic fissures that run right through the body-politic. The post-1977 historical bloc – dominated by Punjabis, but nevertheless containing a diverse amalgam of ethnic-linguistic communities – may have succeeded in inculcating an accomodationist common sense across a wide-cross section of society but this common sense has not displaced the politics of ethnic-national resistance. This is evidence both of the dynamic political subjectivities that exist in contemporary Pakistan, and the resilience of a structure of power that has accommodated those previously excluded from a share of formal state power and the benefits of capital accumulation. It is a matter of fact that the majority of Pakistan's people still remain largely excluded from the 'system'. I turn next to discuss why this majority has imbibed a worldview based on accommodation with the structure of power.

Endnotes

1. Banerjee (2000).
2. Ansari (2005).
3. Axmann (2008).
4. Ali (1970); Ahmed (1973).
5. Initially known as the Muhajir Qaumi Movement (MQM), the name change took place in 1997 as the party sought to forge a more inclusive identity.
6. Talbot (2002).
7. Waseem (2002: 267) points out: 'In spatial term, those regions which were not fully represented in the mainstream politics of the Pakistan movement, or failed to move to centre stage in the emerging State system, did not necessarily share what is otherwise billed as national consensus'.
8. Alavi (1987).
9. Of course the status of Punjabis has changed; they constituted an ethnic minority until the secession of East Pakistan, and have been the majority ethnic group ever since. Whereas the Punjab voted for social change in the 1970 election, from 1988 onwards there is some credence to the claim that Punjab effectively exercises a tyranny of the majority.
10. Smith (1998).
11. Khan (2005).
12. It is important to note that the NAP represented a threat to status quo in part because of its proximity to the Soviet Union, anathema to Pakistan's rulers who were aligned with the US in the Cold War. After 1967, the NAP split into competing pro-Soviet and pro-Chinese factions which adopted differential postures towards the Pakistan state.
13. Muhajirs in Sindh began to perceive of themselves as underrepresented during the 1970s. Muhajir nationalism was arguably precipitated by the 'Sindhi-first' policies of the PPP Government (Ahmed, 1997).
14. Akhtar (2010).
15. Siddiqui (2012a).
16. (Ahmad, 2014).
17. Name withheld on informant's request.
18. The 1857 War of Independence (or Sepoy Mutiny as the British called it) also signalled a clear shift in colonial thinking in terms of recruitment patterns such that the Punjabis, Pakhtuns and Gurkhas – the so-called martial castes – became the recruits of choice. The northwest of India therefore became the heartland of

the army replacing previous recruiting grounds in the eastern and northern parts of India (Cohen, 1998).
19. Tan (2005).
20. Ibid, 219
21. The electoral regime in Punjab was deliberately crafted to ensure that the latent oppositional tendencies of urban areas were subordinated to the pro-establishment vote of the rural areas. More generally the British facilitated 'democratic' institutions in India in the hopes that 'India's democratic urges could be contained and ensnared in these institutions, which served the colonial state's needs; that they were incapable of providing launching pads for a broader oppositional politics and were controllable through networks of resource distribution'. (Washbrook, 1990: 42).
22. Dewey (1988: 148).
23. Pasha (1998).
24. Naveed and Ali (2012).
25. Interview with Afzal Sorraya.
26. Verkaaik (2001).
27. Punjabis were the other major ethnic-linguistic community from north-western India inducted into the British Indian army in large numbers in the latter decades of the nineteenth century in accordance with the 'martial race' theory.
28. Fair and Nawaz (2011).
29. Kennedy (1988).
30. This figure cannot be verified because the last official census completed in the city was in 1998. A country-wide census did take place in 2017 but official figures were not available as this book went to print. Unofficial estimates suggest that Karachi's population is around 20 million, and that Pakhtuns constitute 20 per cent of the total.
31. Hundreds of ANP activists and leaders were target killed between 2008 and 2013 while it occupied the seat of government in Khyber Pakhtunkhwa province. While 'religious militants' reportedly acknowledged responsibility for most of the killings, there is a widespread belief that the state security apparatus, or at least sections of it, patronized at least some of the militant outfits involved in the attacks.
32. See Ali (2013).
33. See http://www.pakistantoday.com.pk/2013/06/17/national/reign-in-the-establishment-or-go-to-hell/
34. Name withheld on request.
35. Interview with Mian Hikmat Shah.
36. Amirali (2015).
37. Name withheld on request.
38. For a detailed study on nationalism, see Anderson (2006); Smith (1998); Gellner (1983); Hobsbawm (1990); Giddens (1985).
39. Siddiqui (2012b).
40. Amirali (2009).

6

The Subordinate Classes
Beyond Common Sense?

I have attempted in this book to demonstrate how the radical political imaginary that thrived in Pakistan through the late 1970s has been virtually banished from the popular consciousness – the 'common sense' of the lower orders of society has shifted away from transformative and towards more accommodative political strategies. This shift has been coeval with dramatic social and economic changes associated largely with the spread of capital and urbanization, and despite the increasingly fragmented practices of state functionaries. All told the twin realities of exclusion and exploitation for the subordinate classes at large, inclusive women, oppressed nations and religious minorities are as pronounced as ever.

As discussed in the introduction, a substantial body of scholarship dealing with different aspects of subordinate class culture, consciousness and politics has been generated over the past few decades. Over time the focus of scholarly efforts to understand subalternity have moved away from the question of whether and to what extent the working class – or any other class – acts as a class-for-itself to much more localized interrogations of events and daily practices.

> [Scholars have] shifted the attention of historians away from intellectual history to ethnography. Now ethnographic studies are no longer concerned with uncovering the implicit conceptual structures that supposedly underlie the practical activities of people who do not produce large bodies of texts of their own, but rather seek to understand embodied practices as activities that people carry out for their own sake.[1]

In this book I have taken what might be considered a somewhat 'traditionalist' look at class, even while I have tried to understand the complex micro-foundations of the prevailing structure of power in Pakistan. One of my primary arguments is that even propertied classes in Pakistan tend to map their fundamental interests in terms of access to state power and resources which *may not* correspond to the understanding of class interests in a traditional materialist schema.

The subordinate classes too have become enmeshed in a system that privileges the building and maintenance of patronage networks often linked to state functionaries. However, the politics of common sense cannot be considered a simple continuity of historical modes of political engagement in the wider social formation that persisted through the British period, and into the post-colonial epoch. Instead, it must be understood as the reassertion of class and state power and the attendant incorporation of new political and economic players into an expanded historical bloc in the post-Bhutto period. This reassertion entailed the articulation of historically rooted political practice with evolving logics of the market, instrumentalization of 'democratic' exercises such as elections, and the forging of ideational innovations congruent with regional and global geo-politics.

Under this backdrop, the present chapter is concerned with two related aspects of subordinate class action. First, I detail the context within which the politics of common sense emerged. I begin with an account of the radical leftist wave that shaped Pakistan's political landscape from the mid-1960s until the military coup that overthrew Zulfikar Ali Bhutto. I emphasize in particular the changes that took place in the consciousness and actual political engagements of the subordinate classes or what has been called the shift from 'interior' to 'exterior' political associations.[2] Second, I show how the politics of common sense has become exactly that; why did the mode of politics that was foisted onto the social formation by the Zia junta and its allies become the dominant form, even while instances of resistance still come to the fore periodically?

'The Politics of the Governed'

It would seem appropriate to begin this chapter by returning to Partha Chatterjee's recent formulations on subaltern politics in the 'majority of the world'.[3] I noted in the introductory chapter my disagreement with Chatterjee's basic contention about the changes to have taken place in subaltern consciousness of, and engagement with, the state in recent years. Here I wish to offer my impressions of Chatterjee's well-known argument on what he calls 'political society', and particularly the primary implication of his work, that political society represents a deepening of democracy in favour of the subordinate classes, alongwith other historically underrepresented segments of Indian society.

Let me start by directly quoting Chatterjee:

> It is true that political society does not offer a transformational narrative threatening the course of capitalist development. It is not a concept of revolutionary politics. Rather, it is a response to the new technologies of government which, by the end of the twentieth century, have developed their own flexible instruments to break up the class-based political solidarities of the high industrial age and create the myriad and changing grids within which population groups could make their demands. Political society represents an altered, even through emergent and often inchoate, response to changed conditions of governmentality.[4]

This is an important admission, and one that needs to be taken seriously. This caveat notwithstanding, a certain romanticism pervades through *The Politics of the Governed* and other related works, and this is what I believe needs to be flagged. Having said this, I share Chatterjee's basic impulse – and others who have been associated with the Subaltern Studies school – to be instantly critical of class or other radical analyses in which it is even implied that oppressed groups of any kind are simply passive recipients of 'dominant class' culture or ideology.

It is this suspicion that informs my basic sketch of the politics of common sense, insofar as I believe that the lower orders of society do not inhabit a unitary consciousness and instead make informed decisions about political alignments based on the constraints and opportunities that exist at any given moment in time.

I have also asserted, however, that the politics of common sense is as much about the strategies and alignments of dominant and intermediate classes as well as state actors. In short, the political alignments of the subordinate classes are shaped by structural forces outside the latter's control.

I have argued that state and class power were reasserted strongly in post-Bhutto Pakistan and that a specific kind of patronage politics came to the fore while transformative imaginaries were almost completely marginalized. It is in this context that the subordinate classes acceded to the politics of common sense; rather than challenge power through durable horizontal collectivities, the subordinate classes negotiated with the state and dominant/intermediate classes through the various and ever-evolving patronage networks that I have discussed in previous chapters.

I do not think that the concept of political society is necessarily inconsistent with the narrative I have sketched through the course of this book. As I demonstrate in this chapter, the most exploited and oppressed segments of Pakistan's society do make sustained and organized efforts to negotiate with the rich and powerful for a share, however small, of political and economic resources that circulate within society. That these negotiations typically take place within the confines of what is still a relatively opaque and exclusive structural environment cannot, at any cost, be neglected. Chatterjee himself notes major structuring forces, including the process of 'accumulation by dispossession'.[5]

Given these structural constraints – or perhaps more accurately *because* of structural changes – some from the lower orders of society have improved their bargaining position *vis-a-vis* classes and institutions higher up in the patronage chain, so much so that elements from the intermediate strata have become part of an expanded historical bloc. Yet, the vast majority of those who remained at the bottom of the social ladder in the previous historical period continue to be excluded and exploited in the present one, even if lived class experience, cultural norms, and modes of political engagement have changed, and continue to do so.

In what follows, I will trace exactly how and why these modes of political engagement have changed. In doing so I hope to make clear Chatterjee's crucial omission of at least some of the immediate historical context within which 'the politics of the governed' has emerged.

The Politics of Resistance and Reaction

The politics of resistance that erupted in the latter half of the Ayub dictatorship persisted throughout the following decade. In effect, the 1960s marked the emergence of class as a major signifier in Pakistan's politics. '[D]uring the Ayub period the industrialization of cities like Karachi, Lahore and Lyallpur had generated new urban forces. Cities were attracting peasants, landless labourers, and tenants from the surrounding countryside and the new industrial and urban climate had created new issues and aroused new expectations'.[6] While industrial labour and increasingly militant student unions were the major protagonists of class politics, there were stirrings in rural areas too as demands for land reform and other radical slogans mobilized landless tenants and small farmers along horizontal lines marking a break from hitherto vertical alignments around landlord-led factions.[7]

The realization of popular discontent in the 1960s was made possible by the enduring struggle of leftist groups through the first two decades of the country's existence. Kamran Asdar Ali and Saadia Toor have chronicled this struggle which carried on despite enormous state repression, especially after the banning of the Communist Party of Pakistan (CPP) in 1954.[8] For my purposes, it is important to emphasize the epic sense of commitment and idealism that guided Pakistan's earliest revolutionaries. An activist of the CPP and NAP who lived and worked both in the Mianwali district of Punjab as well as Karachi offered the following recollections:

> We committed everything in our lives to the cause of revolution. And people responded. Not immediately – we really had to convince them (*bahut zor lagana para tha*) because we were saying things that flew in the face of everything they had learnt. But change was in the air and people were willing to make sacrifices to make it happen. As a young person you felt a bit left out and even selfish if you stayed aloof from everything.[9]

Even while the far left prepared the ground for the emergent challenge to the status quo, it was the PPP and Zulfikar Ali Bhutto that eventually became the face of a populist, Third World nationalism by bringing together large numbers of progressives and working people. The primary demand of the newly mobilized segments of a rapidly changing social formation was a greater share of the pie *vis-a-vis* big capital and the state oligarchy, but this was accompanied by a fierce anti-imperialism, and, in Punjab, the rejection of Indian 'hegemony'.

I have already shown that the upwardly mobile intermediate classes soon chose to align themselves in different ways to the industrial working class and urban and rural poor. Subsequently, students were weaned away from left ideologies while the working class and the peasantry – subject to substantial internal transformation due to the deepening of capitalism – adapted to the imperatives of common sense politics. However, this was not simply a return to 'traditional' matrices of patronage that had hitherto dominated the mainstream political sphere. In fact, it was a fundamental departure from the past.

Jones uses the 'modern' vs. 'parochial' binary to characterize the tension between the divergent forms of politics that existed before and after Ayubian modernization.[10] There was certainly a shift during the 1960s away from what he calls the 'static universe of political absolutes' towards a more dynamic political order in which political engagements came to be made not on the basis of subservience to a traditionally dominant group, but an understanding that the material world can and ought to be changed. Given the idiom of change that was sweeping across large parts of the social formation, the subordinate classes aligned themselves with the parties and ideologies that promised to usher in an egalitarian social order.

However, it is crucial that one avoids taking Jones' argument to its logical conclusion, which would be that the re-emergence of a politics that *appeared* to be based on the same ascriptive ties that characterized the 'parochial' necessarily meant a reversion to the static universe of political absolutes. Instead, I have argued that the state and propertied classes had to acknowledge the emergence of a new, dynamic political universe in the 1960s and tried during the Zia interregnum to shape an acceptable common sense *in the context of this new universe*. Hence demands for inclusion from classes previously excluded from the accumulation of power and capital had to be accommodated lest there be further radicalization and potential rupture of the entire political-economic system.

In the event, the radical upsurge did not completely displace parochial visions of politics, nor was the mere emergence of class-based mobilization sufficient to precipitate structural overhaul. 'So while [the popular mobilization] made a dent in the old structures of the agrarian Punjab, breaking down the *biraderi* (clan), caste, or tribal affiliation....the dominance of rural notables was by no means at an end. Indeed, in Sind the PPP relied on the very *biraderi* and tribal ties that it was trying to rupture in many districts of the Punjab'.[11]

Within leftist circles, the PPP's rise to power was even viewed with suspicion given Bhutto himself had a long association with state power, and because geopolitical interests appeared to be as significant a factor in the PPP's emergence as popular support.[12] An activist associated with the pro-Soviet faction of the Pakistani left told me:

> Don't forget that China was very close to the Ayub Khan regime and a large part of the pro-Chinese left were told not to take the agitation so far as to threaten the edifice of state power (*nizam hi lapaita na jai*). Bhutto played up his Maoist tendencies, even calling himself 'Chairman'. There was more to Bhutto's rise than meets the eye (*andar andar bahut kuch ho raha tha*). If the PPP was as anti-establishment as it claimed it would never have played up the anti-India card so much.[13]

Notwithstanding such suspicions, the rise of the PPP was both cause and consequence of a new culture of popular and democratic politics. The left both within the PPP and outside of it exercised substantial influence across a wide cross-section of society; the potentialities for overhaul of the structure of power were certainly unprecedented. Upon assuming power, however, the

PPP hierarchy became caught between the imperatives of compromise with the powers-that-be and further radicalization as advocated by the left.

> This shift in the class composition of the PPP, once it had formed the government, was neither accidental nor a personal betrayal on Bhutto's part, as it was subjectively experienced by the purged cadres. Changes in the internal class composition of the PPP were objectively determined by the changed position of the party in relation to the state, in other words, PPP had to be an apparatus predominantly of the radical petty bourgeoisie in the pre-election phase when the main objective was to secure a mass base and an electoral majority, particularly in the countryside. Once, however, the PPP had formed the government on the social democratic premise of seeking reform within the predicates of the state as already constituted, thereby becoming the political apparatus of the reactionary state, its Left Wing was faced with the objective choice of either accepting the exigencies of the state or getting liquidated. In the event, the Left was of course liquidated.[14]

In short, while there was a substantial progressive cadre that was produced by the politicization of the late 1960s and early 1970s, 'hundreds of people influenced by the mass movement …had vague ideas of socialism'.[15] These activists may have been mobilized and militant, but were insufficiently autonomous of the PPP government to withstand state repression by the 'people's government'.

While there was a close link between various segments of the mass movement and the PPP – I noted earlier that left-wing student groups like the NSF contributed greatly to the PPP's electoral victory, particularly in Punjab – relations soured shortly after the assumption of power as the left's continued commitment to structural overhaul came to be viewed as too radical. The NSF and other leftist student organizations would eventually be sidelined, and subsequent generations of young people would cease to even recognize the ideological labels of 'left' and 'right'.

A prominent leader of the NSF in the late 1960s and early 1970s had the following to say:

> The whole world seemed to be headed inexorably towards revolution and we thought the PPP's rise was at least a stepping stone in the right direction. But after it took state power the dynamics within the movement changed dramatically. We were accused – sometimes rightly – of being too adventurous. But the real problem was that the government could not decide whether it was willing to trust popular forces or fall back on the crutch of state power.[16]

Similar cleavages developed within the trade union movement. For its part the government created the National Industrial Relations Commission (NIRC) and called Tripartite Conferences to improve the conditions of organized labour. In practice the new institutional framework sought to undermine labour militancy by making strikes and lock-downs 'illegal'. The institution of the collective bargaining agent (CBA) emerged as the sole representative of workers within an enterprise, and, with exception, co-opted labour leaders into administrative and legal entanglements.[17] This marked the beginning of the relationship between the state and a labour aristocracy that has since faithfully served the expanded historical bloc.

During the Zia period, the last remaining vestiges of labour militancy were permanently eliminated. In the subsequent period, the trade union movement has virtually ceased to exist as an autonomous political force. In fact, the vast majority of trade unions are now almost ideal vehicles of common sense politics. The prototypical labour leader distinguishes himself through his connections to influential political factions, his ability to secure *individual* patronage for workers (as opposed to collective betterment through struggle), and, quite paradoxically, for a lifestyle not dissimilar to an upwardly mobile member of the intermediate classes.

The Legacy

Regardless of the chequered nature of the PPP interregnum, there is little doubt about the enormous impact that this period of politicization had on the polity. A non-negligible segment of the labouring poor attributes its political consciousness to this period – and in some cases to the person of Zulfikar Ali Bhutto. Contemporary Sindh remains the heartland of 'Bhuttoism'; many Sindhis still see Bhutto as the martyred Sindhi hero (*shaheed*). In practical terms it was during Bhutto's period that the representation of Sindhis within the administrative apparatus increased substantially; many also availed livelihood opportunities in public industrial enterprises set up in rural parts of the province.[18]

On the whole, however, the first PPP government did not secure substantial material benefits for the subordinate classes across ethnic-linguistic boundaries. The Bhutto period is remembered fondly by segments of the subordinate classes because a permanent transformation took place in their engagement within the wider political field; the development of a consciousness of class and other horizontal solidarities that were opposed to the vertical alignments that had previously been the primary determinant of political practice meant that the world would never be the same.

This is corroborated by a cursory look at the popular media of the time. In contrast to the tone and tenor of newspaper reporting from 1979 onwards, during the previous decade the focus of the print press was decidedly insurrectionary both in terms of the stories that were highlighted, and the implicit or explicit journalistic intent. As already noted, this was a period in which there was a truly global upsurge of left populism/radicalism, and developments around the world garnered significant space in the print media. Reporting on Third World movements and particularly regions where popular movements were proliferating – Indo-China, the occupied Palestinian territories, and Central America – was commonplace. In the post 1979 period, with the exception of the Palestinian cause – which has metamorphosed into an 'Islamic' one – such reporting is conspicuous by its absence.

Reporting on labour and student activism was also widespread in the pre-Zia years, with emphasis placed on the organized class power of workers and political role of students. Not only has reporting on labour and students decreased markedly in the post-79 period, but the little that exists often depicts labour and students as clients of powerful benefactors (whether incumbents or those who are seeking political office). By the 1980s, 'Islamization' in this realm had also become explicit; a report on May Day rallies in a major English daily suggested that 'tributes were paid to Chicago workers and rights and privileges given to the wage earners by Islam were highlighted'.[19]

There has also been a quite marked, albeit gradual, shift in reporting patterns, particularly in the Urdu press, away from country-wide debates and concerns to localized ones. Reporting focuses on the delivery of services and mediation in disputes by individuals and parties, reflecting the restored patronage relation as the defining feature of the polity. The contrast with the 1967-77 period is telling; not only was the reporting in this period far less localized, there was also substantive commentary on competing political systems, and in particular, socialism.[20]

Scholars have documented how this shift from expansive and ideological to localized and functional political frames has taken place since the 1970s.[21] The process of 'localization', institutionalized in the first instance through non-party local body elections, marks a shift in the focus of everyday politics away from confrontation with dominant groups towards implicit acceptance of organized power. Even ascriptive alignments are no longer what they seem: '...a voter or voting group... may vote for a local tribal or *biraderi* leaders, giving the appearance that kinship ties are determining their behaviour. The actual reason, however, is likely to be that the candidate, as a local influential, is linked into the existing patronage network and is therefore able to deliver patronage to supporters'.[22]

As was discussed in Chapter 2, the centrality of the low bureaucracy to this process of 'localization' cannot be understated. If on the one hand the interaction between subordinate classes and the low bureauracy is personalized, on the other hand it can quickly spiral and become coercive and highly oppressive. In either case, it is fundamentally unequal and its persistence reflects only that the subordinate classes remain at the behest of the '*sarkar*', and dominant social groups that the latter privileges.[23]

The politics of common sense and the politics of resistance can accordingly be seen as two ends of a broad spectrum in the post-1960s political field, and the political action of the subordinate classes as dynamic and mutually interdependent on the alignments of the propertied classes, state, and religio-political forces. This spectrum corresponds to two contrasting visions of politics. The first vision is idealistic, and at times epic, reflected in the popular memory of the decade of upheaval as a time of political awakening. This vision privileges collective interests and emphasizes struggle to effect fundamental change in society. The second vision is highly pragmatic, even cynical, premised upon an acceptance of the status quo and, at best, manoeuvring within its confines. One of the overt features of this second vision is the 'vigorous popular condemnation of politics as such'.[24]

It is worth dwelling on this last point; I have argued throughout the course of this book that the Ziaist project can be considered a successful one insofar as the politics of common sense became the dominant mode of political engagement across the social formation. There can be no better indicator of this success than the fact that a large number of people across the social formation consider politics to be a cynical game in which they at least rhetorically want no part.

Yet society is far from 'de-politicized', a common lament of the Pakistani intelligentsia. Zaidi (2005b) argues more persuasively that there exists across the social formation a very active tradition of politics, but not necessarily a democratic politics *per se*. A great number of people across various social divides tend to be well-updated on the latest political developments and are constantly engaged in chatter about various aspects of politics whether at home, in the workplace, or at a *khoka* (roadside tea stall). With the emergence of the TV media since the middle of the 2000s, the urban middle-class has become a captive audience for an endless stream of political talk shows, most reinforcing the notion that politics is the preserve of self-interested and insular elites.

Popular discourse notwithstanding, the politics of common sense has engulfed the entire social formation and characterizes almost every relationship of social exchange, irrespective of whether ordinary people participate in the 'formal' realm of politics. In the event, almost 350,000 Pakistan's citizens with little or no previous experience of electoral contests participated in municipal-level elections across the country in 2015, which is to suggest that, rhetoric aside, ordinary people retain an interest in the political field.[25] That the rules of the political game remain heavily tilted towards those with money and connections was certainly not lost even on those who choose to participate in this game. A candidate for local body elections in Sindh had the following to say:

> We understand that we won't really make a dent in the way things are done. We were never going to win this election, but we thought we could at least get a different point of view across, tell voters that they could still change the course of their lives if they recognized that there is at least one political option that is not tainted by power and money. I think people listened to us – whether they will ever vote for someone that doesn't do *thana* and *katcheri*, and all the other things that is everyday politics in this country (*iss mulk me raij-ul-waqt syasat*) I can't answer.[26]

The Global 'Restoration of Class Power'

I have pointed out already that hegemony is never a discrete or complete event, and that hegemonic claims are almost always disputed. My narrative has emphasized the waning of the anti-systemic challenges to the structure of power that were so prominent in Pakistan – and as I will suggest presently, the whole world – until the 1980s. However, this should not be taken to mean a totalitarian 'dead end', as it were, in which all forms of resistance are eliminated.

Many progressives continue to propagate a transformative politics at various levels of the social formation. Yet, challenging an opaque structure of power is well nigh impossible without making a dent in the 'common sense' that prevails in society at large. Indeed, it is not only in Pakistan that ordinary people harbour cynicism towards the political process, and generally perceive themselves to be powerless to influence the decision-making structures that affect their lives.[27]

The radical political imaginary of the 1960s and 1970s emanated from a mobilized left movement – in the form of class organizations of the industrial working class and peasantry, students and intelligentsia, and political parties. The retreat of this left movement is both cause and consequence of the decline of the radical dimensions of 'common sense' and the increasing sway of its more passive side.

The left remained an important political force through the 1980s, and was the bedrock of resistance to the Zia regime. The resistance was led primarily by workers of the PPP as well as far left political organizations. The politics of patronage championed by the military dictatorship did not immediately displace the politics of resistance, replete the radical political imaginary. The very instrumental 'common sense' that I have outlined in this book has become more and more hegemonic with the passing of time, although one conjuncture demands special mention: the reactionary trends set into motion by the Zia regime were decisively consolidated following the collapse of 'actually existing socialism' between 1989–1991, due to which a large segment of progressives retreated completely from the realm of active politics.

A long-time trade unionist offered the following explanation:

> We had been brought up with the conviction that a working-class revolution was a matter of when, not if (*inqilab ka waqt ana hi tha*). After the Saur Revolution in Afghanistan (1978), something big felt imminent. But the Zia dictatorship took the wind out of our sails and then when the socialist bloc started collapsing, culminating in the disintegration of the Soviet Union in 1991, the feeling of failure became all-encompassing. A large number of leftists, and even trade unionists without any clear sense of left-wing ideology, simply gave up.[28]

To be sure, things did not appear at all bleak when the Zia dictatorship met its demise in 1988 and the PPP returned to power with the country's first female head of government at the helm. However, a changed international context in which the labour and left movements ceased to exercise the bargaining power of the past, as well as changes in the global capitalist order and the emergence of a new 'flexible' division of labour, quickly gave rise to disillusionment within the ranks of the activist community.

The PPP government suffered a legitimacy crisis due to its ultimately futile efforts to reconcile its ideological heritage with the imperatives of accommodation both with multinational capital and the still powerful military establishment. Within 18 months of taking over the reins of the government,

Benazir Bhutto's tenure came to an end, and the incoming pro-business government of the Pakistan Muslim League not only signalled the continuing legacy of the Zia dictatorship, but also confirmed that propertied class power had been decisively restored.

During the 1990s the 'political' became subject to a crisis of imagination with hypotheses such as the 'End of History' proliferating widely. Labour, students and other such previously mobilized and ideologically charged constituencies were particularly affected. Rhetoric aside, the vast majority of student groups, trade unions and other such organizational forms that were the heartbeat of transformative politics of the pre-Zia years metamorphosed into vehicles of patronage, conforming to broader societal trends.

Still, various expressions of resistance to power in Pakistan - and the rest of the world - continue to emerge. For instance, the Occupy Wall Street Campaign 2011, reflected the discontent of a wide cross-section of western societies *vis-a-vis* increasing social and economic inequality. Various forms of resistance to state and corporate power in Pakistan have also risen to prominence since the late 1990s, featuring a new generation of progressives that sees itself both as the inheritance of earlier left movements and an attempt to move beyond those movements' failures.[29]

An Unspectacular Politics of Resistance[30]

In part due to the efforts of this new generation of progressives, everyday acts of resistance continue to litter the social landscape, assuming one has the appropriate lens to see them. Scott's metaphorical 'weapons of the weak' continue to be employed by dependents of all kinds to improve their bargaining power within the exploitative relationships to which they are structurally confined. This idea has been extended by Michel de Certeau's through what he calls 'tactics' – those actions that allow the subordinate classes to secure small victories over their oppressors without challenging the larger system of power within which they are ensconced.[31]

It is important to consider this unspectacular politics of resistance for two related reasons. First, the subordinate classes always have and will continue to engage in acts of resistance, even if such acts do not threaten the prevailing structure of power *per se*. The politics of resistance of the 1960s and 1970s may have been suppressed under the Zia regime, but this did not mean that unspectacular acts of resistance could be eliminated.

Second, there is a need to recognize that even unspectacular acts of resistance can be counter-hegemonic if they defy the logic of patronage which has been outlined in this book. In other words, it is always possible that unspectacular acts of resistance – even if they do not necessarily represent major affronts to the status quo in and of themselves – challenge some aspect of the social order and therefore contain the seeds of a transformative politics.

So, for instance, anecdotal evidence from different parts of Pakistan confirms the gradually increasing role of women in public life, and specifically their greater negotiation with state institutions/functionaries.[32] Women's participation in the labour force is also increasing, even if the majority of working women entering the workforce do so under extremely trying conditions, often at the mercy of subcontractors.[33] Nevertheless, women entering a male-dominated public domain, even to engage in 'common sensical' ways with state functionaries or to navigate the market, constitutes an 'unspectacular' challenge to status quo.

Certainly, the more notable acts of unspectacular resistance are those that privilege some form of expansive *collective* action. In many cases, unspectacular resistance is a personal choice; most women entering the public sphere, for instance, are exercising their agency as individuals. Nevertheless, such individual actions contain within them the potentialities for the emergence of a (relatively) empowered political subject. Inasmuch as such acts of 'resistance' hint at a politics that represents the interests and aspirations of those historically without voice, this is a potentially counter-hegemonic practice.[34]

Having said this, the everyday act of resistance should not and cannot be considered akin to the politics of resistance to which the historical bloc reacted following the Zia coup. What I want to flag in particular is the fetishizing of resistance that is common amongst some post-structuralist thinkers. Everyday acts of resistance in and of themselves are little more than reflections of the subject positions of the lowest orders of society, and the big and ever-increasing gap between aspirations for justice and equality and the dominant political forms that drown out such aspirations.

Contemporary Subaltern Politics

I now move on to the lived political experiences of working people – both to demonstrate the manner in which they have come to imbibe the instrumental 'common sense' inculcated through the 1980s and 1990s and that forms of resistance continue to emerge in the extremely difficult contexts that they inhabit.

Small and Landless Farmers[35]

It is estimated that one of every two rural households in Pakistan is now landless. However, if one adds to the category of landless those that own up to 2.5 acres – in other words, those who survive at barely subsistence levels – one accounts for more than 70 per cent of Pakistan's rural households.[36] Moreover, there has been a steady transformation of the agrarian structure in Pakistan such that traditional share tenancy relationships have been almost completely replaced by wage labour. Even small landholders often supplement their income by working as labour on other farms.

I discuss below the 'land-poor' in the relatively rich, irrigated regions of Punjab and Khyber Pakhtunkhwa. These segments do not represent the diversity of the rural poor more generally; they are relatively better off than, say landless *haris* in Sindh. In this sense alone, Punjabi and Pakhtun farmers tend to have more leeway to choose political strategies that diverge from common sense. The two regions that I document here are ones in which popular movements of small and landless farmers have raged at different times over the past 35 years.

In Punjab's so-called 'canal colonies', small landholdings are the norm; the vast majority of small farmers' forefathers were allotted land by the colonial authorities in the first two decades of the twentieth century.[37] In the Peshawar Valley, large landholdings are more common, but a steady process of fragmentation has reduced land inequality to a degree.

Punjab

The primary social fault line in many Punjabi villages is between agricultural and non-agricultural castes (*zamindar*s and *kammi*s). As discussed in Chapter 5, the British undertook a major social engineering experiment in western Punjab on the basis of their perceptions about what constituted a stable social order. While I have shown in preceding chapters that this social order has changed qualitatively, the divide between *zamindar*s and *kammi*s remains an important one.[38] While some non-agriculturalists have been able to improve their social status by earning income from off-farm sources, distinctions between caste groups remain intact, and are preserved primarily by the practice of endogamy.

On the surface, political alignments of small and landless farmers are often caste-driven in the sense that factions led by powerful members of one caste – Jats, Arains and Rajputs are particularly conspicuous – are constituted largely of less affluent members of the same caste.[39] Such factions often take shape around election-time, but are not necessarily a microcosm of political alignments more generally. Weaker caste members, particularly smallholding and landless households, do not always rely on the same patron in everyday negotiations with the state and/or market.

In fact, small and landless farmers sometimes face victimization – particularly in terms of capture of land and/or other resources such as cattle – by more powerful members of their own caste. In this case, the victimized party may or may not turn to other members of the caste to mediate or intervene on their behalf. Recourse to patrons outside the village with substantive political links of their own, including the *arhti*, traders, and transporters is increasingly common. It is also not uncommon for poorer households to look towards relatively powerful benefactors from different caste backgrounds within the village.

In any case, it is necessary to take seriously Wilder's (1998) observation that what appears to be alignment *only* on the basis of caste – or for that matter other such ascriptive ties – is actually alignment with a patron that is able to effectively mediate in matters of service provision, dispute resolution and employment.[40] In short there is no hard and fast rule *vis a vis* caste and political alignments; all that can be said for certain is that it plays a significant role.

For the most part, the political choices of small and landless farmers reflect their understanding of the existing patronage-based system; they tend to be risk-averse and affiliate themselves with patrons in a manner broadly consistent with the politics of common sense. This often means, as I have suggested is characteristic of patronage ties, ensconcing oneself consciously in an unequal relationship.

However, how is one to explain the conscious and wilfull invocation of state intervention by the rural poor themselves (and particularly the legal and policing apparatuses of the state)? It is common for small and landless farmers to embroil themselves in matters of the *thana* and *katcheri* – or what the colonial administrator Darling called 'addiction to litigation'.[41] For example, disputes over land between *biraderi* members and even blood brothers are widespread, often over a trivially small piece of land, or matters of marriage and inheritance. Such disputes almost inevitably result in the two (or more) parties engaging the state.

Without resorting to cultural essentialism to explain this 'addiction' it is necessary to think through why the subordinate classes 'choose' to undertake such counter-productive exercises given that the litigant and the defendant both incur huge costs and suffer major time lags in the processing of the case.

Lawyers 'representing' the interests of the subordinate classes often play the role of parasitic middleman due to a cumbersome, and sometimes illegible, formal legal code.

An anthropological explanation of such conflicts might emphasise the desire to protect *izzat* – which is often considered synonymous with reducing the enemy's *izzat*.[42] In effect, the constant resort to litigation is a crucial component of the politics of common sense insofar as those who are often victims of state excess themselves invoke the state, thereby granting its legal and policing functions legitimacy.

During the heady politicization of the late 1960s and 1970s 'addiction to litigation' was noticeably displaced as mobilization along class lines overrode pre-existing vertical political alignments. Recently, during a mobilization of landless tenants across 19 villages of state-owned land in Okara district against the imposition of a new rent-in-cash tenure system, not only was considerable unity forged by *zamindar* and *kammi* castes against the military administration, there was also a dramatic decline in litigation by farmers against one another.

The movement began in earnest in the year 2000 soon after the military coup that brought General Pervez Musharraf to power. It quickly became a lightning rod for public resentment against the regime, and particularly the military's vast corporate empire. The so-called Okara military farms are a colonial era legacy – a sprawling 17,000 acre estate controlled by military authorities under the pretext that agricultural output from the farms serves the 'greater national interest'.[43] In 2000, the military administration unilaterally scrapped the share tenancy system that had persisted on the farms since they came into being in the early twentieth century, forcing tenant farmers to sign wage labour contracts that were subject to renewal on an annual basis.

Faced with imminent prospect of eviction, almost 800,000 residents of the area came together under the banner of the Anjuman Mazarain Punjab (AMP) – literally tenant farmers association of Punjab – even though most did not directly till lands themselves. Non-farmers supported the movement on account of shared cultural-historical ties with farmers, as well as a fear that eviction of tenant farmers would harm the overall village economy. Once the mobilization successfully warded off eviction, traditional caste divisions, land-related and other disputes reemerged, resulting in a rehabilitation of the *thana* and *katcheri* 'culture'.

Is there a systematic explanation of the political action of small and landless farmers (and artisans) in Okara from the mobilizations of the 1960s and 1970s to those that took place between 2000 and 2004? In my understanding, the initial mobilizations during the decade of upheaval (1967–77) reflected the dramatic change in the political universe to which Jones refers, whereby small and landless farmers recognized the possibility of actually pressing for a fundamental reconfiguration of the relationship between themselves, propertied intermediaries and the state. This politicization ensured that even after the end of the populist period, small and landless farmers would align politically with the faction most likely to provide benefits of some kind rather than simply pledge allegiance to caste, *biraderi* or any other ascriptive relation.

The politics of common sense became increasingly hegemonic insofar as the alternatives for small and landless farmers to mobilize on horizontal and expansive lines were limited. However, regular recourse to unspectacular acts of resistance – such as collective absconding from rent/harvest payments and social boycott of local influentials – meant that the prospect of expansive political action remained intact. Yet there was no major expression of counter-hegemonic politics in the intervening period because of the larger political environment in which class-based organizations within the peasantry had become largely extinct. Accordingly, Okara's rural poor became increasingly convinced 'that class action to change society [was] unlikely to succeed unless a very significant degree of class unity was to emerge'.[44] As time passed, the politics of common sense became more and more entrenched.

When structural conditions changed, however, a collective consciousness that transcended the fragmentary nature of the politics of common sense did not take long to crystallize. The resistance movement was expansive, bridging class, gender and religious divides,[45] emphasizing ideas of freedom and self-determination as opposed to functionally stressing economic gain, and ultimately challenging the mandate of the state to dictate the 'greater national interest'. One of the organizers of the AMP had the following to say:

> Once we faced the prospect of being evicted from our lands, we forgot all of our own conflicts and came together. We used to file police cases against one another, inflict harm on our neighbours. But that all changed when the movement started. It shows that we can transcend our petty squabbles (*fazool jhagre*) and recognize the collective good.[46]

That this relatively prolonged flirtation with transformative politics once again gave way to the politics of common sense after the threat of eviction was dispelled speaks of a highly repressive political environment, and the highly dynamic nature of subordinate class action.

Khyber Pakhtunkhwa

The irrigated plains of the Peshawar Valley differ from Punjab's canal colonies in two fundamental ways. First, landholdings in the Peshawar Valley are distributed more unevenly, and second, the state is less deeply entrenched into everyday social exchange. Historically rooted social hierarchies in Pakhtun society are also different in important ways. The Pakhtun social order has been described as being more akin to Arab patterns of social organization than it is to that of the Indus or Gangetic plains of the subcontinent. The substantive differences derive from the code of Pakhtunwali which stresses revenge, refuge and hospitality.[47]

The existence of status distinctions maintained by the practice of endogamy nevertheless reminds us that the Pakhtun social order shares similarities with Punjab and Sindh. Most significantly, landholding tribes are distinguished from non-landholding tribes, even though the same tribe need not necessarily have the same occupational status in different locales.[48] In the Charsadda district of Peshawar Valley –the heartland of the historic Hashtanagar peasant movement that emerged in the late 1960s[49] – the main landholding tribe is the Muhammadzai, comprising both larger and smaller landowners. The significant landless population which has historically worked as sharecropping tenants and more recently wage labour hails primarily from the Mohmand tribe.

As in the case of Punjab's canal colonies, this social order is also a relatively recent product of colonial rule and the creation of a hydraulic society. When large-scale irrigation systems were set up in the Peshawar Valley, tribes such as the Muhammadzai were endowed with proprietary rights under the new British legal code. The British encouraged migration from the adjacent Mohmand tribal agency to make the newly irrigated lands arable. The majority of Mohmand farmers in Hashtangar even today maintain homes in the mountain range that separates the tribal agency from the settled Charsadda district.

Aside from the contradiction between landowning Muhammadzais and the landless Mohmands, all agriculturalists, small and landless farmers in particular, have over time come into increasing contradiction with the intermediate classes. Still the major class conflict in the area pits the landless (both tenant farmers and labourers) against large landowners. In this conflict, the small landowner has historically played an ambivalent yet crucial role, vacillating between support for the landless farmers along horizontal, class lines and support for the large landowners on vertical, tribal lines.

The Hashtanagar Movement was arguably the biggest peasant movement in the country during the late 1960s and 1970s, and generated substantial support from radical political groups across the country. It was therefore one of the most symbolic mobilizations during the decade of upheaval (1967–77), not least because some of the landowners who were targeted in the movement were prominent state functionaries and politicians. The movement was largely successful in not only ending the system of *begar* or the system of semi-serfdom, but also in allowing tenants to permanently occupy land and transform power relations within the valley. For the most part land occupations have been maintained in spite of regular eviction attempts on the basis of superior court decisions *against* the tenants.

The Hashtanagar Movement was spearheaded by the Mazdoor Kissan Party (Workers and Peasants Party) which attempted, with some success, to extend the scope of the movement beyond the immediate economistic objective of capturing land to a broader conception of revolutionizing state and society. A long-time activist of a faction of the MKP told me:

> We owe everything to the MKP – we would never even have engaged in land occupations without the ideological commitment that comes with being a member of the party. We were just poor people with no conception of our rights and then Afzal Bangash and Major Ishaq(leaders of the party) came along to waken us from our slumber (*humme jagaya*). The biggest contribution of the party, however, was to make us realize that it was not only us who were suffering at the hands of the landlords, but that we were part of a class with a much grander objective, a class that could change society and, even the world.[50]

In the years following the initial successes of the Hashtanagar movement, the politics of common sense made steady inroads into the local social formation. Social changes engendered by commercialization of agriculture exposed small and landless farmers to the rigours of capital (and the intermediate classes), providing some of them opportunities for upward social mobility while subjecting the vast majority to the atomistic logic of the market.[51] Alongside these objective changes, patronage-based modes of political engagement continued to compete with the collective consciousness generated by the struggles of the early 1970s.

In contemporary Hashtanagar, tribal affiliation remains central to social life. Hence, small farmers from the Muhammadzai tribe remain ambivalent towards the Mohmands, even though their class interests clearly converge more than with the relatively poorer segments of society than more affluent Muhammadzais. This ambivalence is reflected in the fact that small farmers are sometimes complicit with the state in attempts to evict Mohmands from occupied lands. There is conflict and competition within the Mohmands as well, with some have secured opportunities for upward social mobility through out-migration and/or local employment in a government department.

In short, while the symbiotic relationship between tribe and class in Hashtanagar was a major factor in the emergence of a politics of resistance in the area, developments over the past three decades confirm that tribal affiliation is just as likely to be eroded as it is to remain central to social exchanges. This also brings into focus the historical role of the state in Charsadda. As a general rule, the civilian state apparatus has been less interventionist in Pakhtun regions relative to colonial and post-colonial Punjab. Thus, the state has not secured *as hegemonic a status as it has done in Punjab*. Another long-time political activist from district Charsadda offered the following anecdote:

> You have to bear in mind that many Pakhtuns living in settled areas have historical links to the tribal regions where the state does not have such a presence in everyday life. We are used to resolving many disputes amongst ourselves. Pakhtun migration away from villages to secure livelihoods is an old practice, but market forces have only more recently started to penetrate the village economy. With this penetration has come a greater involvement of state institutions in our everyday lives.[52]

Thus, even in regions historically distant from the state, *thanas* and *katcheris* have become constitutive parts of subordinate class lives. Add to this the fact that the Pakhtuns are now over-represented in the civil and military services and changes in the consciousness and posture of ordinary people towards the state are inevitable.

This has not necessarily meant that the historical conflict in Hashtangar has died a slow death. Resistance comes to the fore during the periodic attempts by local state functionaries and displaced landlords to clear occupied lands. In a sense then, the logic of subordinate class action is similar to that in Punjab; it is when the formal state's oppressive face is exposed that expressions of expansive politics take precedence over contemporary common sense.

Katchi abadi dwellers

Katchi abadis are informal squatter settlements, typically located on government land. While there are no authoritative figures available, approximately 35 per cent of Pakistan's urban population resides in *katchi abadis*.[53] By conservative estimates this equates to 30-35 million people across the country. This enormous segment of the urban population is remarkably diverse; *katchi* *abadi*s residents include white-collar professionals (including government employees), members of the intermediate classes, wage labourers and domestic servants. Even so, the majority of *katchi abadi* dwellers hail from historically disadvantaged classes and castes, and represent one of the single biggest property-less agglomerations in society.

A short sketch of the political economy of *katchi abadi* formation sheds light on the informal processes through which state functionaries and intermediate class patrons take advantage of the tenure insecurity of the urban poor. In the absence of affordable housing in cities for migrants from rural areas, land-grabbing middlemen and state functionaries invite those in need of shelter to set up their homes on unoccupied public land – in violation of formal land use laws.[54] The squatters pay under the table for the land as well as unofficial sources of electricity and other basic amenities that are provided to them by state functionaries. The informal land market has its own rules; *katchi abadi* dwellers 'buy' and 'sell' their plots, despite not possessing formal title to the land.

If and when formal policy initiatives require the occupied state property to be resumed, summary evictions are decreed. When faced with the threat of eviction, *katchi abadi* dwellers seek out patrons who can mediate between themselves and the authorities. Even aside from such exceptional moments, *katchi abadi* dwellers are ensconced in patron-client relationships with members of the low bureaucracy and vote-seeking politicians as they lobby for various welfare benefits or attempt to secure legal recognition through regularization.[55] Unsurprisingly, *katchi abadi*s are a favourite of both military rulers and mainstream politicians, the former because the conferment of proprietary rights to *katchi abadi* dwellers helps to garner popular legitimacy and the latter because *katchi abadi*s tend to be amongst the most active voting constituencies in urban areas. In all such cases, the form of political engagement is entirely patronage-based.

The politics of common sense, does, however co-exist alongside sporadic resorts to resistance. The residents of these informal settlements have, on occasion, been able to drum up considerable public pressure for a redressal of elitist planning paradigms, particularly during eviction drives. Over a period of time, *katchi abadi* dwellers' mobilizations have compelled those in power to come to terms with a language of rights and entitlements and thereby take more long-term policy steps to meet the housing needs of the urban poor.

During the Musharraf years, a broad mobilizational effort under the guise of the All-Pakistan Alliance for Katchi Abadis (APAKA) came to the fore after a number of *katchi abadi*s on lands administered by Pakistan Railways were subject to summary evictions. The APAKA's anti-eviction efforts mimicked earlier initiatives such as the Awami Rehaishi Tanzeem that flourished for a while during the early 1970s. Mubashir Hasan, one of the PPP's founding members, was privy to both mobilizations. He explained:

> *Katchi abadis* are a reflection of just how elitist the planning paradigm in Pakistan is. The rich and powerful want poor people to tend to their homes, keep roads clean, build plazas and serve them tea in their offices. They welcome labour into the cities, but make no attempt to provide them shelter. Most of the time *katchi abadi* dwellers accept this flagrant elitism, but from time to time they recognize their strength in numbers and mobilize against the injustices meted out to them, especially when summary evictions are ordered by a bureaucrat or political leader. That is what happened in the early 1970s in Lahore and the same happened in the early 2000s when *katchi abadi* dwellers came together against the excesses of the Railways administration.

For the most part such mobilizations are reactive and therefore do not necessarily precipitate any sustained shift in the way that municipal authorities deal with the issue of low-income housing. Uneven patterns of upward social mobility also explain the inability of *katchi abadi* dwellers to generate momentum for substantive change.[56] In short, while the sporadic episodes of *katchi abadi* mobilization are yet another demonstration of the dynamic nature of the subordinate class action and the fact that counter-hegemonic ideas remain a threat to the historical bloc, their erratic nature also indicates that the politics of common sense remains the dominant mode of subaltern political practice.

The Unorganized Urban Workforce

The informal workforce in urban Pakistan is amongst the most exploited segments of the subordinate classes; it is in the 'informal' sector that the most unbridled effects of Pakistani capitalism are manifest. Other segments of the subordinate classes discussed above still have recourse to historically evolved networks of security, regardless of how much these networks have been eroded by the universalizing tendency of capital.[57] The effects of flexibilization and fragmentation, the two major constitutive elements of the neo-liberal phase of accumulation, become most apparent under conditions of urban informality.[58]

In Chapter 3, I discussed the informal workshops of Sialkot and Faisalabad as well as the sub-contracting system more generally. I emphasized that organizing workers under such working arrangements is fraught with difficulties. At least part of the reason is that the informal workforce is generally not privy to a popular memory of resistance. The organized trade union movement of the 1960s and 1970s was concentrated within large public sector enterprises such as Pakistan Railways and the Water and Power Development Authority (WAPDA). Private sector workers were also radicalized during the decade of upheaval, but the subsequent fragmentation of industry has undermined both collective memory and actual workplace organizing.

As discussed in Chapter 3, intermediate class employers are often seen to be 'doing a favour' for workers by providing opportunities to earn a living. On the one hand, this reflects workers' desperation to escape the impersonalism of the market; on the other hand the personalized nature of the relationship between the worker and the *thekedaar* clearly inhibits resistance against the exploitative system. The feeling of indebtedness to the *thekedaar* is heightened by the immense surplus pool of labour which makes employees' positions highly tenuous. The high percentage of adolescents and even children working in the sector also militates against organization and sustained struggle.

Nevertheless, in this sector too resistance cannot be ruled out entirely. In the early 2000s a mobilization of sweatshop workers in the powerlooms sector in Faisalabad was relatively successful in meeting some of its immediate demands. Going by the name Labour Qaumi Movement (LQM), the effort was spearheaded by former rank-and-file activists of religious organizations whose populist training served them well in a series of confrontations with the Labour Department and powerloom owners.

The LQM was able to bring the powerlooms sector to a halt by mobilising thousands of workers demanding recognition under labour laws to strike. The LQM's demand was that each worker be registered by owners and the Labour Department, given social security cards, guaranteed the legal minimum wage, and that working hours be in accordance with state law. The mobilizations could not persist beyond a period of 24 months on account of internal discord within the LQM, but one powerlooms worker described the movement's impact in that short period of time:

> We had absolutely no rights before the LQM. At least now the other side (*malkaan aur sarkar*) know that we exist. Yes there are still thousands of people who are ready to work in even worse conditions than what we experience, but we had nothing to lose anyways because the managers of the sweatshops could kick us out whenever they wanted. At least now they think twice because they know we are capable of raising a hue and cry *(shor hungama)* and bringing everything to a halt.[59]

Agency versus Structure

In conclusion I return to Chatterjee and 'political society'. Underlying this conceptualization of subaltern political practice is the premise that the *modus operandi* of post-colonial states has been substantively altered over the past few decades, in conjunction with shifts in the global political economy. Specifically, while what has been called 'accumulation by dispossession' – the forcible acquisition of natural resources and environments upon which subalterns rely to reproduce the conditions of their existence – has intensified, a parallel process which seeks to reverse this dispossession has also taken root. Chatterjee attempts to make sense of this reversal by way of the Foucault's well-known writings on governmentality.

In a nutshell, Chatterjee suggests that the structure of power in India has evolved so that a symbiotic relationship has developed between politicians seeking electoral majorities and subaltern populations who have imbibed the discourse of governmental welfare. The engagements between the two political actors take place in political society, a sphere of informal political practices through which the effects of accumulation by dispossession are offset.

I agree with Chatterjee that the contemporary political sphere in many post-colonial countries is different to that which existed only two or three decades ago. I have argued in this book that the most significant shifts relate to the efforts of the powers-that-be to undermine anti-systemic political forces, and to co-opt a wide cross-section of society – including the labouring poor – into status quo arrangements.

Certainly, the structure of power is no longer as insular as in the past, and the exercise of power has also evolved considerably. Under this backdrop Chatterjee's insights about subaltern political strategies and tactics help us make sense of the everyday political sphere. However, it is essential to bear in mind that the collective bargaining power of the lower orders of society has decreased markedly in comparison to a few decades ago. There may be examples of subalterns very skilfully navigating the everyday state and market, but the absence of a wider political consciousness linking all such struggles together cannot be understated.

In the final analysis, the politics of the subordinate classes is most succinctly conceptualized in Marx's famous – some might say notorious – Preface to a Contribution to the Critique of Political Economy: 'In the social production of their life, men enter into definite relations that are *indispensable* and *independent* of their will' (italics added).[60] The subordinate classes undertake political actions within a *given* structural matrix. They are not, therefore, *willingly* ceding to social and political exchanges that are cynical and oppressive. They are instead recognizing the real constraints that they face, including the threat of naked coercion, and the possibility of losing what little they have.

EP Thompson argued for decades that class is not a fixed objective category that magically appears and plays out its role while history proceeds as a teleological stage production.[61] Instead class is a lived experience and the development of consciousness of class, or for that matter any other such expression of solidarity, must be understood in every separate context in its own right. Thus, even as the state and propertied classes impose structural violence upon the subordinate classes, if and when the subjective will to resist or revolt is generated, class – or any other expansive category – becomes operative and the primary identification for political action.

This subjective will was generated in the late 1960s both as a result of structural changes *and* the unique social experiences that evolved coevally with such changes. It was in this period that the subordinate classes experienced a decisive change in the political field. Though the specific challenge to oligarchic rule that emerged in the decade or so between 1967 and 1977 was eliminated, this chapter has attempted to show that the potentialities of counter-hegemonic subordinate class action are not entirely foreclosed.

All of the above-mentioned examples illustrate that class emerges as a shared experience typically in response to overt attacks by the state and dominant classes. Thus, in Gramscian terms, the use of coercive force *alone* actually undermines the hegemonic system. It is for this reason that the state and its allies have attempted to institutionalize a submissive common sense by robbing politics of its potentially revolutionary meaning, whilst also inculcating a certain cynicism within the wider social formation, Islam acting as the ultimate demobilizational tool.

This hegemonic project has also been directed by the objective structural changes that shape the evolving social order. The deepening of capitalism and the newer forms of organization and consumerism to which it has given rise have been crucial factors in facilitating the state-led project of demobilization. All of which is to say that the resilience of the structure of power 'from above' is both cause and consequence of the absence of a transformative politics 'from below'.

Endnotes

1. Chatterjee (2012).
2. Jones (2003: 424).

3. For a good summary of these criticisms and variations, including a response by Chatterjee himself, see Gudavarthy (2012).
4. Chatterjee (2011: 148).
5. Chatterjee (2008).
6. Sayeed (1980: 151).
7. Herring (1983: 46–49).
8. Ali (2015); Toor (2011).
9. Interview with Malik Lal Khan.
10. Jones (2003).
11. Jalal (1994: 162).
12. Bhutto himself proclaimed on more than one occasion that his coming to power represented a guarantee to western powers that communism would be contained. See for example, Jones (2003: 473).
13. Interview with Noor Baloch.
14. Ahmad (1978: 481).
15. Leghari (1979: 158).
16. Interview with Ovais Abid.
17. Shaheed (1983).
18. Ahmed (1998: 61-88).
19. *The Pakistan Times*, May 2, 1984.
20. There were even full-page write-ups on Latin American revolutionaries such as Che Guevara (Jang, July, 20, 1968). This is unthinkable in the present-day climate.
21. Wilder (1998); Waseem (2006).
22. Wilder (1998: 194).
23. See Roy's (2004) revealing discussion of the popular term *sarkar* in India, distinguishing *sarkar* (government) from the public, confirming not only the coercive nature of the state, but also its paternalism (*maibaap*).
24. Verkaaik (2004: 8).
25. See http://www.ecp.gov.pk/Documents/LG%20Elections/LGE2015_Report.pdf
26. Interview with Mehr-un-Nisa.
27. The Occupy movement and its various offshoots in rich countries confirmed the deep sense of alienation from formal politics felt by the mass of working people – the '99%'.
28. Manzoor Razi.
29. Akhtar (2015: 102–14).
30. The use of the term 'unspectacular' owes itself to an unpublished manuscript of a lecture delivered by Sudipta Kaviraj to the American Association of South Asian Studies in 2004.
31. de Certeau (1988).
32. See, for example, Cheema et al (2014).
33. See Khattak and Sayeed (2001).
34. A version of this argument is made by Bayat (2009) in his work on street and other forms of resistance politics in the Muslim Middle East.

The Subordinate Classes   159

35. I define the landless here as either wage labourers or sharecropping/cash-in-rent tenants. Both are distinct from the increasingly large number of the rural landless who are involved in non-agricultural occupations.
36. Gazdar (2003).
37. Most of the canal-colonists were originally given short-term tenancies, but following riots in 1907 the policy of successive British – and following partition in 1947, Pakistani – regimes was to issue occupancy tenants proprietary rights to the land (Ali, 1988).
38. Gazdar's (2003) study of villages in three Punjabi districts, namely Attock, Hafizabad and Faisalabad, confirms that 'significant cases of mobility have occurred among the poorer segments of the traditional cultivators, while the traditional "non-cultivators" continue to face social and economic disadvantage'.
39. This corresponds to the factional model prevalent in Punjab villages outlined by Alavi (1971; 1972a; 1973).
40. Wilder (1998).
41. Chaudhary (1999: 26).
42. Chaudhary (1999); Lyon (2002); Nelson (2011).
43. Specifically, the farms produced milk and cheese that was sent to troops on the frontline, whilst also being a breeding ground for horses and mules. For more information about the history of the Okara military farms, along with the farmers' movement, see Akhtar (2006b).
44. Khan (2000: 578).
45. In Okara, as in much of Punjab, Christians are low-caste menials and remain more alienated than Muslim *kammi*s. During the mobilization between 2000 and 2004, the Christian-Muslim divide, although latent, was dramatically bridged.
46. Interview with Chaudhry Mukhtar.
47. Lindholm (1982).
48. Importantly, there is also always a distinction between members of the tribe in terms of land ownership; some members of landowning tribes may even be landless due to fragmentation of holdings over the span of generations. More generally, Pakhtun tribes distinguish themselves from non-Pakhtuns such as Gujjars in regions like Malakand.
49. Hashtanagar refers to an area that spans three districts, namely Mardan, Peshawar and Charsadda. For more information on the Hashtanagar movement, see Laghari (1979: 213–22).
50 Interview with Salaar Ahmad Ali.
51. Migration of working-age males is not uncommon in Charsadda – almost every family has at least one male member of the household working either in Rawalpindi, Peshawar, Karachi or in one of the Gulf states.
52. Interview with Pervez Khan.
53. Hasan (2002b).
54. In the immediate post-partition period, land was available in many parts of the city and thus many *katchi abadis* developed in and around city centres. In the current

period land has become scarce and *katchi abadis* are now springing up on natural drains, physically depressed pieces of land, and the outskirts of the city.
55. Many municipal and development authorities have *katchi abadis* cells, including the Capital Development Authority (CDA) in Islamabad. The Punjab government has a department dedicated to *katchi abadis* headed by a Director-General, while Sindh boasts the highest level of institutionalization in the form of the Sindh Katchi Abadis Authority (SKAA). It is the members of these departments, along with functionaries of the encroachment cells that generate the most benefits from their interactions with *katchi abadis* dwellers.
56. Patronage tends to be distributed not along the lines of any particular social identity, but rather reflects historically developed links between factions within *katchi abadis* (organized along party and trade union lines for example) and politicians/ state functionaries. Religion, however, remains a major fault line within *katchi abadis*. Menial caste Christians who typically take up cleaning jobs in government departments or elite homes live in *katchi abadis* in big numbers, and their highly depressed social status explains their regular search for powerful patrons.
57. The agricultural wage labourer is arguably just as vulnerable to the dictates of the market as the informal sector workers in urban areas.
58. Harvey (1992).
59. Interview with Rana Tahir.
60. Marx (1977).
61. Thompson (1966).

7

Epilogue
What does a Counter-hegemonic Politics Look Like?

The narrative presented in this book has featured a dialectic of 'order' and 'change' that is deeply imbricated in the post-colonial structure of power, as it was during the colonial period. For the most part, the state has upheld the imperative of order even while privileging the logic of capital and the inevitable transformation that a deepening capitalism brings with it. The result has been both substantial continuity in that entrenched classes and institutions have maintained power and privilege, and transformative change as mobility 'from below' has allowed newer, nativized segments of society to push their way into an expanded 'historical bloc'.

This basic dialectic of order and change – and the contradictions to which it invariably gives rise – is not unique to Pakistan's case. In many other post-colonial societies the structure of power is distant and coercive yet permeable and personalized, while the deepening of capital has greatly altered the dynamics of a previously insular political-economic system. Certainly the trajectories of what I have called the politics of common sense must be thoroughly contextualized, yet the conceptual parallels in Pakistan's and other cases are considerable, particularly in the era of 'globalization'.[1]

In conclusion, I will provide a brief summary of the argument that has been presented in the book, detail developments since the beginning of the millennium, and offer some tentative projections on the prospects of rupture in the structure of power moving forward. In doing so I will once again bring into focus the heuristic method adopted throughout this book; an understanding of contemporary political forms in Pakistan requires explication of a dynamic and expanding structure of power *and* a recognition of the fact that this structure is, in some measure at least, legitimated from below. As I have argued throughout the preceding chapters, these two levels of analysis should not be considered mutually exclusive; coercion and consent are two sides of the same coin.

When All is Said and Done

Despite the immense changes that have taken place throughout society, particularly from the 1960s onwards, the configuration of power in Pakistan continues to feature the 'steel frame' which has survived by propagating the imperative of order. However, I have argued that the historical bloc – the dominant coalition of interests – has undergone transformation and that the steel frame itself has become porous and subject to parochial capture in a manner that was unthinkable under the British.

The everyday state thinks and operates in very different ways to how it is often imagined. Yet, somewhat counter-intuitively, the fact that the composition and practice of state institutions and functionaries has become less coherent has also permitted the 'steel frame' – the military institution, to be precise – to remain the arbiter of power while potential challenges to its preeminence have been defused through a vast patronage machine.

Certainly the threat and occasional use of coercive power remains necessary to disarm those political forces – particularly ethnic-nationalist militants – that do not accede to the politics of common sense.[2] In fact, coercion is a fact of life in all parts of the country, including Punjab where the relationship between the state and relatively underprivileged segments of society has been far more consensual than in the peripheries.

I have emphasized the role of two social forces that have been crucial to the stability of the expanded historical bloc which emerged during the 1980s, namely the intermediate classes and religio-political forces. These two groups have been the agents of a retrograde populism, which functions as the shell through which the subordinate classes have been co-opted into the sphere of common sense politics.

I will now consider the extent to which the power equation 'from above' may be changing on account of the emergence of new claimants to both material resources and ideological influence beyond those that constituted the post-Zia historical bloc. I will then offer my impressions about whether or not these new claimants undermine the established structure of power or in fact are reinforcing it, again linking this question dialectically to the potential erosion of consent 'from below'.

Whence the 'Establishment'?

Amongst the words most often bandied about in contemporary Pakistan is 'establishment'. The term is typically understood to refer to the military and its various agencies, along with elements of the high bureaucracy, sections of the propertied classes and the state's 'organic intellectuals'. I have demonstrated in this book that the notion of a relatively insular 'establishment' exercising almost exclusive control over society cannot be sustained by the evidence. Nevertheless, the military-led historical bloc has managed to sustain a structure of power that is exclusionary and exploitative by engaging intermediaries that can generate everyday consent 'from below'. Meanwhile, the military continues to depict itself as the sole embodiment of the 'state-idea' that undergirds the everyday politics of common sense.

A body of opinion has emerged in Pakistan and beyond that the power of the military-led 'establishment' has dissipated through the 2000s and early 2010s. I have dealt at length with the hypothesis of state fragmentation, and rejected the notion that less coherence in the exercise of power necessarily means the proliferation of counter-hegemonic ideas and attendant political challenges to status quo.

The proposition that the military-led establishment's dominance has been challenged in recent times is a distinct argument that needs to be dealt with in its own right. According to this line of thinking, the military's arbiter role has been undermined by the rise of competing centres of power, both at the level of the state and in what has rather vaguely been termed as 'civil society'.[3]

The impetus for this growing perception can be traced to the lawyer-led mobilization against the regime of General Pervez Musharraf. This movement began in early 2007 and eventually culminated in Musharraf relinquishing the presidency in August 2008. The movement crystallized around the person of the Chief Justice of the Supreme Court, Iftikhar Mohammad Chaudhry, who had been deposed by Musharraf and his close circle in March 2007. The slogans of 'rule of law' and 'independence of the judiciary' featured prominently during the agitation, which also saw the coming of age of a young private TV media. During and after the movement, the superior judiciary and media were hailed as new centres of (popular) power that had significantly changed the dynamics of the political field.[4]

There are at least three reasons to be skeptical of this proposition. First, the movement brought together a reasonably wide cross-section of social and political forces in its initial phase when the immediate objective was to bring down the Musharraf dictatorship. It fractured considerably in its subsequent phase after the Pakistan People's Party (PPP) won the general election of February 2008. In this second phase the movement became much more parochial, with a predominantly anti-PPP and right-wing face.

Second, the 'state-idea' with which the military is so closely identified has been largely reinforced by the superior judiciary and corporate media. Both of the latter institutions, as well as the urban middle-classes to whom they appeal most, generally fortify established ideas about both 'national security' and Islam as the glue that binds all the people of Pakistan together. Then CJ Iftikhar Chaudhry went on record in 2010 to ask the following rhetorical question during a hearing in the Supreme Court challenging constitutional amendments: '[S]hould we accept if tomorrow parliament declares secularism, and not Islam, as the state polity?'[5]

Third, the military has historically suffered a distinct fall from grace towards the end of prolonged stints in government, but has always managed to resuscitate its image by retreating out of the political spotlight in the subsequent period. I noted in Chapter 2 that the military has never suffered as much public humiliation as in December 1971 following the dismemberment of the country. However, it was restored to its position as the 'guardian of the state' relatively soon afterwards.

It can plausibly be argued that the same general pattern has played out in the years following the end of the Musharraf dictatorship. The post-Musharraf top brass appears to have once again adopted the 'Sher Ali' formula, originally devised in the late 1960s by a close confidante of then army chief General Yahya Khan, according to which the military maintains its larger-than-life image in society by remaining distant from the public eye and allowing politicians to become the target of public ire for all of the country's failings.[6]

In a sense, I am drawing attention to the continued dynamism of the post-Bhutto historical bloc. This dynamism does not sit well with triumphant predictions of the ascendance of 'genuine' democracy based on snapshots of the formal power equation frozen in time and space. After all, the diverse means and practices of patronage that have been discussed throughout the book have not emerged despite, but *through* formal democratic procedures. Earlier chapters have confirmed that the emergence of new and variegated contenders for power has been facilitated by increasingly localized electoral contests, a favourite strategy of military dictators, and particularly Zia ul Haq.

The few examples I have mentioned from neighbouring India through the course of the book confirm that there can be no romanticizing of 'democracy' in the contemporary period. Political patronage – and all its discontents – is a defining feature of Indian democracy.

Still, it would be misleading to understate the extent to which Pakistan's long experiences with unelected rule have stunted the democratization of society more generally, at least insofar as democracy is not only to be equated with procedural exercises such as elections. I have argued that the very meaning of politics in Pakistan has been reduced over the past three decades to a highly cynical set of practices in which substantive notions of equal entitlements and basic freedoms are conspicuous by their absence.[7]

Hence, precisely because the military has been the arbiter of power 'from above' in the post-Zia period, that it remains the symbol of an ethnically skewed structure of power, and because it is so synonymous with the 'state-idea', I subscribe to the broad line of reasoning that a dissipation of the military's power would constitute a central plank of a counter-hegemonic politics in Pakistan.

The military's burgeoning economic interests have brought it into contact with the subordinate classes in a manner that has undermined its myth, even in Punjab where it has historically maintained a consensual relationship with a wide cross-section of society.[8] The military's ever-expanding corporate empire is also a potential source of disharmony within the historical bloc itself, which has negotiated change in the social formation on the basis of relatively stable power-sharing principles. It can therefore be surmised that, if and when the military institution encroaches decisively on the domains/interests of other members of the historical bloc, it endangers the survival of the bloc itself.

Can Democratic Forces of Pakistan Unite?

Towards the end of the Musharraf dictatorship, the military top brass' brazenness in confronting criticism of its exclusionary practices in the political, economic and wider social realms had reached unprecedented proportions:

> The defence societies everywhere are the top societies of Pakistan ... now, why are we jealous of this? Why are we jealous if somebody gets a piece of land, a kanal of land, cheap when it was initially, and because of the good work done by the society, the price rises by 100 times and the man then earns some money. What is the problem? Why are we jealous of this? There's no problem at all.[9]

As noted above, the post-Musharraf military top brass toned down the rhetoric so as to rehabilitate its battered image, but the institutional drive to accumulate capital and power was hardly tamed. This is in large part because the military has continued to enjoy the implicit consent of 'junior partners' in the historical bloc, all of whom are beneficiaries of the structure of power and share the fear of a counter-hegemonic politics that would threaten their privilege.

However, the military cannot accumulate recklessly lest some of the other players in the power-sharing arrangement break ranks. So, for example, if the military's incessant drive to capital accumulation crowds out private industry, the latter may refuse a steadily reduced share of the spoils. I have pointed out that the propertied classes, old and new, tend not to act as corporate groups with coherent interests, the preferred approach being to build factions with proximity to state power. It is therefore unlikely that the military's growing *economic* ambitions on their own could alienate a significant enough segment of any of the propertied classes to precipitate a rupture.

A more likely possibility is the military's exclusionary *political* ambitions leading to discord within the historical bloc. Here it is necessary to think beyond both the 'old guard' as well as the post-Bhutto entrants into the power equation and consider the prospect of a much wider cross-section of democratic forces generating a consensus over curbing the military's power.

During the Musharraf tenure, both of the two major political parties, the PML-N and the PPP, were frozen out of the power-sharing arrangement. Both parties remained at the forefront of the opposition to the Musharraf regime, but there was no major rupture of the system because significant numbers of politicians representing the propertied classes at large were co-opted by the regime as was the coalition of the religio-political parties, the MMA. It was only when the wider democratic community came together – by which I mean professional associations such as the bar, journalists, as well as political and community activists outside the mainstream – that the dictatorial regime was forced into retreat.

Following the 'success' of the anti-Musharraf movement, the military's status of 'sacred cow' has been steadily rehabilitated. For the first couple of years after Musharraf's ouster in August 2008, the military institution remained subject to public censure on various accounts, including criticism of its economic empire, its manipulation of the formal political process, its alleged involvement in the disappearance and killings of activists associated with ethnic-national movements, and its selective patronage of right-wing militants. The PML-N which formed the government after the 2013 general elections even attempted to try Musharraf for subverting the constitution – an unprecedented step, even if not very politically sagacious.

Predictably, Musharraf was eventually allowed to leave the country, and the PML-N government's initial bravado *vis-a-vis* the 'establishment' eventually gave way to a much more familiar posture of deference. 'Public opinion', as manufactured by the corporate media via the captive audience of the urban middle classes, slowly but surely metamorphosed so that the military – and its chief, Raheel Sharif – was yet again cast into the role of 'saviour', singularly capable of guiding Pakistan towards peace, progress and stability, untainted as it was by the 'corruption' which is said to be an endemic feature of Pakistan's politics.

Many mainstream parties – the Pakistan Tehrik-e-Insaf foremost amongst them – reinforced this 'anti-politics' narrative, and almost pleaded with the military to facilitate 'regime change'.[10] This confirms that the political choices of the military's 'junior partners' in the historical bloc are generally conditioned by the tenor of public discourse. When the image of the military as the guardian of the state falters, political contenders across landed, industrialist, intermediate class and religio-political backgrounds remake themselves as apparently principled opponents of praetorianism.[11]

However, when the narrative cycle is such that 'national security' imperatives rear their head and sympathetic swathes of 'public opinion' are generated in favour of the military, mainstream parties tend to join in the chorus; crucial in this regard has been the 'consensus' forged in and around the so-called 'war on terror', the prosecution of which has accorded extraordinary power to the state security apparatus.[12]

Related to the 'war on terror' is another potential fault line within the historical bloc that demands interrogation. Throughout this book, I have emphasized the steady 'nativization' of the structure of power, as the westernized, secular successors to the British have had to cope with the rise of a much less urbane, conservative element within the corridors of power. This element emerges 'from below' to be inducted into the unelected apparatuses of the state, seeks elected political office at various levels, and with time garners greater influence in the day-to-day lives of ordinary people.[13]

Until 2001, this process of nativization did not necessarily produce any serious contradictions within the structure of power. However, under a changed global environment, and especially in the context of the American-led war against right-wing militants in Afghanistan and parts of Pakistan with long-term ties to the state's security apparatus, there has been evidence to suggest growing tensions between 'progressive' and 'reactionary' factions within the historical bloc.

The murder of the Governor of Punjab, Salman Taseer, by one of his bodyguards in early 2010 is indicative of such fissures within the structure of power. Taseer was in many ways the symbol of the westernized 'old guard', a businessman-cum politician with a history of supporting liberal causes. His death was mourned by secular elites, especially as he was killed for taking up the cause of a poor Christian girl sentenced to death under the draconian

Blasphemy Law. On the other hand, his killer was celebrated openly by the religious right, and more reservedly by conservative elements within the state apparatus.

Taseer had been the Governor of Punjab in the later period of the Musharraf dictatorship and retained the post under the PPP Government that triumphed in the 2008 general election, which itself confirms that the epithets 'progressive' and 'reactionary' have less meaning for the occupants of political office than might otherwise be assumed. Taseer's politics and the various reactions to his death were a microcosm of the tensions as well as hybrid political alignments within state and society that have unfolded under the backdrop of the so-called 'war on terror'.

The uneasy relationship between the old incumbents and the relatively new 'vernacular interests' in the corridors of power is not likely to result in rupture, not least of all because both segments ultimately recognise their interests are best served by a relatively stable historical bloc. And to the extent that the fault lines between the 'secular' and the 'religious' exist in society at large, I have already discussed how the imperatives of accumulation for those with money and power, and survival for those without it, trump many an ideological contradiction.[14]

The United States and other western governments have of course been at the forefront of the ostensibly epic battle between the forces of 'civilization' and 'global terrorism'. I noted in the introduction that I would not probe the role of external powers in conditioning Pakistan's structure of power at length. Suffice it to say that Washington openly patronized the Zia regime and the development of a *jihadi* infrastructure that has generated an interminable spiral of hate and violence. The US has on the whole played a far from progressive role in Pakistan's history.

In the post-Musharraf period, some policy initiatives have suggested that Washington's traditional positioning is being reconfigured. Yet western governments, and particularly the United States, will continue to pursue narrow geo-political goals; their predominantly strategic objectives in the region continue to militate against any meaningful commitments to a long-term process of democratization.[15]

A case can be made that China is now competing with the US to become the most influential benefactor of the state of Pakistan. The Chinese Government's pledging of more than US$50 billion in economic aid in the form of the China-Pakistan Economic Corridor (CPEC) in 2015 has been hailed by officialdom and much of the intelligentsia as a 'game-changer' for the country.[16] Chinese aid and assistance may reduce or reinforce Pakistan's traditional dependency on superpower states. It has, however, already allowed the military to consolidate its arbiter role. The Chinese government appears to have more confidence in the military rather than the elected government to protect its various investments, particularly in insurgency-affected Balochistan.[17]

In the final analysis, thinking about the imperative of 'democratic' forces both home and abroad uniting to force a rupture in the military's power must be put into broader context. Mainstream political parties, even if they do contest aspects of the military's historic dominance, have no necessary commitment to challenging the patronage-based order in which they too have considerable stakes. Certainly, they will benefit in the long-run from a dissipation of the military's power inasmuch as this increases their relative position *within the historical bloc*. However, it is important to bear in mind that the post-Bhutto power nexus 'from above' has survived, however tenuously, with the military acting as a unifying force. Mainstream political parties would be best served by a deepening of the formal democratic process which will increase their *relative* power within the historical bloc *vis a vis* the military, but without a fundamental reordering of class and state power which would represent a challenge to their own interests.[18]

Are We All Middle Class?

A genuine overhaul of Pakistan's structure of power is only possible if and when a critical mass is created with a commitment to challenging contemporary common sense. Contesting the military's arbiter role in the economy, polity and wider society may be a necessary condition in this regard, but the truly sufficient condition is the emergence of an alternative imaginary and practice of politics through the agency of the lower orders of society.

I have emphasized repeatedly that a wide cross-section of society across the ethnic, class and other divides tends to a certain cynicism when it comes to the idea of politics. There are notable exceptions to this rule, particularly in peripheral regions where ethnic-nationalism is the dominant political idiom, but a substantive political project of and by the subordinate classes is conspicuous by its absence. The latter cultivate political relationships to navigate everyday state and market, but while maintaining a rhetorical distance from 'politics', which is considered to be the monopoly of the rich and powerful, and therefore disdained.[19]

As such, a counter-hegemonic politics would have to be preceded by a regeneration of a culture of politics itself. Even the instances of resistance outlined in the previous chapter were referred to by many of the protagonists themselves as 'non-political' undertakings. Many informal workers, landless farmers and slum dwellers alike insist that the struggle for their 'rights' should not be construed as an attempt to achieve 'political' objectives. In other words, there is not only a disassociation of everyday questions of social justice with politics, but a disinclination to be perceived as being involved in 'politics' itself. This posture changes somewhat during election cycles, but only so that functional alignments corresponding to contemporary common sense are reinforced.

In my estimation, the common sense rhetoric against politics has much to do with the virtual disappearance of class from the political lexicon. Both in Pakistan and around the world, those who would in a previous generation readily describe themselves as working class now have little pretence of being part of any class at all. Young, educated segments of society once attracted to leftist ideology have little awareness of the difference between 'left' and 'right' – in similar vein working people have little association with a class identity, let alone a politics that represents their class interests.

This disappearance of class idiom is due to objective changes in the structure of work, particularly the related phenomena of flexibilization and informalization. It is also explained by the fact that class-based organizations such as trade unions have become increasingly marginal to the everyday experience of working people. That explicitly left-of-centre political parties are on the fringes of society is both cause and consequence of the decline of the labour movement.[20]

However, there is another related set of developments that I would like to highlight in this regard, namely the increasingly 'middle-class' character of political discourse. So, for instance, the slogan of the anti-Musharraf movement – aside from the fundamental demand that the dictator restore the democratic process – was for the establishment of 'rule of law', which, by any estimation, has only a vague relation to the everyday struggles of working people. In the post-Musharraf period, the imperative of ending the rule of 'corrupt' individuals in government has been the pet phrase of every opposition movement, which is again a somewhat vacuous slogan that glosses over the fact that the entire political-economic system is 'corrupt' inasmuch as it discriminates against those without money and influence.

In effect, issues that affect working people on a daily basis – particularly those related to employment, as well as access to basic amenities such as education, health and housing are virtually absent from the political and intellectual mainstream. The once-powerful idea that informed the twentieth-century welfare state, namely that the public sector should provide for the basic needs of every citizen, is conspicuous by its absence. Politicians seeking votes offer the promise of service-delivery, but the operative logic is one of functional exchange between those with access to state power and those without it.

On the whole, the imperatives of neo-liberal globalization and the information economy are such that the very idea of social collectivities – including those conceptualized in class terms – possessing immutable political, economic and cultural freedoms is an increasingly marginal one. We are witnessing the emergence of a public sphere comprised of discrete individuals, all of whom seek access to a globalized wealth of information, and with it a desire to consume commodities available across time and space.

As I have suggested at different junctures, individuals 'from below' are continually seeking ways and means to graduate into superior social strata, quite irrespective of the fate of others who share their class and/or status background. The rise of a smart phone 'culture' – there are now 133,908,192 registered mobile phone users in Pakistan[21] – would suggest that the experience of shared class backgrounds in the context of the workplace or residential neighbourhoods is likely to become even more displaced by the highly individualized experience of navigating a globalized world.

The proliferation of gated housing communities in urban Pakistan is an apt example of just how much the imagination of upward mobility – at the level of the individual and the family that he heads – is gaining credence. It is the dream of every 'middle-class' citizen of Pakistan to buy a plot in gated housing communities. I noted in Chapter 3 that close to 60 million people in the country could now be designated 'middle-class', and it is increasingly the case that those below them on the social ladder have similarly middle-class aspirations even if they do not yet possess the means.

Since a plethora of real estate schemes are run by the military – or at the very least use its name – the symbiotic link between a growing middle-class unaware or unconcerned with the plight of the mass of working people unable to partake in the globalized culture of consumerism, and a corporate military that also cultivates an impeccable image of patriotism is likely to grow stronger. Conversely, working people in all their various manifestations, unable to find their specific class concerns addressed in the political and intellectual mainstream, are left only with the possibility of seeking out patrons to continue surviving the system – and occasionally putting in their lot with right-wing populism to boot.

Only a small fraction of those with the requisite political and economic savvy are actually successful in making their way up the social ladder. The patronage-based order cannot guarantee even survival for most working people, especially given the ever more dramatic encroachments on basic livelihoods, homes and the like by corporate capital. A new political imaginary therefore requires a break from the politics of common sense beyond idealized notions of the 'Islamic' state and 'anti-corruption' populism. Given how deeply rooted the patronage-based order has become, this will take time.

Perhaps most importantly, such a new political imaginary requires the rehabilitation of the idea of a radical political subject that is not bound by apolitical 'middle class' aspirations. I have shown that various forms of resistance proliferate in Pakistan, even while the larger environment continues to be stultifying. It is not necessarily the case that each such instance of resistance culminates in an egalitarian outcome, but as I have argued throughout this book, counter-hegemonic expressions of politics can never be entirely muted.

As counter-hegemonic claims continue to emerge, systemic domination will be increasingly challenged. And, as Gramsci reminds us, common sense will evolve, perhaps even in ways that can form the basis of a free and egalitarian social order.

Endnotes

1. Gooptu (2007); Levitsky (2003).
2. The 'blowback' of *jihadi* militants nurtured by the state security apparatus is a separate case; it is beyond the scope of this book to consider the extent to which the state is actually rolling back its historical policy of patronage for such militants.
3. The concepts of state and civil society are of course part of a well-established theoretical tradition within western political philosophy that can be traced as far back as Hegel; Gramsci too employed this terminology extensively. I have discussed at length the novel theoretical framework proffered by Partha Chatterjee but not the classic expositions. For a good summary of both classical and contemporary usage of 'civil society', see Kaviraj and Khilnani (2001).
4. Zaidi (2014).
5. *Dawn* (2010).
6. Haqqani (2005).
7. Amongst the most obvious long-term effects of undemocratic rule in Pakistan is the virtual absence of women from the public realm; India's public sphere may not be very women-friendly, as is proven by the coming to prominence of numerous cases of sexual assaults against women, but the fact that women occupy public space and are free to do things as innocuous as ride motorcycles astounds Pakistanis who are not at all used to such a spectacle in their own country.

8. Khan and Akhtar (2014).
9. General Pervez Musharraf speaking at the launch of a Defence Housing Authority (DHA) desalination plant in 2004, quoted in Siddiqa (2007: 194). Having said this, the military is clearly sensitive to public censure: The launch of Ayesha Siddiqa's book, which is the first documented account of the 'military economy', was greeted with a massive public relations exercise by the military to defame the author and reject her findings as concoctions. In an interview with a private TV channel, General Musharraf even went so far as to accuse Siddiqa of being involved in anti-state activities at the behest of India.
10. Grare (2015).
11. Javed Hashmi of the PML-N stands out as an example of a politician made by the military who has now become an anti-military stalwart. Hashmi was an activist with the IJT during the early Zia period distinguishing himself by his virulent anti-PPP polemic. He made his way up through the local body elections and then became a cabinet member following non-party elections in 1985. Hashmi remained with the PML between 1988-99, acquiring ministerial positions in both of the PML governments that ruled through the period. Under the Musharraf regime, Hashmi was imprisoned for a little under 4 years for 'defaming the armed forces' and publicly apologized for his past association with military rule. He later joined and left the PTI under the pretext that the latter had colluded with the establishment to undermine the democratic process.
12. The manner in which the 'war on terror' empowers the military is no more evident in the passing of the 21st constitutional amendment in January 2015 through which special military courts were created giving the institution powers to arrest, prosecute and execute whomever it chooses to label a 'terrorist' without any oversight. For details, see HRW World Report (2016).
13. Eqbal Ahmad (1974) presciently foresaw the 'nativization' of the power structure, replete with the ideological propensity of emergent classes within the state towards a reactionary form of political Islam.
14. See Akhtar (2016) for a detailed interrogation of the 'secular-religious' divide in contemporary Pakistan.
15. The Kerry-Lugar Bill, passed in 2009, promised an overturning of the traditional emphasis on military as opposed to civilian aid. See Ahmad (2010).
16. Zaidi (2016).
17. Panda (2016).
18. Akhtar (2010a).
19. I have already pointed out that significant segments of the urbanized 'elite' are just as prone to demonize politics, and particularly politicians.
20. For a theoretical explanation of the decline of twentieth century orthodoxies inspired by Marxism, see Therborn (2008). For a more general discussion of various critical theorizations on the left, including contemporary formulations of the revolutionary political subject, see Keucheyan (2013).
21. According to the Telecom Indicators issued by the Pakistan Telecommunications Authority (PTA) as of August 2016.

Glossary

Arhti	A middleman in agricultural commodity markets with a permanent presence in the *mandi* area; networked with the wider agrarian community so as to ensure debtors pay back loans
Bania	Commercial caste performing various functions in the agrarian economy, most notably moneylending at high rates of interest
Biraderi	Patrilineal lineage group, the insularity of which is sustained through endogamous marriage practices, sometimes confused with caste
Hari	Landless tenant farmer whose family is often enmeshed in a patron-client relationship with a landlord over a number of generations
Jihad	A political movement that came to prominence in the 1970s employing violent means to defend 'Islam' against 'enemies' of the faith
Kammi	Traditional artisans in the caste/*biraderi*/*qaum* hierarchy, ranking below *zamindars* but distinguishable from the 'untouchable' castes occupying the bottom-most rung
Katcheri	A courthouse in which all cases pertaining to law and order, dispute resolution and property transfers/conflicts are prosecuted within any given jurisdiction, typically *tehsil* or district
Katchi abadi	A squatter settlement on public land with a minimum of forty residential dwellings
Madrassah	A religious seminary typically operating on state funds; hundreds of thousands mushroomed in Pakistan from the 1980s onwards
Mandi	An exchange hub for agricultural produce in which primary growers come into contact with middlemen and others involved in the marketing process

Maulvi/mullah	A Muslim cleric that performs various functions; social status was enhanced greatly by the Zia regime via opportunities to acquire power and cultural/economic resources
Mujahideen	The exponents of *jihad;* popularized and feted around the world during the Afghan war in the 1980s; criminalized after the collapse of the Soviet Union, and particularly after 9/11
Numberdar	A village headman designated so by local officialdom; usually hailing from the dominant agricultural caste/tribe in the village
Panchayat	A male-only decision-making body at the local (typically village)-level; the modern variant often draws on practices and ideas from the pre-modern period
Patwari	The keeper of land records at the sub-district level responsible for sale, purchase and other land-based transactions
Qaum	Typically signifies ethno-linguistic background, but in the official narrative refers to the epithet 'Pakistani'; colloquially used at the local level synonymously with *biraderi* /caste
Rishwat	Cash or in-kind transfers in exchange for personal favours; typically refers to bribes given to state functionaries in exchange for a bending of formal rules
Sahurkar	generally synonymous with *bania*, although in some cases the terms connotes the status of merchant rather than moneylender
Sarkar	Strictly a man of authority; more widely used to refer to the government
Shagird	Apprentice who learns a trade, usually linked via his teacher (*ustad*) to a specific artisanal group
Sifarish	The doing of favours on the basis of established norms of public conduct; a favour done today will be reciprocated at a later date
Tehsildar	The administrative functionary who oversees revenue, law and order and other affairs of the state bureaucracy at the sub-district level of *tehsil*
Thana	A police station headed by the Station House Officer (SHO) and manned by Inspectors, sub-inspectors and constables
Thekedaar	A sub-contractor typically operating in the 'informal' sector, enjoys power over an available supply of dependent workers without legal protection
Ulema	Religious scholars with the institutional backing of established Islamic centres of learning; the most well-known of such centres in the subcontinent is that of Deoband

Ummah	The global community of Muslims that is invoked by scholars and political leaders alike, but not possessing institutional form
Ustad	A mentor in a unique artisanal trade that is sustained through the institution of apprenticeship
Wadero/a	A hereditary landlord/owner generally enjoying a symbiotic relationship with the local institutions of the state
Zaildar	An administrative position created by the British to help oversee revenue collection and other matters in a group of villages
Zamindar	A landed proprietor who commands the authority of the tenants/landless labourers who till his fields

Bibliography

2005. 'Protest against Removal of Religion Column.' *Dawn*, 10 March. Accessed on 1 October 2016. Available at: http://www.dawn.com/news/384845/protest-against-removal-of-religion-column.
2007. 'Loya Jirga Asked to Consider One-day Strike.' *Daily Times*, 23 May.
2010. 'SC's Responsibility?' *Dawn*, 18 August. Accessed on 4 October 2016. Available at: http://www.dawn.com/news/846079/sc-s-responsibility.
2013. 'Reign in the Establishment or Go to Hell!' *Pakistan Today*, June 17. Available at: http://www.pakistantoday.com.pk/2013/06/17/.
2014. 'Missing Persons Case: Army Man Offered "Last Chance" to Record Statement.' *Express Tribune*, 11 March. Accessed on 12 February 2016. Avaiable at: http://tribune.com.pk/story/681348/missing-personscase-army-man-offered-last-chance-to-record-statement/.
2014. 'Missing Persons: 21-year-old in ISI Custody, SC Told.' *Express Tribune*, 13 February. Accessed on 12 February 2016. Available at: http://tribune.com.pk/story/671121/missing-persons-21-year-old-in-isi-custodysc-told/.
2015. 'Senior Educationist Dr Bernadette Leaves Pakistan after Receiving Death Threats.' *Dawn*, 12 May. Accessed on 1 October 2016. Available at: http://www.dawn.com/news/1181357.
Abrams, Philip. 1988. 'On the Difficulty of Understanding the State.' *Journal of Historical Sociology* 1 (1): 58–89.
Addleton, Jonathan. 1992. *Undermining the Centre: The Gulf Migration and Pakistan*. Karachi: Oxford University Press.
Ahmad, Aijaz. 1978. 'Democracy and Dictatorship in Pakistan.' *Journal of Contemporary Asia* 8.4: 477–512.
———. 2000. 'Democracy and Dictatorship in Pakistan.' *Lineages of the Present: Ideological and Political Genealogies of Contemporary South Asia*. London: Verso.
Ahmad, Eqbal. 1974. 'Signposts to a Police State.' *Journal of Contemporary Asia* 4: 123–46.
———. 1980. 'Post-Colonial System of Power.' *Arab Studies Quarterly* 4: 350–63.
———. 2006. 'Roots of the Religious Right.' In *The Selected Writings of Eqbal Ahmad*, edited by C. Bengelsdorf, M. Cerullo and Y. Chandrani. New York: Columbia University Press.
Ahmad, Ishtiaq. 2010. 'The U.S. Af-Pak Strategy: Challenges and Opportunities for Pakistan.' *Asian Affairs: An American Review* 37: 191–209.
Ahmad, Mahvish. 2014. 'Home Front: The Changing Face of Balochistan's Separatist Insurgency.' *The Caravan: A Journal of Politics and Culture*, July.

Ahmad, Mumtaz. 1998. 'Revivalism, Islamisation, Sectarianism and Violence in Pakistan.' In *Pakistan 1997*, edited by C. Baxter and C. Kennedy. Delhi: Harper Collins Publishers.

Ahmad, Sadaf. 2009. *Transforming Faith: The Story of Al-Huda and Islamic Revivalism among Urban Pakistani Women*. New York: Syracuse University Press.

Ahmad, Saghir. 1977. *Class and Power in a Punjabi Village*. New York: Monthly Review Press.

Ahmed, Akbar S. 1986. *Pakistan Society: Islam, Ethnicity and Leadership in South Asia*. Karachi: Oxford University Press.

Ahmed, Amineh. 2006. *Sorrow and Joy among Muslim Women: The Pukhtuns of Northern Pakistan*. Cambridge: Cambridge University Press.

Ahmed, Feroz. 1973. 'The Structural Matrix of the Struggle in Bangladesh.' In *Imperialism and Revolution in South Asia*, edited by Kathleen Gough and Hari Sharma. New York: Monthly Review Press.

———. 1998. *Ethnicity and Politics in Pakistan*. Karachi: Oxford University Press.

Ahmed, Manzoor. 2003. 'Pakistan: Aporia of its Kind.' In *Pakistan: The Contours of State and Society*, edited by Soofia Mumtaz, Jean-Luc Racine and Imran Ali. Karachi: Oxford University Press.

Akhtar, Aasim S. 2006. 'The State as Landlord in Pakistani Punjab: Peasant Struggles on the Okara Military Farms.' *Journal of Peasant Studies* 33 (3): 479–501.

———. 2010a. 'Crisis of a Frontline State.' *Journal of Contemporary Asia* 40 (1): 105–22.

———. 2010b. 'Islamism as Ideology of Tradition and Change: The "New Jihad" in Swat, Northern Pakistan.' *Comparative Studies in South Asia, Africa and the Middle East* 30 (3): 595–609.

———. 2010c. 'What is Really Happening in Pakistan?' *Economic and Political Weekly* 45 (10).

———. 2015. 'The Socialist Imperative: Left Politics in Contemporary Pakistan.' *Capitalism Nature Socialism* 26 (3): 102–14.

———. 2016. 'Dreams of a Secular Republic: Elite Alienation in Post-Zia Pakistan.' *Journal of Contemporary Asia* 46 (4): 641–58.

Akhtar, Aasim S., Asha Amirali and Muhammad Ali Raza. 2006. 'Reading between the Lines: The Mullah-Military Alliance in Pakistan.' *Contemporary South Asia* 15: 383–397.

Alavi, Hamza. 1971. 'The Politics of Dependence: A Village in West Punjab.' In *South Asian Review* 4: 272–95.

———. 1972a. 'Kinship in West Punjab Villages.' *Contributions to Indian Sociology* 6: 98–112.

———. 1972b. 'The State in Post-Colonial Societies: Pakistan and Bangladesh.' *New Left Review* 74: 59–81.

———. 1973. 'Peasant Classes and Primordial Loyalties.' *Journal of Peasant Studies* 1: 78–94.

———. 1983a. 'Class and State in Pakistan.' In *Pakistan: The Unstable State*, edited by Hasan Gardezi and Jamil Rashid. Lahore: Vanguard Books.

———. 1983b. 'Elite Farmer Strategy and Regional Disparities in Agricultural Development.' In *Pakistan: The Unstable State*, edited by Hasan Gardezi and Jamil Rashid. Lahore: Vanguard Books.

———. 1987. 'Pakistan and Islam: Ethnicity and Ideology.' In *State and Ideology in the Middle East and Pakistan*, edited by Hamza Alavi and Fred Halliday. New York: Monthly Review Press.

———. 1990. 'Authoritarianism and Legitimation of State Power in Pakistan.' In *The Post-colonial State in Asia: Dialectics of Politics and Culture*, edited by S. K. Mitra. New York: Harvester Wheatsheaf.

Ali, Imran. 1988. *Punjab under Imperialism*. Karachi: Oxford University Press.

———. 2001. 'Business and Power in Pakistan.' In *Power and Civil Society in Pakistan*, edited by Anita Weiss and Zulfikar Gilani. Oxford: Oxford University Press.

———. 2003. 'Past and Present: The Making of the State in Pakistan.' In *Pakistan: The Contours of State and Society*, edited by Soofia Mumtaz, Imran Ali and Jean-Luc Racine. Karachi: Oxford University Press.

Ali, Kamran A. 2005. 'The Strength of the Street Meets the Strength of the State: The 1972 Labour Struggle in Karachi.' *International Journal of Middle East Studies* 37 (February).

———. 2015. *Surkh Salam: Communist Politics and Class Activism in Pakistan 1947–1972*. Karachi: Oxford University Press.

Ali, Manzoor. 2013. 'Tracing ANP's Trajectory: From Nationalist to Pro-establishment?' *Express Tribune*, March 11. Accessed on 11 March 2016. Available at: http://tribune.com.pk/story/518857/tracing-anps-trajectory-from-nationalist-to-pro-establishment/.

Ali, Nosheen. 2008. 'Outrageous State, Sectarianized Citizens: Deconstructing the "Textbook Controversy" in the Northern Areas, Pakistan.' *South Asia Multidisciplinary Academic Journal* 2.

Ali, Tariq. 1970. *Military Rule or People's Power*. London: Verso Books.

———. 1983. *Can Pakistan Survive?: The Death of a State*. London: Verso Books.

Amin Khan, Tariq. 2012. *The Post-Colonial State in the Era of Capitalist Globalization: Historical, Political and Theoretical Approaches to State Formation*. New York: Routledge.

Amirali, Alia. 2009. 'Political Culture of the Baloch National Movement.' MPhil Thesis, Department of Anthropology, Quaid-i-Azam University, Islamabad.

———. 2015. *Balochistan: A Case Study of Pakistan's Peacemaking Praxis*. New Delhi: Sage Publications.

Amjad, Rashid. 1982. *Private Industrial Investment in Pakistan, 1960–1970*. Cambridge: Cambridge University Press.

Anderson, Benedict. 2006. *Imagined Communities: Reflections on the Origin and Spread of Nationalism*. London: Verso Books.

Ansari, Sarah. 1992. *Sufi Saints and State Power: The Pirs of Sind, 1843–1947*. Cambridge: Cambridge University Press.

———. 2005. *Life after Partition: Migration, Community and Strife in Sindh: 1947–1962.* Karachi: Oxford University Press.

Appadurai, Arjun. 1996. *'Modernity at Large: Cultural Dimensions of Globalization.'* Minneapolis: University of Minnesota Press.

Arif, G. M., and Mohammad Irfan. 1997. 'Population Mobility across the Pakistani Border: Fifty Years Experience.' *Pakistan Development Review* 36 (4): 989–1009.

Arif, G. M., and Hassan Irfan. 1997. 'Return Migration and Occupational Change: The Case of Pakistani Migrants Returned from the Middle East.' *The Pakistan Development Review*, 36 (1): 37.

Arnold, David. 1984. 'Gramsci and Peasant Subalternity in India.' *Journal of Peasant Studies* 11 (4): 30.

Arrighi, Giovanni. 2005. 'Hegemony Unravelling – I.' *New Left Review* 32: 23–80.

Axmann, Martin. 2008. *Back to the Future: The Khanate of Kalat and the Genesis of Baloch Nationalism, 1915–1955.* New York: Oxford University Press.

Ayubi, Nazih. 1995. *Over-stating the Arab State: Politics and Society in the Middle East.* London: I. B. Tauris.

Aziz, Mazhar. 2007. *Military Control in Pakistan: The Parallel State.* New York: Routledge.

Banerjee, Mukulika. 2000. *The Pathan Unarmed: Opposition and Memory in the North West Frontier.* James Currey.

Barrow, Clyde W. 2002. 'The Miliband-Poulantzas Debate: An Intellectual History.' In *Paradigm Lost: State Theory Reconsidered*, edited by S. Aronowitz and P. Bratsis. Minneapolis: Minnesota University Press.

Bayat, Asef. 2009. *Life as Politics: How Ordinary People Change the Middle East.* Stanford: Stanford University Press.

Bayart, Jean Francois. 1991. 'Finishing with the Idea of the Third World: The Concept of the Political Trajectory.' In *Rethinking Third World Politics*, edited by James Manor. London: Longman.

———. 1993. *The State in Africa: The Politics of the Belly.* New York: Longman.

———. 2000. 'Africa in the World: A History of Extraversion.' *African Affairs* 99.

Berger, Peter L., and Samuel P. Huntington. 2002. *Many Globalizations: Cultural Diversity in the Contemporary World.* New York: Oxford University Press.

Berry, Sara. 1992. 'Hegemony on a Shoestring: Indirect Rule and Access to Agricultural Land.' *Africa* 62 (3), July.

Blom, Amelie. 2005. '"Qui a le bâton, a le buffle": Le corporatisme économique de l'armée pakistanaise.' *Questions de Reserche* 16. Paris: Centre d'études et de Recherches Internationals.

Blundo Giorgio. 2006. 'Corruption in Africa and Social Sciences.' In *Every Day Corruption and the State, Citizens and Public Officials in Africa*, edited by G. Blundo and J-P Olivier de Sardan. London: Zed Books.

Brenner, Robert. 1976. 'Agrarian Class Structure and Economic Development in Pre-industrial Europe.' *Past & Present* 70: 30–75.

Burki, Shahid J. 1969. 'Twenty Years of the Civil Service of Pakistan: A Re-evaluation.' *Asian Survey* 9: 239–54.

———. 1976. 'The Development of Pakistan's Agriculture.' In *Rural Development in Bangladesh and Pakistan*, edited by Hamza Alavi, R. Stevens and P. Bertocci. Honolulu: University of Hawaii Pressm.

———. 1980. *Pakistan under Bhutto 1971–1977.* Basingstoke: Macmillan.

Burki, Shahid J., and Craig Baxter. 1975. 'Socio-Economic Indicators of the People's Party Vote in the Punjab: A Study at the Tehsil Level.' *Journal of AsianStudies* 34: 222–44.

Cassan, Guilhem. 2011. 'Caste Identity Manipulation and Land Ownership in Colonial Punjab.' *Actors, Markets, and Institutions in Developing Countries: A Micro-empirical Approach, Working Paper.* Paris: Paris School of Economics.

deCerteau, Michel. 1988. *The Practice of Everyday Life.* Berkeley: University of California Press.

Chadda, Maya. 2000. *Building Democracy in South Asia: India, Nepal, Pakistan.* Boulder: Lynne Reiner Publishers.

Chakrabarty, Dipesh. 2000. 'Subaltern Studies and Postcolonial Historiography.' *Nepantla: Views from the South* 1: 1.

Chatterjee, Partha. 1986. *'Nationalist Thought and the Colonial World: A Derivative Discourse.'* London: Zed Books.

———. 2008. 'Democracy and Economic Transformation in India.' In *Economic and Political Weekly* 43 (April).

———. 2011. *Lineages of Political Society: Studies in Postcolonial Democracy.* New York: Columbia University Press.

———. 2012. 'After Subaltern Studies.' *Economic and Political Weekly* 47 (35).

Chaturverdi, Vinayak (ed.) 2000. *Mapping Subaltern Studies and the Postcolonial.* London: Verso.

Chaudhuri, Ajit. 1988. 'From Hegemony to Counter-Hegemony: A Journey in a Non-imaginary Unreal Space.' *Economic and Political Weekly* 23.5: 19–23.

Chaudhary, Muhammad A. 1999. *Justice in Practice: Legal Ethnography of a Pakistani Punjabi Village.* Karachi: Oxford University Press.

Cheema, Ali. 2003. 'State and Capital in Pakistan: The Changing Politics of Accumulation.' In *Corporate Capitalism in Contemporary South Asia: Conventional Wisdoms and South Asian Realities*, edited by Ananya Mukherjee Reed. Basingstoke: Macmillan.

Cheema, Ali and Shandana Mohmand. 2003. 'Local Government Reforms in Pakistan: Legitimising Centralisation or a Driver for Pro-Poor Change.' *Working Paper.* Lahore: Lahore University of Management Sciences.

Cheema, Ali, Shandana Mohmand and Ali Asjad. 2006. 'History, Land Settlement and Semi-Formal Local Governance Structures in Sargodha.' *Working Paper.* Lahore: University of Management Sciences.

Cheesman, David. 1997. *Landlord Power and Rural Indebtedness in Colonial Sind, 1865–1901.* Richmond: Curzon.

Cloughley, Brian. 2008. *War, Coups and Terror: Pakistan's Army in Years of Turmoil.* New York: Skyhorse Publishing.

Cohen, Stephen. P. 1998. *The Pakistan Army.* Karachi: Oxford University Press.
———. 2011. *The Future of Pakistan.* Washington: Brookings.
Cohn, Bernard .S. 1996. *Colonialism and its Forms of Knowledge: The British in India.* Princeton: Princeton University Press.
Crehan, Kate. 2013. 'Living Subalternity: Antonio Gramsci's Concept of Common Sense.' In *The Political Philosophies of Antonio Gramsci and B. R. Ambedkar: Itineraries of Dalits and Subalterns,* edited by Cosimo Zene. New York: Routledge.
Dahrendorf, Ralf. 1959. *Class and Class Conflict in Industrial Society.* London: Routledge.
Devji, Faisal. 2013. *Muslim Zion: Pakistan as a Political Idea.* London: Hurst and Co. Publishers.
Dewey, Clive. 1988. *Arrested Development in India: The Historical Dimension.* London: Riverdale.
Dirks, Nicholas. 2001. *Castes of Mind: Colonialism and the Making of India.* Princeton: Princeton University Press.
Dobb, Maurice. 1963. *Studies in the Development of Capitalism.* London: Routledge and Kegan Paul.
Durr-e-Nayab. 2011. 'Estimating the Middle Class in Pakistan.' *The Pakistan Development Review,* 1–28.
Eisenstadt, Shmuel N. 2000. 'Multiple Modernities.' *Daedalus* 129.1: 1–29.
Ekeh, Peter P. 1975. 'Colonialism and the Two Publics in Africa: A Theoretical Statement.' *Comparative Studies in Society and History* 17.
Esposito, John L. 1988. 'Islam: Ideology and Politics in Pakistan.' In *The State, Religion, and Ethnic Politics: Afghanistan, Iran, and Pakistan,* edited by Banuazizi, Ali, and Myron Weiner. New York: Syracuse University Press.
Fair, Christine C. 2014. *Fighting to the End: The Pakistan Army's Way of War.* New York: Oxford University Press.
Fair, Christine C., and Shuja Nawaz. 2011. 'The Changing Pakistan Army Officer Corps.' *The Journal of Strategic Studies* 34.
Feenberg, Andrew. 1995. *Alternative Modernity: The Technical Turn in Philosophy and Social Theory.* Berkeley: University of California Press.
Fernandez, Bina. 2003. *(En)gendering Poverty Policy in India: Towards a New Feminist Theoretical Framework.* D.Phil, University of Oxford, Oxford.
Fox, Richard G. 1984. 'Urban Class and Communal Consciousness in Colonial Punjab: The Genesis of India's Intermediate Regime.' *Modern Asian Studies* 18 (3): 459–89.
Fuller, Chris J., and J. Harriss. 2001. 'For an Anthropology of the Modern Indian State.' In *Everyday State and Society in Modern India,* edited by C. J. Fuller and Veronique Benei. London: Hurst & Co.
Fuller, Chris. J., and Veronique Benei. 2001. *Everyday State and Society in Modern India.* London: Hurst & Co.
Gadi, Mushtaq. 2003. 'Re-colonising the Indus Basin Irrigation System.' In *The Politics of Managing Water,* edited by Kaiser Bengali. Karachi: Oxford University Press.
Gayer, Laurent. 2014. *Karachi: Ordered Disorder and the Struggle for the City.* New York: Oxford University Press.

Gazdar, Haris. 2003. 'The Land Question.' Unpublished Paper. Karachi: The Collective for Social Science Research.
Gellner, Ernst. 1977. 'Patrons and Clients.' In *Patrons and Clients*, edited by Ernst Gellner and John Waterbury. London: Gerald Duckworth & Co.
———. 1983. *Nations and Nationalism*. Ithaca: Cornell University Press.
Giddens, Anthony. 1985. *The Nation-State and Violence, Volume 2*. Berkeley: University of California Press.
Gilmartin, David. 1979. 'Religious Leadership and the Pakistan Movement in the Punjab.' *Modern Asian Studies* (July): 485–517.
———. 1988. *Empire* and *Islam: Punjab and the Making of Pakistan*. London: Tauris.
———. 2014. 'The Paradox of Patronage and the People's Sovereignty.' In *Patronage as Politics in South Asia*, edited by Anastasia Piliavsky. Delhi: Cambridge University Press.
———. 2015. *Blood and Water: The Indus River Basin in Modern History*. California: University of California Press.
Gohain, Hiren. 2012. 'Subaltern Studies: Turning around the Perspective.' *Economic and Political Weekly* 47 (39).
Gooptu, Nandini. 2007. 'Economic Liberalisation, Work and Democracy.' *Economic and Political Weekly* 42 (21).
Government of Pakistan. 2007. *Economic Survey 2005–6*. Islamabad: Ministry of Finance and Economic Affairs.
Gramsci, Antonio. 1971. *Selections from the Prison Notebooks*. London: Lawrence and Wishart.
Grare, Frederic. 2016. 'The Challenges of Civilian Control Over Intelligence Agencies in Pakistan.' In *Intelligence, National Security and Foreign Policy: A South Asian Narrative*, edited by A. S. M. Ali Ashraf. Dhaka: Bangladesh Institute of Law and International Affairs.
Gudavarthy, Ajay. (ed.) 2012. *Re-framing Democracy and Agency in India: Interrogating Political Society*. London: Anthem Press.
Guha, Ranajit. 1983. *Elementary Aspects of Peasant Insurgency in Colonial India*. Delhi: Oxford University Press.
———. 1997. *Dominance without Hegemony: History and Power in Colonial India*. Cambridge: Harvard University Press.
Gunes-Ayata, Ayse. 1994. 'Clientelism: Pre-modern, Modern, Postmodern.' In *Democracy, Clientelsim, and Civil Society*, edited by Luis Roniger and Ayse Gunes-Ayata. Boulder: L. Rienner Publishers.
Gupta, Akhil. 1995. 'Blurred Boundaries: The Discourse of Corruption, the Culture of Politics, and the Imagined State.' *American Ethnologist* 22 (2): 375–402.
Habib, Irfan. 1995. *Essays in Indian History*. Delhi: Manohar.
Haines, Daniel. 2013. *Building the Empire, Building the Nation: Development, Legitimacy, and Hydro-Politics in Sind, 1919–1969*. Karachi: Oxford University Press.
Haq, Ikramul. 1996. 'Pak-Afghan Drug Trade in Historical Perspective.' *Asian Survey* 36 (10): 945–63.

Haqqani, Hussain. 2005. *Pakistan: Between Mosque and Military.* Washington: Carnegie Endowment for International Peace.

Harriss-White, Barbara. 2003. *India Working: Essays on Society and Economy.* Cambridge: Cambridge University Press, 2003.

Harvey, David. 1992. *The Condition of Postmodernity: An Enquiry into the Origins of Cultural Change.* Boston: Blackwell.

———. 2003. *The New Imperialism.* New York: Oxford University Press.

———. 2005. *A Brief History of Neoliberalism.* New York: Oxford University Press.

Hasan, Arif. 2002a. 'The Roots of Elite Alienation.' *Economic and Political Weekly* November 2–9: 4550–53.

———. 2002b. *The Unplanned Revolution: Observations on the Process of Socio-Economic Change in Pakistan.* Karachi: City Press.

Herring, Ronald J. 1983. *Land to the Tiller: The Political Economy of Agrarian Reform in South Asia.* New Haven: Yale University Press.

Hobsbawm, Eric J. 1990. *Nations and Nationalism since 1780: Programme, Myth, Reality.* Cambridge: Cambridge University Press.

Hoodbhoy, Pervez, and A. H. Nayyar. 1985. 'Rewriting the History of Pakistan.' In *Islam, Politics and the State: The Pakistan Experience*, edited by M. Asghar Khan. London: Zed Books.

Hull, Matthew S. 2012. *Government of Paper: The Materiality of Bureaucracy in Urban Pakistan.* London: University of California Press.

Human Rights Watch. 'World Report 2016.' Accessed on 4 October 2016. Available at: https://www.hrw.org/sites/default/files/world_report_download/wr2016_web.pdf.

Hussain, Asaf. 1979. *Elite Politics in an Ideological State: The Case of Pakistan.* Folkestone: Dawson.

Hussain, Zahid. 2007. *Frontline Pakistan: The Struggle with Militant Islam.* London: I.B. Tauris.

International Crisis Group. 2002. 'Pakistan: Madrasas, Extremism and the Military.' *ICG Asia Report* 36.

Iqbal, Nasir. 2010. 'Parliament doesn't have Unfettered Powers: CJ.' *Dawn*, 17 August. Accessed on 1 March 2017. Available at: https://www.dawn.com/news/553879.

Iqtidar, Humeira. 2011. *Secularizing Islamists? Jama'at-e-Islami and Jama'at-ud-Da'wa in Urban Pakistan.* London: University of Chicago Press.

Jalal, Ayesha. 1985. *The Sole Spokesman: Jinnah: The Muslim League and the Demand for Partition.* New York: Cambridge University Press.

———. 1990. *The State of Martial Rule: The Origins of Pakistan's Political Economy of Defence.* Cambridge: Cambridge University Press.

———. 1994. 'The State and Political Privilege in Pakistan.' In *The Politics of Social Transformation in Afghanistan, Iran and Pakistan*, edited by Ali Banuazizi and Myron Weiner. Syracuse: Syracuse University Press.

———. 1995. *Democracy and Authoritarianism in South Asia: A Comparative and Historical Perspective.* Cambridge: Cambridge University Press.

Javid, Hasan. 2011. 'Class, Power and Patronage: Landowners and Politics in Punjab.' *History and Anthropology* 22.

Jeffrey, Craig, and J. Lerche. 2000. 'Stating the Difference: State, Discourse and Class Reproduction in Uttar Pradesh, India.' *Development and Change* 31: 857–87.

Jha, Prem S. 1980. *India: A Political Economy of Stagnation*. Bombay: Oxford University Press.

Johnson, Dale. 1985. *Middle Classes in Dependent Countries*. Beverly Hills: Rutgers University Press.

Jones, Philip. E. 2003. *The Pakistan People's Party: Rise to Power*. Karachi: Oxford University Press.

Kalecki, Michael. 1969. *Selected Essays on the Economic Growth of the Socialist and the Mixed Economy*. Cambridge: Cambridge University Press.

Kaviraj, Sudipta. 1994. 'On the Construction of Colonial Power: Structure, Discourse, Hegemony.' In *Contesting Colonial Hegemony: State and Society in Africa and India*, edited by Dagmar Engels and Shula Marks. London: British Academic Press.

———.1997. 'The Modem State in India.' In *Dynamics of State Formation: India and Europe Compared*, edited by S. Kaviraj and Martin Doornbos. New Delhi: Manohar.

———. 1998. 'A Critique of the Passive Revolution.' *Economic and Political Weekly* 23 (45–47): 2429–44.

———. 2005a. 'An Outline of a Revisionist Theory of Modernity.' *European Journal of Sociology* 46 (3).

———. 2005b. 'On the Enchantment of the State: Indian Thought on the Role of the State in the Narrative of Modernity.' In *European Journal of Sociology* 46: 263–96.

Kaviraj, Sudipta, and S. Khilnani. 2001. *Civil Society: History and Possibilities*. Cambridge: Cambridge University Press.

Kemal, A. R. 1999. 'Patterns and Growth of Pakistan's Industrial Sector.' In *50 Years of Pakistan's Economy: Traditional Topics and Contemporary Concerns*, edited by Shahrukh Rafi Khan. Karachi: Oxford University Press.

Kemal, Muhammad A., and Ahmed Waqar Qasim. 2012. 'Precise Estimates of the Informal Economy.' *Working Paper*. Islamabad: Pakistan Institute of Development Economics.

Kennedy, Charles. 1988. *Bureaucracy in Pakistan*. Karachi: Oxford University Press.

Keshavarzian, Arang. 2006. *Bazaar and State in Iran: The Politics of the Tehran Marketplace*. Cambridge: Cambridge University Press.

Keucheyan, Razmig. 2013. *Left Hemisphere: Mapping Contemporary Theory*. New York: Verso Books.

Khan, Adeel. 2005. *Politics of Identity: Ethnic Nationalism and the State in Pakistan*. Delhi: Sage.

Khan, Mahmood H. 1999. 'Agricultural Development and Changes in the Land Tenure and Land Revenue Systems in Pakistan.' In *50 Years of Pakistan's Economy: Traditional Topics and Contemporary Concerns*, edited by Shahrukh Rafi Khan. Karachi: Oxford University Press.

Khan, Mushtaq. 2000. 'Class, Clientelism and Communal Politics in Bangladesh.' In *The Making of History: Essays Presented to Irfan Habib*, edited by K. N. Panikkar, T. J. Byres and U. Patnaik. New Delhi: Tulika.

Khan, Naveeda. 2009. 'The Martyrdom of Mosques: Imagery and Iconoclasm in Modern Pakistan.' In *Enchantments of Modernity: Empire, Nation, Globalization*, edited by Saurabh Dube. New Delhi: Routledge.

Khan, Shahrukh R., and A. S. Akhtar. 2014. *The Military and Denied Development in the Pakistani Punjab*. London: Anthem.

Khan, Shahrukh R., Foqia Sadiq Khan, and Aasim Sajjad Akhtar. 2007. *Initiating Devolution: Ignoring the Power Structure*. Karachi: Oxford University Press.

Khan, Shahrukh R., Saba Gul Khattak, and Sajid Kazmi. 2005. *Hazardous Home-based Sub-contracted Work: A Study of Multiple Tiered Exploitation*. Karachi: Oxford University Press.

Khan, Zia. 2014. 'Missing Persons: UN Fact-finding Mission Points Finger at Agencies.' *Express Tribune*, September 21. Available at: http://tribune.com.pk/story/440082/missing-persons-un-fact-finding-mission-points-finger-at-agencies/. Accessed on 12 February 2016.

Khory, Kavita. 1997. 'The Ideology of the Nation-State and Nationalism.' In *State, Society and Democratic Change in Pakistan*, edited by Rasul Bakhsh Rais. Karachi: Oxford University Press.

Kochanek, Stanley. 1983. *Interest Groups and Development: Business and Politics in Pakistan*. New York: Oxford University Press.

———. 1996. 'Ethnic Conflict and the Politicization of Business.' In *Pakistan 1995*, edited by Charles Kennedy and Rasul Bakhsh Rais. Colorado: Westview Press.

Kurin, Richard. 1985. 'Islamisation in Pakistan: A View from the Countryside.' *Asian Survey* 25: 115–28.

LaPorte Jr., Robert. 1975. *Power and Privilege: Influence and Decision-Making in Pakistan*. Berkeley: University of California Press.

Lefebvre, Alain. 1999. *Kinship, Honour and Money in Rural Pakistan: Subsistence Economy and the Effects of International Migration*. Richmond: Curzon.

Leghari, Iqbal. 1979. 'The Socialist Movement in Pakistan: An Historical Survey, 1940–1974.' Unpublished PhD thesis. Montreal: Laval University.

Levitsky, Steven. 2003. 'From Labor Politics to Machine Politics: The Transformation of Party-Union Linkages in Argentine Peronism, 1983–1999.' *Latin American Research Review* 38 (3).

Leys, Colin. 1976. 'The "Overdeveloped" Post-Colonial State: A Re-evaluation.' *Review of African Political Economy* 3: 39–48.

Lieven, Anatol. 2011. *Pakistan: A Hard Country*. London: Allen Lane.

Lindholm, Charles. 1982. *Generosity and Jealousy: The Swat Pukhtun of Northern Pakistan*. New York: Columbia University Press.

Low, D. A. 1988. *The Political Inheritance of Pakistan*. Basingstoke: Macmillan.

Lyon, Stephen. 2002. 'Power and Patronage in Pakistan.' PhD thesis, University of Kent, Canterbury.

Maddison, Angus. 1971. *Class Structure and Economic Growth: India and Pakistan since the Mughals*. London: Allen and Unwin.

Mahmood, Shafqat. 1988. *Bureaucracy in Pakistan: An Historical Analysis*. Lahore: Progressive Publishers.

Malik, Hasnaat. 2014. 'Missing Persons' Case: SC asks Balochistan about Mode of Proceedings.' *Express Tribune*, March 8. Accessed on 12 February 2016. Available at: http://tribune.com.pk/story/680268/missing-persons-case-sc-asks-balochistan-about-mode-of-proceedings/.

Mamdani, Mahmood. 1976. *Politics and Class Formation in Uganda*. London: Heinemann Educational.

———. 1996. *Citizen and Subject: Contemporary Africa and the Legacy of Late Colonialism*. Princeton: Princeton University Press.

———. 2005. *Good Muslim, Bad Muslim: America, the Cold War and the Roots of Terror*. Lahore: Vanguard Books.

Martin, Nicholas. 2013. 'The Dark Side of Political Society: Patronage and the Reproduction of Social Inequality.' *Journal of Agrarian Change* 14 (3).

———. 2015. Politics, *Landlords and Islam in Pakistan*. New York: Routledge.

Marx, Karl. 1977. *A Contribution to the Critique of Political Economy*. Moscow: Progress Publishers.

Medard, Jean-Francois. 1982. 'The Underdeveloped State in Tropical Africa: Political Clientelism or Neo-patrimonialism.' In *Private Patronage and Public Power: Political Clientelism in the Modern State*, edited by Christopher Clapham. London: St. Martin's Press.

Mellema, R. L. 1961. 'The Basic Democracies System in Pakistan.' *Asian Survey* 1 (6): 10–15.

Metcalf, Barbara. 2001. 'Piety, Persuasion and Politics: Deoband's Model of Islamic Activism.' New York: Social Science Research Council.

Mitchell, Timothy. 1991. 'The Limits of the State: Beyond Statist Approaches and Their Critics.' *American Political Science Review* 85: 77–96.

Miliband, Ralph. 1997. *Marxism and Politics*. Oxford: Oxford University Press.

Moj, Muhammad. 2015. *The Deoband Madrassah Movement: Countercultural Trends and Tendencies*. London: Anthem Press.

Mussadaq, Maha. 2014. 'Missing Loved Ones: Baloch Caravan Stages Protest Outside the National Press Club.' *Express Tribune*, March 2. Accessed on 12 February 2016. Available at: http://tribune.com.pk/story/677869/missing-loved-ones-baloch-caravan-stages-protest-outside-the-national-press-club/.

Naveed, Arif and Nazim Ali. 2012. 'Clustered Deprivation: District Profile of Poverty in Pakistan.' *Policy Paper*. Islamabad: Sustainable Development Policy Institute.

Nadvi, Khalid. 1990. *Employment Creation in Urban Micro-Enterprises in the Manufacturing Sector in Pakistan*. Bangkok: ILO/ARTEP.

Nadvi, Khalid. 2003. 'Social Networks in Urban Punjab: A Case Study of the Sialkot Surgical Instrument Cluster.' In *The Post-Colonial State and Social Transformation in India and Pakistan*, edited by S. M. Naseem and Khalid Nadvi. Karachi: Oxford University Press.

Nasr, Seyyed V. R. 1994. *Vanguard of Islamic Revolution: Jama'at-e-Islami of Pakistan*. Berkeley: University of California Press.

———. 2001. *Islamic Leviathan: Islam and the Making of State Power*. New York: Oxford University Press.

———. 2002. 'Islam, the State, and the Rise of Sectarian Militancy in Pakistan.' In *Pakistan: Nationalism without a Nation*, edited by Christophe Jaffrelot. London: Zed Books.

Neale, Walter C. 1969. 'Land is to Rule.' In *Land Control and Social Structure in Indian History*, edited by R. E. Frykenberg. Madison: University of Wisconsin.

Nelson, Matthew J. 2011. *In the Shadow of Shari'a: Islam, Islamic Law, and Democracy in Pakistan*. New York: Hurst & Co.

Noman, Omar. 1988. *Pakistan: Political and Economic History since 1947*. London: Kegan Paul International.

———. 2001. 'An Uncivil Society: The Role of Shadow Privatization, Conflict and Ideology in the Governance of Pakistan.' In *Power and Civil Society in Pakistan*, edited by Zulfikar Gilani and Anita Weiss. Karachi: Oxford University Press.

O'Hanlon, Rosalin and David Washbrook. 1992. 'After Orientalism: Culture, Criticism and Politics in the Third World.' *Comparative Studies in Society and History* 34 (1).

Pakistan Telecom Authority's Telecom Indicators. Accessed on 4 October 2016. Available at: http://www.pta.gov.pk/index.php?Itemid=599.

Panda, Ankit. 2016. 'Pakistan's Army Seeks Greater Authority over China-Pakistan Economic Corridor Administration.' *The Diplomat*, April 20. Accessed on 4 October 2016. Available at: http://thediplomat.com/2016/04/pakistans-army-seeks-greater-authority-over-china-pakistan-economic-corridor-administration/.

Papanek, Gustav F. 1968. *Pakistan's Development: Social Goals and Private Incentives*. Karachi: Oxford University Press.

Pasha, Mustafa K. 1992. 'Islamisation, Civil Society, and the Politics of Transition in Pakistan.' In *Religion and Political Conflict in South Asia: India, Pakistan, and Sri Lanka*, edited by Douglas Allen. Westport: Greenwood Press.

———. 1997. 'The "Hyper-Extended" State: Civil Society and Democracy.' In *State, Society and Democratic Change in Pakistan*, edited by Rasul Bakhsh Rais. Karachi: Oxford University Press.

———. 1998. *Colonial Political Economy: Recruitment and Underdevelopment in the Punjab*. Karachi: Oxford University Press.

Pastner, Carol L. 1996. 'Introduction' In *Marginality and Modernity: Ethnicity and Change in Post-Colonial Balochistan*, edited by Paul Titus. Karachi: Oxford University Press.

Paul, Thazha V. 2014. *The Warrior State: Pakistan in the Contemporary World*. New York: Oxford University Press.

Perlez, Jane and Pir Zubair Shah. 2010. 'In Violent Karachi, Insurgency Finds a Haven.' *New York Times*, May 21. Accessed on 2 March 2016. Available at: http://www.nytimes.com/2010/05/22/world/asia/22karachi.html?_r=0.

Piliavsky, Anastasia. (ed.) 2014. *Patronage as Politics in South Asia*. Delhi: Cambridge University Press.

Pirzada, Sayyid A. S. 2000. *The Politics of the Jamiat Ulema-i-Islam Pakistan, 1971–1977.* Karachi: Oxford University Press.
Poulantzas, Nicos. 1980. *State, Power, Socialism.* London: Verso.
Prakash, Gyan. 1990. 'Writing Post-Orientalist Histories of the Third World: Perspectives from Indian Historiography.' *Comparative Studies in Society and History* 32 (2).
———. 1992. 'Can the "Subaltern" Ride? A Reply to O'Hanlon and Washbrook.' *Comparative Studies in Society and History* 34 (1).
Qadeer, Muhammad. 2000. 'Ruralopolises: The Spatial Organisation and Residential Land-Economy of High-Density Rural Regions.' *Urban Studies* 37: 1025–44.
Rahman, Taimur. 2012. *The Class Structure of Pakistan.* Karachi: Oxford University Press.
Ranger, Terence and Eric Hobsbawm (eds.) 1983. *The Invention of Tradition.* Cambridge: Cambridge University Press.
Raza, Rafi. 1997. *Zulfikar Ali Bhutto and Pakistan, 1967–77.* Karachi: Oxford University Press.
Rehman, Shafiq-ur. 1998. *Who Owns Pakistan? Fluctuating Fortunes of Business Mughals.* Islamabad: Aelia Communications.
Richter, William L. 1978. 'Persistent Praetorianism: Pakistan's Third Military Regime.' *Pacific Affairs* 51: 406–26.
Rittenberg, Stephen A. 1988. *Ethnicity, Nationalism, and the Pakhtuns: The Independence Movement in India's North-West Frontier Province.* Durham: Carolina Academic Press.
Rizvi, Hasan A. 2003. *Military, State and Society in Pakistan.* Lahore: Sang-e-Meel Publications.
Rouse, Shahnaz. 1983. 'Systematic Injustices and Inequalities: "Maalik" and "Raaiya" in a Punjab Village.' In *Pakistan: The Unstable State,* edited by Hassan Gardezi and Jamil Rashid. Lahore: Vanguard Books.
Roy, Arundhati. 2004. 'Public Power in the Age of Empire.' Lecture delivered to 99th Annual Meeting of American Sociological Association. San Francisco, August 16.
Sanyal, Kalyan. 2007. *Rethinking Capitalist Development: Primitive Accumulation, Governmentality and Post-colonial Capitalism.* London: Routledge.
Sayer, Andrew. 2001. 'For a Critical Cultural Political Economy.' *Antipode* 33: 687–708.
Sarkar, Sumit. 2000. 'Orientalism Revisited: Saidian Frameworks in the Writing of Modern Indian History.' In *Mapping Subaltern Studies and the Postcolonial,* edited by Vinayak Chaturvedi. London: Verso.
Saul, John S. 1974. 'The State in Post-colonial Societies-Tanzania.' *The Socialist Register.* London: Merlin Press.
Sayeed, Asad U. 1995. 'Political Alignments, the State and Industrial Policy in Pakistan: A Comparison of Performance in the 1960s and 1980s.' Unpublished PhD Dissertation, University of Cambridge.
Sayeed, Khalid B. 1980. *Politics in Pakistan: Nature and Direction of Change.* New York: Praeger.
Schwarz, Henry. 2002. 'Subaltern Studies: Radical History in the Metaphoric Mode.' In *Reading Subaltern Studies: Critical History, Contested Meaning and the Globalisation of South Asia,* edited by David Ludden. London: Anthem Books.

Scott, James. 1976. *The Moral Economy of the Peasant: Rebellion and Subsistence in Southeast Asia*. New Haven: Yale University Press.
———. 1985. *Weapons of the Weak: Everyday Forms of Peasant Resistance*. New Haven: Yale University Press.
Shafqat, Saeed. 1997. *Civil-military Relations in Pakistan: From Zulfikar Ali Bhutto to Benazir Bhutto*. Boulder: Westview Press.
———. 2003. 'Democracy and Political Participation in Pakistan.' In *Pakistan: The Contours of State and Society*, edited by Soofia Mumtaz, Jean-Luc Racine and Imran Ali. Karachi: Oxford University Press.
———. 2011. 'Praetorians and the People.' In *Pakistan: Beyond the Crisis State*, edited by Maleeha Lodhi. Karachi: Oxford University Press.
Shah, Aqil. 2014. *The Army and Democracy: Military Politics in Pakistan*. Cambridge: Harvard University Press.
Shaheed, Zafar. 1983. 'The Role of the Government in the Development of the Labour Movement.' In *Pakistan: The Unstable State*, edited by Hassan Gardezi and Jamil Rashid. Lahore: Vanguard Books.
Shaikh, Farzana. 2009. *Making Sense of Pakistan*. New York: Columbia University Press.
Sharma, Aradhana, and Akhil Gupta. 2006. *The Anthropology of the State: A Reader*. Oxford: Blackwell Publishers.
Shivji, Issa G. 1976. *Class Struggles in Tanzania*. London: Heinemann Educational.
Siddiqa, Ayesha. 2007. *Military Inc: The Politics of Military Economy in Pakistan*. London: Pluto Press.
Siddiqi, A. R. 1996. *The Military in Pakistan: Image and Reality*. Karachi: Vanguard Books.
Siddique, Osama, and Z. Hayat. 2008. 'Unholy Speech and Holy Laws: Blasphemy Laws in Pakistan – Controversial Origins, Design Defects and Free Speech Implications.' *Minnesota Journal of International Law* 17 (2).
Siddiqui, Farhan H. 2012. 'Ethnopolitics, Ethnic Conflict and the State in Pakistan: The Mobilization of Hazara and Seraiki Ethnic Identites.' Paper presented at Conference entitled Federalism in Pluralistic Developing Societies: Learning from the European Experiences, University of Karachi.
———. 2012. *The Politics of Ethnicity in Pakistan: The Baloch, Sindhi and Mohajir Ethnic Movements*. UK: Routledge.
Smith, Anthony D. 1998. *Nationalism and Modernism*. London: Routledge.
Sobhan, Rehman. 2003. 'State and Governance as Factors in Development.' In *The Post-Colonial State and Social Transformation in India and Pakistan*, edited by S. M. Naseem and K. Nadvi. Karachi: Oxford University Press.
Spear, Thomas. 2003. 'Neotraditionalism and the Limits of Invention in British Colonial Africa.' *Journal of African History* 44: 3–27.
Spencer, Jonathan. 1997. 'Post-colonialism and the Political Imagination.' *The Journal of the Royal Anthropological Institute* 3 (1).
Steinmetz, George. 1999. *State/Culture: State Formation after the Cultural Turn*. Ithaca: Cornell University Press.

Talbot, Ian. 1996. *Freedom's Cry: The Popular Dimension in the Pakistan Movement and Partition Experience in North West India.* London: Oxford University Press.

———. 2002. 'The Punjabization of Pakistan: Myth or Reality?' In *Pakistan: Nationalism with a Nation*, edited by Christophe Jaffrelot. London: Zed Books.

Tan, Tai Yong. 2005. *The Garrison State: Military, Government and Society in Colonial Punjab, 1849–1947.* London: SAGE.

Therborn, Goran. 2008. *From Marxism to Post-Marxism?* New York: Verso.

Thompson, Edward P. 1966. *The Making of the English Working Class.* New York: Vintage-Random House.

———. 1971. 'The Moral Economy of the English Crowd in the Eighteenth Century.' *Past and Present* 50.

———. 2015. *Customs in Common: Studies in Traditional Popular Culture.* New York: The New Press.

Toor, Saadia. 2011. *The State of Islam: Culture and Cold War Politics in Pakistan.* London: Pluto Press.

Tsakok, Isabelle. 1986. 'The Export of Manpower from Pakistan to the Middle East.' In *Pakistan's Development Priorities: Choices for the Future*, edited by Shahid Javed Burki and Robert LaPorte Jr. Karachi: Oxford University Press.

Tudor, Maya. 2013. *The Promise of Power: The Origins of Democracy in India and Autocracy in Pakistan.* Cambridge: Cambridge University Press.

Verkaaik, Oskar. 2001. 'The Captive State: Corruption, Intelligence Agencies, and Ethnicity in Pakistan.' In *States of Imagination: Ethnographic Explorations of the Postcolonial State*, edited by Thomas Blom Hansen and Finn Stepputat. Durham: Duke University Press.

———. 2004. *Migrants and Militants: Fun and Urban Violence in Pakistan.* Princeton: Princeton University Press.

Wacquant, Loic J. D. 1985. 'Heuristic Models in Marxian Theory.' *Social Forces* 64: 17–40.

Waseem, Mohammad. 1994. *Politics and the State in Pakistan.* Islamabad: National Institute of Historical and Cultural Research.

———. 2002. 'The Dialectic of Domestic Policy and Foreign Policy.' In *Pakistan: Nationalism without a Nation*, edited by Christophe Jaffrelot. London: Zed Books.

———. 2006. *Democratisation in Pakistan: A Study of the 2002 Elections.* Karachi: Oxford University Press.

Washbrook, David. 1990. 'South Asia, the World System, and World Capitalism.' *Journal of Asian Studies* 49: 479–508.

Wright, Erik O. 1985. *Classes.* London: Verso.

Wilder, Andrew. 1998. *The Pakistani Voter: Electoral Politics and Voting Behaviour in the Punjab.* Karachi: Oxford University Press.

Weiss, Anita. 1991. *Class, Culture and Development in Pakistan: The Emergence of an Industrial Bourgeoisie in Punjab.* Boulder: Westview Press.

———. 1994. 'The Consequences of State Policies for Women in Pakistan.' In *The Politics of Social Transformation in Afghanistan, Iran and Pakistan*, edited by Ali Banuazizi and Myron Weiner. Syracuse: Syracuse University Press.

White, Joshua T. 2008. 'Pakistan's Islamist Frontier'. *Religion & Security Monograph Series*, 5.

White, Lawrence J. 1974. *Industrial Concentration and Political Power in Pakistan*. Princeton: Princeton University Press.

Witsoe, Jeffrey. 2013. *Democracy against Development: Lower-caste Politics and Political Modernity in Postcolonial India*. London: University of Chicago Press.

Wright Jr, Theodore. P. 1974. 'Indian Muslim Refugees in the Politics of Pakistan.' *Journal of Commonwealth and Comparative Politics* 12.

Zaidi, S. Akbar. 2002. 'Dismal State of Social Sciences in Pakistan.' *Economic and Political Weekly* 37 (August).

———. 2005a. *Issues in Pakistan's Economy*. Karachi: Oxford University Press.

———. 2005b. 'State, Military and Social Transition: Improbable Future of Democracy in Pakistan.' *Economic and Political Weekly* 40 (49): 1122–40.

———. 2014. 'Rethinking Pakistan's Political Economy: Class, State, Power and Transition.' *Economic and Political Weekly* 49.

———. 2016. 'The New Game Changer in Pakistan.' *The Hindu*, 28 May. Accessed on 4 October 2016. Available at: http://www.thehindu.com/opinion/lead/chinapakistan-economic-corridor-the-new-game-changer-in-pakistan/article8656498.ece.

Zaman, Qasim. 1998. 'Sectarianism in Pakistan: The Radicalization of Shia and Sunni Identities.' *Modern Asian Studies* 32: 689–716.

Ziring, Lawrence.1974. 'Militarism in Pakistan: The Yahya Khan Interregnum.' *Asian Affairs* 1 (6): 402–20.

———. 1997. *Pakistan in the Twentieth Century: A Political History*. Karachi: Oxford University Press.

Index

Achakzai, Mahmood Khan, 127
Ahmad, Sadaf, 108
Ahmadi riots, 1953, 98
Ahmed, Sheikh Rasheed, 54
Alavi, Hamza, 4–5, 32
Ali, Kamran Asdar, 18, 135
Ali, Niaz, 37, 126
Ali, Nosheen, 7
All-Pakistan Alliance for Katchi Abadis (APAKA), 153
All-Pakistan Federation of Transporters, 84
Anjuman Mazarain Punjab (AMP), 148
anti-Musharraf movement, 166, 170
*arhti*s, 76–80
    functions of, 79
    influence in wholesale grain and seed markets, 77
    interactions of, 78
    local, 77
    recovery of outstanding debts, 78–79
    relationships between farmers and, 77
    relative power of, –78
Awami League (AL), 13, 100, 117
Awami National Party (ANP), 85, 127

Baluchistan, 13, 67, 116, 118, 120–122, 124, 127–128, 169
    NAP regime in, 117–118
Baluch nationalism, 122, 128–130
bania, 77
Bhutto, Zulfikar Ali, 117, 120, 136, 139
Bhutto regime, 48–49
    anti-India sentiment, 120–121
    civil service reforms of the 1970s, 35, 41
    collusion between intermediate classes and state functionaries, 76
    contemporary Sindh, 139
    labour and student activism, 135–142
biraderi structures, 24–25
Blasphemy Law, 102, 168
Brenner, Robert, 65
bureaucratic paternalism, 26
business community (industrial bourgeoisie) of Pakistan, 69–73
    Chinioti business families, 70
    Karachi-based business families, 70–71
    Pashtun intermediate classes, 72
    Punjabi entrepreneurial class, 72–73
    Punjabi urban entrepreneurs, 72
business community in India, 70

Capital Development Authority (CDA), 7
Chatterjee, Partha, 133–135
    political society, 133–134, 156
    process of 'accumulation by dispossession,' 135
Chaudhry, Iftikhar Mohammad, 163–164
China, 168–169
coercion-consent dialectic, 28, 80, 89, 105, 125, 161–162
Cohen, Stephen, 54
common sense, understanding of, 5–6, 15–19
Communist Party of Pakistan (CPP), 136
contemporary political practice in Pakistan, 161–162
counter-hegemonic politics, 28, 121, 128–129, 149, 165–166, 170, 172

de Certeau, Michel, 144
Devji, Faisal, 96
Dobb, Maurice, 65

Ekeh, 44–45

ethnic-nationalism, 116–118
　ethnic-linguistic identity, 118
　and infusion of 'Islam,' 121–122
　intensification of, 128
　and 'intra-ethnic' conflicts, 127–130
　Pashtun, 116, 125–127
　politics of ethnic-nationalist resistance, 121–124
　symbiotic relationship between class and, 119–121
　in theory and practice, 118–119
　west *vs* east, 116–117
ethnic-nationalist movements, 27
ethnic-national movements, 121
everyday state, 37

Fahim, Makhdoom Amin, 50
Federally Administered Tribal Areas (FATA), 85
Federal Shariat Court and Council of Islamic Ideology, 99

Gramsci, Antonio, 2, 3
　common sense, understanding of, 5–6, 16–17
　hegemony, 15
　historical bloc, concept of, 10–11
　trajectory of culture and politics in materialist tradition, 5, 7
Great Revolt of 1857, 9
Green Revolution, 13, 67
Gulf labour migrations, 73–75

Haq, Zia ul. *see* Zia regime
Hashtanagar land rights movement, 127–128
Hashtanagar Movement, 151–152
high bureaucracy, 41–43, 45
　Bhutto's civil service reforms, 41
　democratic interregnum of 1988-1999, 42
　erosion of the elitist spirit, 43
　practice of installing loyalists, 42
　process of 'nativisation,' 43
　under Zia regime, 42
historical bloc, 10–15, 10–16, 22, 168, 169

Hull, Matthew, 7
hundi system, 91n48

ideology of Pakistan, 116
imagined community, 122, 129
impersonal civic public sphere, 44
informal economy, 63, 66, 75–76, 83–84, 89n5
intermediate classes, 112, 123, 155, 162, 171
　*arhti*s, 76–80
　contradictions between subordinate and, 68–69
　differentiation, 64–65
　historical migrations of, 66–69
　Pashtun, 72
　shopkeeper/trader, 86–88
　socio-economic changes, 67
　state functionaries and, collusion between, 75–76
　thekedaar (sub contractor), 80–84
　in theory and history, 64–66
　transformation, 88–89
　transporters, 84–86
Iqtidar, Humeira, 18, 108
Islam
　as an idiom of political mobilisation, 95
　in the context of geo-political developments, 95
'Islamic' essence of Pakistan
　global discourse of 'anti-terrorism' and, 109–110
　influence in the social and political mainstream, 94
　'Islam-pasand' programmes, 100
　religio-political organizations and movements, influence of, 88, 94, 96—102, 104–110
　religious right's politics, 94–95
　Zia regime, 98–100
'Islamic' ideological state, 96–99
　association of Islam in defence of nation, 98
　Islamic symbols, use of, 97
Islami Jamhoori Ittehad (IJI), 99

Islami Jamiat-e-Tulabah (IJT), 100–101
'Islamisation' drive during Zia period, 17, 27, 51–52, 98–100, 140
    Blasphemy Law, 102, 168
    cultural expression, impact on, 101
    declaring Ahmadis as non-Muslims, 98
    differences within the 'non-elite' and, 105–109
    duality in private and public life, 103–104
    educational institutions, impact on, 101–102
    Hudood Ordinances, 102
    impact of, 100–105
    local mullah in dealing with domestic dispute, role of, 107
    secular elites, impact on, 102–103
    social life, impact on, 102, 105–106
    in urban areas, 104
    women, impact on, 102

Jalal, Ayesha, 95
Jamaa't-e-Islamic (JI), 96, 99, 101, 109, 113n32
Jamiat-e-Ulema-e-Hind (JUH), 95
Jamiat-e-Ulema-e- Islam (JUI), 95, 109, 117
Jinnah, Muhammad Ali, 116–117

Karachi Labour Movement, 18
Katchi abadis, 152–154, 159n54, 160n55–56
Kaviraj, Sudipta, 6, 8
Khan, Ayub, 12, 35–36
    civil service during, 41
    high bureaucracy during, 45
    intermediate classes, role in ending regime of, 67
    military regime, 51
    process of social transformation, 36
Khan, Naveeda, 7
Khanis, Aga, 110
Khudai Khidmatgars, 116, 127
Khyber Pakhtunkhwa province, 67, 104, 108, 126
    small and landless farmers, 150–152

Labour Qaumi Movement (LQM), 155
Lalu Prasad regime in the Indian state of Bihar, 44
land-to-own, notion of, 9
localisation, 140–141
low bureaucracy, 43–46, 46, 141
    post-Bhutto period, 45–46
    practice of giving and receiving favours, 44
    social control, 46
    Zia regime, 46

Mahmud, Maulana Mufti, 100
Marxist theory of the state, 57n8
Masood, General (Retired) Talat, 55
Maudoodi, 97
Mazdoor Kissan Party (Workers and Peasants Party), 151
middle-class. *see* intermediate classes
migrants, role in state, 97
military, 165–166, 166
    Army, Navy and Air Force, relationship between, 52
    Bhutto period, 54–55
    civil-military relations, 53–54
    corporate activities of, 53
    dialectical relationship between Islam, Pakistan and, 51
    dominated structure of power, 54
    economic autonomy, 52
    encroachment into politics, 51
    higher and lower ranks, relationship between, 52–53
    ideological, economic and political power of, 55
    intelligence apparatus, 55
    involvement in domestic politics, 55
    during Musharraf tenure, 166
    'Pakistani generation' of soldiers, 54–55
    post Musharraf tenure, 166–167
    privatisation, 53
    socialisation within, 52
    Yahya Khan regime, 55
    Zia regime, 54

Movement for Restoration of Democracy (MRD), 74
Muhajirs, 97–98, 118, 130n13
Musharraf, General Pervez, 148, 163–164
Muttahida Majlis-e-Amal (MMA), 111
Muttahida Qaumi Movement (MQM), 104, 109, 118, 130m5

National Awami Party (NAP), 13, 109, 117–118
National Industrial Relations Commission (NIRC), 139
National Labour Federation (NLF), 102
National Logistics Cell (NLC), 85
National Students Federation (NSF), 120, 138
'nativisation' of state institutions, 43, 75
Nizam-e-Mustapha, 87
'non-elite' culture of politics, 105–109
non-western modernity, 21

Objectives Resolution, 97
Occupy Wall Street Campaign, 144
'overdeveloped' state, theory of, 32

Pakhtunkhwa MilliAwami Party (PkMAP), 127
Pakistan, 1
   as an 'establishment,' 162–165
   Bhutto regime's civil service reforms, 14
   Chinese aid and assistance, 168–169
   contemporary social order, 3–5, 163
   east, 13
   militarism in post-colonial, 11
   patronage structures, 19–23
   political power, 12
   politics of common sense in, 2
   post-Bhutto military regime, 15
   principle of 'personalisation of power,' 15
   rise of smart phone 'culture,' 171
   sifarish and *rishwat*, 15
   state formation in, 11
   west, 12
   during Zia period, 2
   Zia regime's 'Islamisation' drive, 17, 27
   Zia years, 13–15
Pakistani society, 62
Pakistan Muslim League (PML), 173n11
Pakistan Muslim League (PML)-N, 166
Pakistan National Alliance (PNA), 48, 87, 109
Pakistan People's Party (PPP), 13, 67–69, 100, 117–118, 120, 137–138, 143, 166
   Benazir Bhutto's tenure, 143–144
   class composition of, 138
   emergence as popular support, 137–138
   legacy of, 139–142
   link between mass movement and, 138
Pakistan Tehrik-e-Insaf (PTI), 113n29, 167
Pashtun Loya Jirga, 85
Pashtun nationalism, 116, 125–127
Pashtun transporters, 86
patriarchal societies, 4–5
patronage-based political economy, 31–32
patronage structures, 19–23
   in Attock district of Pakistani Punjab, 20–21
   Zia regime, 42, 54, 71
patron-client relations, 21, 25–6, 68
pre-British India, 10
Peshawar Valley, 24, 116, 120, 125, 146, 150
Pillavsky, Anastasia, 19–20, 22
power structure in India, 156
power structure in Pakistan, 142
   Alavi's basic contention, 32
   Ayub Khan's decade, 35–36
   colonial influence, 31
   contenders, 63–64
   direct or indirect control over land, 34
   emergence of intermediate classes, 36
   'from below,' 32
   Green Revolution, impact of, 35, 36
   high bureaucracy, 41–43
   landed notables, influence of, 34–35
   low bureaucracy, 43–46
   military-bureaucratic oligarchy, 32
   military establishment, 31
   nativisation of, 27, 43, 75, 106, 167

patronage politics, 31–36, 46
post 1959 land reforms, 35–36
relationship between civil
    administrators and landed
    notables, 34–35
role of 'big men,' 34–36
state bourgeoisie, 33
of state functionaries, 36–39
pre-British India
    agrarian economy, 9
    logic of capital, 8–10
    patron-client relations, 10
    politics during, 8
    property rights, 9
    social power, 10
    state in, 8–10
    transformation of landlord to
    landowner, 9
Prison Notebooks, 11
public sphere in post-colonial Africa, 44
Punjab, 130n21, 162
    agricultural and non-agricultural
    castes (*zamindar*s and *kammi*s),
    146–149
    under British, 122–123
    canal colonies, 150
    economy, 123–124
Punjab Alienation of Land Act 1901, 9
Punjabi society, 124–125, 130n9

Quaid-i-Azam University, 40

Rahman, Mujibur, 117
religio-political organizations and
    movements, 3, 13, 18, 52, 63, 88, 94,
    96–99, 101–102, 104–110, 162
religious right, 48, 75, 110–112
    bases, 109
    charitable foundations and, 109
    'counter-elite' narrative, 107–108
    intermediate classes and, 63
    'Islam-pasand' programmes of, 100
    military's overt patronage of, 51
    political discourse of, 105–106
    role in making and breaking elected
    governments, 99–100
    role in undermining radical political
    environment, 94–95
    student and trade union activities,
    influence on, 102
    targeting of left populism, 101
    working-class women, influence on, 108
right-wing during the Zia years, 27

Shariatisation, 105
Sharif, Nawaz, 72
Sharif, Raheel, 167
shopkeeper/trader, 86–88
Sindh, 13, 24, 50, 67, 74, 86
    *arht*is of, 77
    ethnic-national movements in, 121
    Islamisation, 105
    Muhajir community of, 118
    poverty in, 124
    PPP dominance in, 120, 139
Sindh Encumbered Estates Act 1878, 9
Sindh *Katchi Abadis* Authority (SKAA),
    160n52
Siraikis, 121
state, role in Pakistan, 36–39
    capitalist development, 39
    civilian state institutions, 38
    employment in the public sector, 39–40
    idealized and abstract conception, 38
    involvement of state functionaries in
    'informal activities,' 47
    Miliband-Poulantzas debate on relative
    autonomy, 57n8
    in moulding the social formation, 47
    Niaz Ali's insights on state-society
    binary, 37
    relationship between state and labour
    aristocracy, 139
    in social exchange, 37–39
    in social life, 48
    state-society divide, 37
    for working people, 38
state-capital relation, 57n10
subaltern politics, 133–134, 145, 156
subordinate classes, 68, 73, 112, 124,
    132–133, 165

Bhutto period, 139–140
Katchi abadis, 152–154
political alignments of, 134–137
politics of resistance and reaction, 135–139
small and landless farmers, 146–154
unorganized urban workforce, 154–155
unspectacular politics of resistance by, 144–145

Tablihghi Jamaa't (TJ), 108
Taseer, Salman, 167–168
9/11 terrorist attack, 1
thekedaar (sub contractor), 80–84, 92n70, 155
 affluent, 81
 background of, 81
 as collective bargaining agent (CBA), 83
 in informal manufacturing, 83–84
 links with *patwari,* 82
 in manufacturing industries, 82
 networks of labourers and artisans, 81–82
 nexus of owner-*thekedaar*-state functionary, 83
 Pashtun, 83–84
 relationship with worker, 83–84
 symbiotic relationship between purchase/sale/renting of land, 80, 82
 urban, 81
Third World nationalism, 136
Thompson, E. P., 157
Toor, Saadia, 3, 135
trade unionism, 83
transporters ('transport mafia'), 84–86
Tripartite Conferences, 139
two-nation theory, 11

unorganized urban workforce, 154–155
urbanisation in Pakistan, 49–50
urban politics, 38

1857 War of Independence, 130n18
Water and Power Development Authority (WAPDA), 155
Waziristanis, 84–85
Weberian rationality, principles of, 22
Witsoe, Jeffrey, 44

Zia regime, 2, 13–15, 48–49, 74, 121, 137
 Afghan war, 100
 collusion between intermediate classes and state functionaries during, 75–76
 distribution and expansion of state patronage, 47, 99
 educational institutions, transformation of, 101
 entrepreneurial class, 63–64, 71
 Federal Shariat Court, 105
 high bureaucracy's bureaucratic paternalism, 42
 induction of religious organisations into state institutions during, 99–100
 intermediate classes, 48, 64
 'Islamisation' drive, 17, 27, 51–52, 98–105
 labour militancy, 139
 Martial Law Regulation 51, 101–102
 patronage politics, 42, 54, 71
 religio-political organizations and movements, 52, 63, 88, 94, 96–99, 101–102, 104–110
 role of the *mujahideen,* 100
 scope of local state's functions, 46
 smuggling of contraband during, 85
 state's coercive power under, 89